Jewish Roots

A Foundation of Biblical Theology

Dan Juster

Destiny Image® Publishers, Inc.
P.O. Box 310
Shippensburg, PA 17257

"Speaking to the Purposes of God for this Generation
and for the Generations to Come"

ISBN 1-56043-142-3
(Previously ISBN 0-937831-00-X)
Library of Congress Catalog Card Number 94-074707

For Worldwide Distribution
Printed in the U.S.A.

Third Edition: 2001   Fourth Printing: 2003

This book and all other Destiny Image, Revival Press, MercyPlace, Fresh Bread, Destiny Image Fiction, and Treasure House books are available at Christian bookstores and distributors worldwide:

For a U.S. bookstore nearest you, call **1-800-722-6774**.
For more information on foreign distributors,
call **717-532-3040**.
Or reach us on the Internet:

www.destinyimage.com

Dedication

To the two most special women in my life:

First of all, my mother, *Edith Christensen Juster*, whose kindness and love toward Jewish people has been a major factor in my life;

And to my wife *Patty*, whose love and devotion in hard times and good times has been extraordinary; she is a remarkable wife and mother to our four children.

Table of Contents

Preface to the Third Edition

The third edition of *Jewish Roots* is essentially un-
changed. There are corrections of statement but not basic
content. The preface to the second edition is still important,
in my view, in rightly approaching *Jewish Roots* from my
present perspective.

Since the last edition, David Stern's *Jewish New Testament*, a new translation, has been printed. The *Jewish New
Testament Commentary* has also been published by David
Stern. I believe that these are monumental publishing
events for the Messianic Jewish Movement.

There are pros and cons to the *Jewish New Testament*.
First of all, it should be noted that, in my view, it is a good
translation. Some sections do bring out the intended meaning in its first century context better than other translations.
Dr. Stern has decided to use Yiddish in the translation of
various words and concepts. This, of course, is not accurate
since Yiddish is a recent language that did not exist in the
first century. Yiddish language and culture is not universally Jewish or first century. However, it is the cultural root-
ing of most Jews, though this cultural background is being
left behind by many Israelis. On the other hand, the use of
Yiddish shouts that the New Testament is Jewish in a way
that mere first century Hebraisms would not. Dr. Stern was
fully aware that this was a judgement call. Yiddishisms
make this edition of the New Testament a great outreach
tool. Whether or not one appreciates Dr. Stern's decision in
this regard is a matter of perspective.

I have to note that I am very excited by the *Jewish New
Testament Commentary*. Any corrections I could mention
would be minor and unworthy of mention. This commentary
is an excellent piece of work. It is supportive of the interpretive thrust of *Jewish Roots* in almost every Biblical theology
issue. No Jewish believer should be without a copy. Actually, I wish all believers would own it and consult it.

The Messianic Jewish movement continues to grow in the States and in foreign lands. Growth has been slower of late. However, in Russia, growth is explosive. We are beginning to see significant growth in Israel as well. Court cases have gone against Messianic Jews in Israel with regard to the Law of Return. However, we are going to ultimately win. Good theology is needed more than ever. We are seeing some good theology from such writers as Michael Shiffman, Raimon Bennet's *When Day and Night Cease*, and others. Keith Intrater and I have been privileged to publish other Messianic works. These include *Israel, the Church, and the Last Days*; *Revelation: the Passover Key*; and *From Iraq to Armageddon*. *Jewish Roots* is foundational to the rest. *Growing to Maturity, a Messianic Jewish Guide*, is also in its third printing. We praise God for this and that the Messianic Jewish Movement grows. May we avoid heresy and foolishness on the base of a solid theology.

Preface

This preface is mainly for the purpose of expressing new perspectives and changes in viewpoint since the first edition. I believe that it is very important for the reader to carefully examine the content of this preface if he or she is not to be misled concerning the positions I espouse today. I believe that it is better that I clearly write concerning the development of my perspective in this preface than to actually rewrite the content of the book itself. In this way the reader can compare the past viewpoint with the changes and developments reflected in this preface. This I hope, will be a more significant learning experience.

Messianic Judaism and Messianic Jewish Biblical theology are not of significance only to those who are part of Messianic Jewish congregations. Indeed because the destiny of Israel and the Church are bound together, Messianic Jewish theology has implications of great importance for all. If the Church consists of those grafted into a Jewish olive tree, the issues discussed here are of no mere parochial concern.

Since the first edition of this book, the Messianic Jewish movement has continued to grow both here in the North American continent and abroad. There is still a great need for clear Biblical thinking on many of the issues discussed in those pages. It is my conviction that the content of *Jewish Roots* is trustworthy except for those corrections which I will note in this preface. I stand by the central thrust of the book on all major issues; the nature of the covenants, the call of

Jewish people in the Messiah to maintain a Jewish life, the relationship between grace and law and much, much more. I believe that the basic application of the Law in the New Covenant order of existence is as outlined in the text and as reflected in the appendix on the 613 laws. The following is an outline of developments and changes.

THE PROPHETIC MEANING OF THE FEASTS

Since the first edition I have come to a greater appreciation of the Biblical feasts of Israel. However, more than was reflected in the first edition, I have come to see all the feasts as having great future prophetic reference awaiting fulfillment. Hence each feast has historic reference to God's salvation to ancient Israel, to the meaning of fulfillment in Yeshua who brings out the deepest meaning of the feast, to agricultural significance in celebrating God as the provider, and reference to the last days and the millenial age to come. The book adequately covered the first three dimensions of the feasts. I now add my sense of still future prophetic significance.

Passover definitely looks forward to the last great exodus of the people of Israel from all the lands to which they have been scattered. Jeremiah 16 and Jeremiah 23 look forward to a day in which Israel will no longer say the LORD who brought us out of the land of Egypt, but the LORD who brought us out of all the countries in which He has scattered us and brought us back into our own land. This great return to the land of Israel is one of the most amazing prophetic happenings in our time. Much more of this regathering is yet to come. It is reflected throughout the prophets. This is a fulfillment of the meaning of Passover. There is more yet to come out of the meaning of Passover! I believe that Passover in its millenial context will emphasize this great exodus. Messianic Jews today do well to celebrate Passover with a great deal of reference to these prophetic events. Furthermore, the plagues of the book of Revelation are parallel to the Exodus plagues and are part of God's working to effect this exodus.

It may also be correct to see references to the gathering of the saints out of all the nations of the earth in the Passover themes. This of course relates to the return of the Messiah Jesus to earth.

It should be noted that the feasts do not provide exclusive meanings, but overlapping themes so that some themes are emphasized more in one feast than another. This will become clear in our discussion of additional feasts.

The feast of Shavuot, or Pentecost, has reference *not only* to the early harvest in Israel, and to the giving of the Law but also the pouring out of the Spirit upon the first disciples in Jerusalem. This feast also looks forward to a much greater outpouring of the Spirit both in the last days revival of the people of God, what Joel calls the early and the latter rain together, and also to the great outpouring that shall determine the whole character of the Age to Come. In New Testament theology, the Age to Come has broken into this age through Yeshua. Hence we note the fulfillment of Joel 2:28-30 in which the Spirit has been poured out upon all flesh and all can prophecy. So in the Age to Come, the knowledge of the LORD shall cover the earth as the water covers the beds of the seas. The Age to Come is an age of the Spirit. We partake of its realities now and are heralds of the coming age. As we are faithful to the divine mandate, we, as Peter says, hasten the day of his coming. So Messianic believers need to celebrate this feast with a real prophetic cutting edge in the Holy Spirit.

The Day of the blowing of the Shofar in the fall certainly looks forward to the return of Yeshua the Messiah. The preaching and teaching on this day should be full of last days meanings. If the shofar of I Thes. 4:16, 17 and I Cor. 15 is the same as the seventh trumpet in the book of Revelation, and I believe it is, then our service calls upon our people to be ready for his return, for our translation into glory, for the pouring out of the bowls of God's wrath, and for the establishment of his Kingdom. In the Jewish tradition, Rosh Hoshana looks toward the judgment of God. In the light of the book of Revelation, this certainly is a correct emphasis.

The fall cycle of feasts are tied together coherently in prophetic meaning. The return of the Messiah (Yom haShofar) leads to the fast of Yom Kippur. This is because his return produces the mourning and repentance in Israel spoken of in Zechariah 12:10, and the mourning over the face of the whole earth predicted in Matthew 24 and Revelation 1:7. Yet this great repentance is not without fulfillment, for there is a great fountain open for the cleansing of sin (Zech. 13) and the nations come to the knowledge of God. Hence Yom Kippur, for those who know Yeshua, is a feast of intercession for the salvation of Israel and the nations of the world. These prophetic meanings are a significant part of our celebration.

Once cleansing has taken place, we may celebrate the universal feast of God. Yom Kippur leads to the great feast of Sukkot in which the Kingdom of God is established all over the earth in the reign of the Messiah. All nations will send representatives to celebrate this feast. It is this feast, more than any other, which testifies that God is the provider and the King over all the earth. We who live in the reality of his Kingdom today look forward to the fullness of the Kingdom in the future.

Of course the Sabbath has great future reference. The Age to Come is the age of Shalom or peace over all the earth. It is the seventh age on earth in Jewish reckoning. It also is a foreshadowing of that bliss that belongs to those who are resurrected in the Messiah.

It is my firm belief that Messianic Jewish worship and celebration should reflect all of the multifaceted meanings of the feasts, but especially the meaning of fulfillment in Yeshua and the great work of God yet to come as predicted in these feasts. None of the feasts have been fulfilled in the sense of their meaning being already completed in history. There is more to come, even continuing unto the new heavens and the new earth.

THE RABBINIC SPIRIT AND MESSIANIC JUDAISM
Sometimes Messianic Jews, in seeking to recapture their

Jewish roots, become enamored of Ra' _inic custom and Rabbinic worship. Indeed I shared this tendency in the early days of my Messianic Jewish life. The first edition of *Jewish Roots* reflects a positive appreciation of some dimensions of classical Judaism that I can no longer endorse. I believe that the Spirit of God has definitely spoken to me about these matters, but unless the Spirit so speaks to the reader, my recounting of such experiences may not be particularly convincing. Therefore, I will try to put into reasons the leading of God in my life.

First of all, I have become convinced that Rabbinic Judaism is a more severe departure from Biblical faith than I had ever realized in my early days of Jewish recovery. Although there are good things to be found in Rabbinic Judaism, and true wisdom from the Rabbis need not be rejected, I believe that the heart essence of Rabbinic Judaism is the rejection of the prophetic Spirit that forms the essence of the Hebrew Scriptures and the New Covenant Scriptures. The atmosphere of the New Testament carried on the Spirit of the Hebrew Scriptures pervasively and profoundly. The essence of Rabbinism is a severe departure, replacing revelation with human reason. The rationalistic decisions of a majority of the rabbis using even hellenistic models of reasoning becomes authority in the Jewish community. This development preceded the coming of Yeshua (see M. Hengel, *Hellenism in Judaism*), and came to its full fruition when the first century Jewish religious leadership rejected the witness of Jewish Apostles. This witness which gave irrefutable testimony to the resurrection of Jesus and which was confirmed with extraordinary signs and wonders, made the generation of that day without excuse. Although God continues to love Israel and will call them to himself and will restore them to their Biblical roots, Rabbinic Judaism is the child of the first century pharisees who added the prayer of condemnation against Jewish believers and Jesus to the Synagogue liturgy. This all took place long before the Church become paganized and rejected its Jewish roots. Hence, as Jewish followers of Jesus, we must be very careful in copying the Synagogue as a source of identification. Can we be comfortable using the traditions of those who inherited the stance of those who rejected Yeshua? Some traditions are so Biblical by clear implication that we can answer, "yes." But for others we may well answer, "no." Furthermore, a Messianic Jewish congregation is a congregation of Jews and Gentiles in the Messiah that is rooted in its Jewish Biblical heritage and in which Jewish continuance is encouraged as willed by God. A Messianic congregation is not merely a national organization, but is a partaker of the international character of the people of God as well. We must therefore project ourselves as we truly are, not as a synagogue that is like other synagogues except that we have added Yeshua. We can not say too strongly, we who are Jewish are Biblical New Covenant Jews, not Rabbinic Jews!

How does this work out practically? First of all, I am convinced to no longer use post first century Rabbinic prayers. Prayer is the deepest chamber of intimacy with God. As good as a Rabbinic prayer may seem on the surface, I have to note that it was created by a people who said no to Yeshua. Indeed that beauty of the very prayer itself may produce an aesthetic satisfaction that covers the void in the life of a person who might otherwise seek Yeshua. The intimacy of our worship experience with God, I believe, must only include prayer material that we are convinced comes out of the faith community that was walking in the true revelation of God. Messianic Jews are therefore much more shut up to seeking God and creatively producing material that fully reflects the fullness of their faith.

Lest I be misunderstood, I should note that I am not saying that cultural traditions that have became universal usages of our people are to be discarded. Each custom needs to be prayerfully weighed as people are led by the Spirit. In my view there is much that is valid and remains. The simplicity of Jewish burial practices is so much more Biblical than western practices. Jewish dance, Jewish foods and the Hebrew language especially are certainly legitimate. Lighting eight lights during the time of Channukah, having Purim celebrations, plays, and readings while making great noise at the name of Hamen are worthwhile customs. Recognizing the stage of sexual development at the age of thirteen in a ceremony that gives young people a chance to profess faithfulness to the covenants and personal responsibility can be done meaningfully. Marrying under a hupah and drinking red covenantal wine to seal the wedding is ancient and worthy. We could go on and on. However, the prayer content at such events needs to truly reflect who we are in the Messiah.

With regard to worship, I see no problem in combining new Messianic music with old tunes. The forms of blessings and prayers are pre-first century. These forms can be filled with content that reflects our faith. However, we need to return to the Bible to express the fullness of what we believe. This means that all will be seen through a New Covenant perspective. A great bulk of Jewish worship consists of singing the Psalms and other parts of the Scripture. These aspects of Jewish worship belong to us and can be used as the Spirit leads. The section on Jewish worship in *Jewish Roots* needs to be revised with these considerations. I can no longer say that eighty per cent of the Siddur is Biblical as stated in *Roots*. However there is a great amount of material that simply consists of Biblical quotation and interweaving Biblical passages. This Biblical material along with pre-first century material may of course be used as the Spirit leads. The material in the Holiday and Festival prayer book includes much more material that is not Biblical but is the creation of the post first century Jewish community. I have great reservations about using such material and definitely prefer creating our own material in the forms of Jewish prayer and worship.

All Jewish practices need to be evaluated in the light of our faith and the leading of the Spirit. It is well to ask the question, "Is this the kind of practice that Messianic Jews would have likely come up with?" If the answer is "no," perhaps it is best we depart from it. We are not seeking to simply copy the synagogue. However, if the answer is "yes," we need not foolishly try to rid ourselves of what looks like the synagogue!

For example, would Messianic Jews have had such symbols as a seven branched candelabra and an eternal light? I believe it is not at all unlikely. Indeed, the Church adopted such symbols. Would the Messianic Jews have had an ark? I believe they did. We historically know that they read the Torah. In the first century Torahs were kept in an ark! Did they keep New Testament Scriptures in the Ark? We do not know. However, we do know that ancient eastern Churches that stem back to the Syrian Church have ark like structures in which they keep the Scriptures. Perhaps we will keep the whole Bible in the Ark with the Torah. The Torah, a scroll of the Prophets, and the New Covenant Scriptures may all be displayed in the Ark!

We know that the early Church fathers wore fringes. However, when togas were no longer in use, would Messianic Jews have developed a tallit? (Church vestments were developed with fringes.) Possibly they would have, but the fringes would have been blue as prescribed. They wouldn't have followed the Rabbinic prescriptions of tying the knots! However, there is a foundation for apt symbolism in the Biblical concept of a garment of praise. I would like to see our own distinct garments and fringes!

We need not be aesthetically impoverished because the Church and the Synagogue had 1800 years of creativity to come up with rich symbols and patterns and Messianic Jews have had an 1800 year decline, even a cessation from significant existence! Church and Synagogue developed many ideas and symbols that would naturally follow from the Bible. Where this is the case we may copy, reform, change and adapt as is fitting to what the LORD is leading us to do and to profess. We need not be lacking in a rich texture because those who preceded us in Church and Synagogue already created or adapted what we might have come up with!

How about the mazuzah? I believe that God really meant us to write his word on our doorposts or at least hang something upon which His words could be seen. Would a real appropriation of Biblical intentionality cause us to depart from Rabbinic applications in some cases while seeing in other cases that they sometimes hit upon what is right? I believe this is so.

Overall Messianic expression should be a full bodied expression of the New Covenant faith. It should be clearly apparent that we are not Rabbinic Jews! We must be fully up front concerning what we are and who we are. We must also avoid every temptation of pride that we might fulfill our servanthood calling in God. I believe that there is enough in the Bible with regard to Jewish calling, and enough creativity in the Spirit that we are in no danger of losing our identity because we leave behind post first century Rabbinic prayers and practices that are not in accord with the Spirit of the New Covenant. God did truly transfer his authority from the Sanhedrin to the Apostolic leaders of the New Covenant. We are Apostolic believers through and through who express our calling in Torah as applied to the New Covenant order of existence. Let our expression be truly in Spirit and truth and clear in intent in every way. We look to the Bible for the meaning of our identity or calling, not to the Synagogue. We seek to appropriate that which truly conveys life and truth.

DAVID STERN'S *A MESSIANIC JEWISH MANIFESTO*

Recently, my friend David Stern published a noteworthy book. Much of his content is complementary to our treatment. His call for an application of Torah in the New Covenant is similar to mine and is dear to my heart. However, I believe the tone is too positive concerning that which we have to gain from Rabbinic Judaism. Where his book veers from the comments above I would be critical. However, much within his book I highly recommend.

THE KINGDOM NOW MOVEMENT

Since the publication of *Jewish Roots,* a movement called the Kingdom Now Movement has gained great impetus in the Charismatic movement. In my home town of Washington, D.C., this movement has spread widely. I have sought to relate to these brothers in the faith since they are such a significant flow in the Charismatic Movement. They cannot be ignored. Some have wondered whether I have become a Kingdom Now person. Have I changed my theology? Let me assure you that my theology of the Kingdom is the same as reflected in this book. The Kingdom Now people have warmly and humbly received me and my criticism. Some have received the words of correction and some have not. I have come to them humbly both with agreement and disagreement. I have come as a brother with love.

It is still too early to know where this movement will head. Outsiders mistakenly think that this movement is all of a piece, but it is not so. Within this movement there are pre-millenialists (Jesus returns before he establishes a literal age of peace of earth), post-millenialists (Jesus returns after the Church has discipled the nations and ruled for an age), and a-millenialists (this is the age of Jesus' rule through the Church which will end with his return and the inauguration of the New Heavens and New Earth). Most of these folks are a-millenialists. Some brethren have dismissed the Kingdom Now people as heretics. However, every position these folks hold has been a classic position in the Church. Finney was a post-millenialist; some think Jonathan Edwards was as well. A-millenialism was the classic position of reformed theology.

The Kingdom Now people are held together not by a single eschatology, but by agreement in the following areas. First, they believe that the Kingdom has come in a significant sense with the coming of Jesus. Most do not believe that the Kingdom will come in fullness until the Lord returns. However, the post-millenial brethren, who have gained the most notoriety but are the minority, do believe that through the power of the Spirit the Church will establish a fullness of the Kingdom on earth before the return of Jesus.

George Ladd, in *Jesus and the Kingdom*, rightly hit the balance on this issue when he taught the New Testament perspective on the Kingdom is "already" but also "not yet." To blunt either the edge of the paradox is an error. Some

Kingdom Now people have reacted to dispensationalism and its emphasis on the future Kingdom to such an extent that they have lost the "not yet" dimension. This age is one in which the future age of God breaks in, but never fully until the return of Jesus. Of course, as a pre-millenialist, I would, in love, criticize the eschatology of my brethren who hold other viewpoints.

The Kingdom Now movement believes that it is not necessary to view the Church as declining in the end of this age. They look for a great revival and restoration of the true Church before Jesus comes. I believe that this emphasis is correct and Biblical according to Jesus' prayer in John 17 for the Church and the role of the Church in the last days in bringing Israel to God (Romans 11) and gaining a great harvest from all of the nations of the world.

The Kingdom Now movement believes that believers should demonstrate the principles of the Kingdom of God in every realm of life, not just in personal piety. Hence we are to be witnesses of righteousness in the business world, the world of government, the world of art, education, science, the family, medicine and much more. I agree with this emphasis. Actually, the Kingdom Now people have unknowingly recovered the Puritan revivalist perspective on many issues.

I am troubled by some trends in the Kingdom Now movement, however. At times, the emphasis on the role of the Church becomes so stressed that the role of Israel is lost from view. This is a serious problem since the future of Israel and the Church are bound together. The replacement theory, wherein the Church becomes the new and true Israel, replacing fully old national Israel, has made its reappearance in some Kingdom Now circles. (Even many of the Puritans saw a significant place for Israel and wrote concerning the crucial role of the Church in Israel's salvation leading to world redemption. *The Puritan Hope* by Murray deals with this.) Some do not realize that you can believe in God's covenant with Israel without being a dispensationalist. My comments in *Roots* on replacement theology deal with this issue.

Some Kingdom Now people have, in line with the above error, adopted a subjective mode of interpretation and have lost touch with authorial intent as the ultimate meaning of a text. This text meaning forms an objective basis for testing doctrine. Although the Spirit of God may say many things to many people through a text, doctrinal foundations must be based on the writer's intent in context. When a-millenial symbolic exegesis is combined with a revelatory subjective approach to the text, we could be in for great danger. The bedrock of authorial intent is crucial.

In dialogue with Kingdom Now people, some of these criticisms have been well received by some. It remains to be seen whether Messianic Jews can enter into loving dialogue with Kingdom Now folks for their and our mutual enrichment and correction. We need to approach these folks as brothers, not heretics, who have discovered much in the way of Biblical truth, but who need to hear and receive as well what God has shown us. I believe that the jury is still out on this movement. However, if they can recover a clear place for Israel in their theology, avoid being enamored with worldly success, and recover an emphasis on authorial intent for Biblical interpretation, the Kingdom Now people could bring significant revitalization to the whole Church. These folks dearly love the LORD and the moving of His Spirit. We must pray and trust that God will reveal more of his truth to them.

CHAPTER ONE

The Biblical Meaning of Israel

Torah Foundations

It is no accident or mistake that the Synagogue has given a special recognition to Torah, the first five Books of Moses. Some wrongly believe that the Synagogue thereby depreciates the value of the rest of the Bible. This is not the case. Rather, the early Jewish community properly sensed the *foundational* nature of Torah. The Torah records God's basic covenants with Israel; therefore, all further revelation must be in accord with these foundational revelations. Consistency to Torah-teaching was a standard by which further revelation was to be judged as God-given or not (Deuteronomy 13).

The Torah is the pivot of Judaism, for in the Torah is recorded the Creation, the Flood, the call of Abraham, the lives of the Patriarchs, the sojourn in Egypt, the rescue from Egyptian bondage and the revelation of the priestly sacrificial system which foreshadow the work of Messiah Himself. Any Messianic Jewish perspective, therefore, must be clear in its understanding of Torah and the early covenants God made with Israel. Our understanding is, of course, retrospective through the person of Yeshua; but it is an understanding that seeks to be fair to the original utility of the covenants as well.

The Call of Abraham

Jewish history begins with Abraham. Although the term *Jew* is derived later from the tribe of Judah, it has come to refer to all Israelites: the descendants of Jacob—or Israel—Abraham's grandson. God's covenant with Israel begins with Abraham, so we might say Abraham, in this sense, was the first Jew.

We know little of Abraham's early life. He came from Ur of the Chaldeans with his father, Terah; he settled in Haran, whence he was later called forth. Was Abraham's family completely "pagan?" Or did Abraham's family carry on a tradition of reverence for the living God, albeit distorted with certain pagan influences? These are questions we cannot now answer. We do know that there were some in the Middle East who worshipped the creator God—or the sky God above other gods—but we do not find any monotheists at this time.[1] We are on much firmer ground in seeking to understand, instead, *the nature* of God's call to Abraham.

Abraham recognized the voice of God and obeyed when he was told, "Go from your country and your kindred and your father's house to the land that I will show you" (Genesis 12:1). God came to Abraham with a call and command which he accepted: (v. 4) "So Abraham went as the Lord had told him." This first statement underscores tremendous promises. We read of seven: "I will make you a great nation; I will bless you; I will make your name great; you will be a blessing; I will bless those who bless you; him who curses you I will curse;" and "by you all the families of the earth will be blessed" (vv 1-3).

A nation must have a land. We soon find that the promise of land is part of the covenant material of these chapters. In Genesis 12:7, God says that He will give this land—the land of Israel—to Abraham's seed forever or as an everlasting possession. We consistently read that this promise is eternal (Genesis 13:14-15; 15:18; 17:19; 26:1-4; 28:12-14). The covenant is passed down through Abraham's son, Isaac, and then to Jacob—whose name was changed to Israel—and to his twelve sons.

God's covenant is offered by His grace, not as a response to works. From the recipient, God required faith, issuing in obedience. Hence we find that "Abraham believed the Lord and he reckoned it to him as righteousness" (Genesis 15:6). This verse becomes essential to New Testament teaching. Paul consistently shows that right standing with God is achieved by a faith response, not by works of self-righteousness and he points to this Abrahamic covenant as the key to this doctrine (Romans 4; Galatians 3). Of what did this faith consist? Firstly, it was a faith sufficient for Abraham to travel onward with God for the sake of the promise God had given. It was also manifest in the fact that Abraham believed God when told that his descendants would be as the stars of heaven when, as yet, his wife Sarah was barren.

The whole story of Abraham and the eventual birth of Isaac is miraculous and points to Messiah Yeshua. Isaac, like Yeshua, is the only son of his father, miraculously conceived, and offered up as a sacrifice to God for the sake of obedience to his Father and for the benefit of others (Genesis 22). Sarah was supernaturally enabled to bear this child just as Miriam (Mary) supernaturally conceived by God's Holy Spirit. What a joy to read these accounts and compare them, for Isaac, the ancestor of our Messiah, foreshadows Yeshua.

The practice of circumcision is also of note as part of the revelation of this covenant. Abraham is told that he is to circumcise all males in his household; all male children are to be circumcised the eighth day. Circumcision is a *sign* of the covenant of God with Abraham. As Paul argues, Abraham was justified before God gave this sign of the covenant. Circumcision is a sign of response to the covenant, not an act which makes us righteous with God. The same can be said of the new Covenant mikvah bath or baptism. Several things should be noted about circumcision which are crucial to understanding Messianic Judaism.

Circumcision is a sign of a gracious covenant that is astounding for its offer of grace and promise. Abraham's seed will be a blessing; his heirs will possess the land as an everlasting possession, etc. Hence, Paul, in Galatians, sees the Abra-

hamic Covenant as a statement of the good news in a way that
points to God's grace in Yeshua. This Abrahamic Covenant is
the primary covenant of God with Israel. As Paul rightly
argues, no later covenant (e.g., Mosaic) can annul the basic
principles of this covenant; the Abrahamic Covenant includes
the good news of God's salvation by grace (Galatians 3:8).
Circumcision is not only the sign of being under the Mosaic
"constitutional" covenant, but, rather, of being part of the
covenant of grace and the promise that God has given to
Israel!

Circumcision is performed on the penis. Nothing could be
clearer in showing that it was God's intention for this covenant to be carried on through Abraham's physical descendants. (We will later find that one can join the community of
Israel through conversion and assimilation into the national-
physical people). Circumcision emphasizes the national-
physical application of this covenant to Abraham's descendants. Only the male receives the covenant sign; for, in
ancient times, the father determined the religious identity of
his seed. When Israel took non-Israelite wives—with God's
approval—during the days of Joshua, the children were
automatically considered Israelites. Later Jewish thought
confuted this biblical precedent by identifying a child as Jewish through his mother, pointing both to the influence of a
mother on her children and Ezra's specific injunctions to the
Jews (fifth century B.C.E.) to put away their foreign wives.
Ezra's decision was a response to a specific problem and does
not change the essence of circumcision pointing to the father
as the source of covenant identity.

Eighth-day circumcision was a unique practice. Other
peoples practiced circumcision as a puberty rite signifying
the entrance of the male into adult life (a rite of passage).
Circumcision on the eighth day divorces the sign from the
rites of passage so that it has a distinct covenant meaning. The
children of Abraham exhibit the sign of the covenant of grace
from the eighth day. It is amazing to note that the eighth day
is the safest day for infant circumcision, for on this day the body
possesses a superior blood-clotting ability.

We might note that circumcision in these Scriptural passages (Genesis 17) is four times called an everlasting sign, an unconditional sign to be performed as a covenant-sign forever among Jewish people who affirm God's covenant with the house of Israel. To forego this sign is to deny that we are part of Israel. Israel, in its identity, is the people descended from Abraham who are given the promise of land and blessing and the promise of bringing a blessing to the world. It is a covenant of grace. Israel is a nation constituted and preserved by God's covenant promise; this, we believe, is the central meaning of Israel's identity. We cannot forego the physical sign of these truths (circumcision) without foregoing our part in the meaning of Israel.

This, of course, leads to a question: Does Israel retain a special meaning under God's covenant promises? If so, what is that meaning? This question will occupy a major part of our attention.

No New Testament passage confutes the continuation of the Abrahamic Covenant, an unconditional and everlasting covenant. As Paul says, "the gifts and call of God are irrevocable"; Israel remains "beloved for the father's sake" (Romans 11:28-29). The salvation of individual Jews is not assured simply by their being part of Israel, but Israel, as a nation, still is part of this covenant which promises to give and receive blessing, preservation, land and purpose as a national instrument of God's purposes.

We need to emphasize that God's choice of Abraham—and Israel—was not for a narrow or limited purpose. Rather, His blessing for the whole world is the keynote. Israel might be chosen, but that choice is for service, to bring blessing to all. The covenant is universally inclusive. Traditionally, the choice of special individuals or nations was called the "scandal of particularity," for the human mind recoiled at such unfair privilege. Yet the "scandal of particularity" is the way with a truly historical faith. God works through people, accommodating Himself to people and situations in ways we cannot fully fathom. Even the Church, although universal in scope, moved out from Jerusalem and spread to others over time within the limitations of travel and communication. Those who were near to Jerusalem had an advantage. The scandal is here as well. Messianic Jews—although one with all believers—are criticized because the flesh of man recoils at a chosenness that is not theirs, even if it is for the purpose of service and even if it is accompanied by trial and suffering. Hence, some criticism arises because the Messianic Jew sees himself as part of the universal people of God, while yet playing a role in God's purposes through the nation Israel.

THE MOSAIC REVELATION

The patriarchs died and the descendants of Israel found themselves in bondage to a king who did not know their ancestor, Joseph. This grievous slavery of the chosen people is the background setting for the Mosaic revelation. The revelation was an incredible demonstration of God's grace and salvation. Part of this revelation was a new national covenant from God, found in Exodus 20, Leviticus 19-26 and the whole of Deuteronomy. This covenant did not alter nor do away with the earlier Abrahamic Covenant; but it provided a constitution for the ancient nation. Hence all of the Mosaic revelation—Exodus, Leviticus, Numbers, and Deuteronomy— takes on the character of covenant literature, recording God's work and His will for Israel.

It is significant that God's historic revelation is manifested through a program to rescue a dispossessed slave people. The consistent picture of God revealed in the events of the Exodus—as well as by the prophets—is a God who cares for the poor, the needy, the dispossessed, the aged, the orphaned and the widowed, that is, for all who are defenseless, God is their defender. Yeshua Himself announces His ministry in these terms, quoting Isaiah: "The Spirit of the Lord is upon me, because he hath anointed me to preach the gospel to the poor; he hath sent me to heal the broken-hearted, to preach deliverance to the captives, and recovering of sight to the blind, to set at liberty them that are bruised . . ." (Luke 4:18).

The Mosaic legislation which followed the Exodus gives

special attention to strangers, for Israel was a stranger in Egypt (Leviticus 19:33, Psalm 69:32-33). Although Christians have often heard of the legal stringency of the Mosaic revelation, it is incumbent upon Messianic Jews to point out the incredible level of compassion found in the Mosaic revelation as well.

The exodus events began with the call of Moses. God revealed His name to Moses, stating that he would always be known as the God of Abraham, Isaac, and Jacob (Exodus 3). Further revelation of God's name is given in response to Moses' request so that the people might believe him. God here reveals Himself in the phrase variously translated "I Am Who I Am," or "I act as I act," or "I am He who causes to be."

Interpretations of this passage are myriad.[3] It is probable, however, that God was not speaking of His eternity (a Greek concept) but of His nature as defined by all His actions in revelation. He is the God of revelation. This phrase is caught up in meaning with the covenant name of God, spelled with the consonant yod, he, vav, he, a name that Jews do not pronounce. This is the most prevalent name of God in Scripture, especially when Scripture speaks of God in His Covenant context.

The Exodus story continues with the well-known accounts of Moses going to Pharoah. He demands the release of his people, and, under instruction from God, calls down plagues upon Egypt. Finally, when the magicians can no longer duplicate the plagues—especially the death of all first born males in the land of Egypt—Pharoah lets the Israelites go.

The plagues, although grievous physical trials to the Egyptians, represent far more: The plagues undercut faith in the Egyptian gods and show the powerlessness of the Egyptian gods to protect Egypt from the God of Israel. The Nile, for example, is a "god"; it turns rancid. Hupi is the frog "god" and Egypt is given enough frogs to feast on frog legs for decades to come! The sun is a chief "god"; it is blotted out by darkness. Most alarming is the death of the first born—especially of Pharoah's own first born—who would have been considered an incarnation of the sun god!

Egyptian religion was a very sophisticated pagan ritual of magic and superstition. Egypt was the most powerful nation of that age. Therefore, the exodus of this enslaved people was truly a defeat of paganism, of all false gods of all superstition and magic, a defeat authored by the one Creator—God! The defeat of Egypt and its gods by the Israelites could only lead to the conclusion that God is the Lord of all the earth. The exodus of Israel struck terror into the hearts of the decadent, utterly corrupt Canaanite peoples whom Israel was to conquer.

The Passover in which Israel escaped the angel of death who destroyed Egypt's first born also teaches a great lesson, since it was the blood on the door posts from a sacrificial lamb which caused the angel of death to pass over Israelite homes. Within these homes, the families ate lamb meat and fellowshipped with God and one another. Nothing speaks quite like the Passover in regard to sacrificial blood being the means of avoiding the penalty of death for sin.

And so Israel leaves Egypt, crosses through the sea miraculously, and the pursuing Egyptians drown as the parted waters return!

The Exodus foreshadows the greatest act of God's grace in all of history, Yeshua's death and resurrection: It is the event which foreshadows the exodus from sin and death experienced by all Yeshua's followers (I Corinthians 10:1-4).

Because the Exodus was an event whereby God worked through a nation to defeat the nations and paganism, it is to us a symbol and foretaste of the future world redemption spoken of by the prophets.

Well do the psalmists recount the Exodus as a totally unique event of world history (Psalm 46:8-11, Psalm 47:8-10— vv. 7-9 in some versions). Who ever heard of a rag-tag bunch of slaves defeating the mightiest nation in the world! Of all the events of Israel's history, the Exodus becomes the pivotal, formative event in Israel's concept of God: God is gracious and merciful. Israel's judgment, declared by the prophets, is not primarily a condemnation for breaking the law; rather Israel's breaking of the law is symptomatic of her spurning God's love and grace.

The Exodus is at the heart of the Torah, just as God's love and grace is at the heart of the Exodus. This is the true and full nature of the Mosaic revelation and the whole of the Tenach (Old Testament).

As we continue in the Book of Exodus we read the history of Israel's approach to the promised land, the tragedies of rebellion, and, in Numbers, the refusal to enter and possess the land of Canaan. Forty years of wandering followed. This history, as well as legislative material, is part of the covenant documents found from Exodus through Deuteronomy. God desired the behavior and faith of future generations under His covenants to be based on the revealed lessons of history: the accounts of His grace and the disaster following the unfaithfulness of the people. In this history we begin to discern the purpose of God for choosing Israel both to fulfill His promise to Abraham and to be a blessing to the nations. This supersedes Israel's purpose as an instrument of judgment. Israel illustrates God's truth.

Hence we read in Exodus 19:6 that God chose Israel to be a kingdom of priests. What is the function of a priest? The priest is a mediator between God and man. Nothing could be more foolish than to say that Judaism sees no need of a mediator. The whole Torah and its system of priests interceding for the people with sacrifices refutes this gross untruth. By his mediation the priest brought God and the people together. Therefore, if Israel's purpose was to be *a nation* of priests, then she is to be a national mediator between God and the peoples of the world. She was to bring the nations to God and God to the nations. How? By being a nation under God, under His rule or Covenant, so that life would be blessed, just and healthy. Remember, Israel was promised none of the diseases of Egypt if she followed the Covenant; no, she was promised prosperity and joy!

God desired there to be a nation among the nations to demonstrate His lordship. And He has never changed this purpose. He created nations with their variety; but nations

need to come under His lordship (Acts 17:26). The purpose of
the universal Church is different: The Church is not (strictly
speaking) a nation; rather it is a people-movement that transcends all nations gathered from all nations.

God, however, has never given up His purpose of preserving a nation among the nations to demonstrate His
lordship.

As Walter Kaiser stated, "He will yet have victory over
the nations through Israel"![4]

This, of course, brings us to the nature of the Mosaic
revelation. We have already showed the centrality of the
Exodus to the whole of this revelation. However, in recent
years it has been shown by biblical scholars that there are—
within the books from Exodus through Deuteronomy—
specific "covenant documents." Central among these documents are Exodus 20 (the Ten Commandments), Leviticus
19-26 (the holiness code) and the whole Book of Deuteronomy.
The other laws and instructions in the books are expansions
and additions to these basic covenant materials and are to be
understood in the light of these inspired covenants. The present writer is firmly convinced that the work of George Men-
denhall and Meridith Kline in this field should revolutionize
our understanding of the Torah and that we can never again
see Torah as providing us with a "dispensation of law" in the
sense of a legalistic system of works-righteousness.

The Covenant documents within Exodus through
Deuteronomy provide Israel with a *national constitution*
under God, a treaty between God and the nation. This treaty
is the basis for Israel's morality and social-legal system as
well as its system of worship, priesthood and sacrifice. Every
nation has a social-legal system. However, Israel's system is
totally unique. Kline demonstrates that the structure of the
Covenant documents, especially Exodus 20 and Deuteronomy (which is a revised Covenant treaty given before Israel
entered the land), parallel the structure of other treaty documents from the 15th century B.C.E. Furthermore, he
showed that this structure carries with it meanings which
enhance our understanding of the whole Bible. These mean-

ings would have been apparent to the generation which received the Torah, but are hidden to modern readers. A cardinal rule of biblical interpretation is that we must interpret the Scriptures according to their historically intended meaning, as given to the people to whom they were originally addressed. This is the only objective control restricting us from interpreting the Scriptures however we like.

The true meaning of Scripture is discovered through the original languages in the context of culture in which the concepts of that language found their meaning. When Scripture is thus understood, its application to us becomes clear.

The following paragraphs are an attempt to properly understand Torah in this way. What is the structure of the 15th century B.C.E. treaties which help us define the terminology and conceptual nature of the Torah?

The first characteristic of the 15th century B.C.E. treaty form is the fact that the king of a powerful nation offered a treaty to the other nations under its influence. The treaty was always couched as a gracious offer to be under the rule of the ancient king, called a suzerain. The king may have been a heartless tyrant. However, the form of the treaty required that he appear to be a gracious, benevolent ruler. Hence the deeds of the ruler for the people were first recounted. On the basis of the king's grace, the subject people were expected to respond in faith and obedience. This obedience included respect for and obedience to the king's governing representatives. The treaty went on to describe the great benefits of obedience, that is, the blessings that would follow. It also emphasized the great punishment which the king would bring upon his disobedient subjects, called *cursings*. We can see how such a treaty was an ideal form for God's communication, since God truly was the beneficent king who saved Israel by grace and called Israel as a nation to faith and obedience. Such a treaty context is an ideal setting for Israel's national legislation which includes the heights of the call for love in human relationships, "love thy neighbor as thyself," as well as everything from the judicial system; a means for the redistribution of wealth; honesty in business; and to care for the poor, the needy, the orphan, the widow and the stranger. The religious sacrificial sytem which is integrally related to this whole constitution also finds its meaning in this context.

It is fascinating to see the parallels in covenant form in these treaties and in the Book of Deuteronomy and the Exodus 20 passage (the Ten Commandments). The whole of the Book of Deuteronomy fits the ancient treaty form precisely. It begins with a *preamble* 1:1-5. The preamble is simply the introductory paragraph such as "We the people of the United States . . ." The *second section* is the *historical prologue*— 1:6—4:49. The prologue is a brief summary history which, in the ancient treaties, recalled the gracious work of the ancient king (suzerain) for the people. In Deuteronomy's case, the acts of God's grace are recalled as well as the history of the response of the people. This prologue recounts the mighty exodus from Egypt, God's provision of supernatural food in the wilderness (manna), the people's rebellion against God and Moses as well as God's judgment (disciplinary measures) and mercy (forgiveness). The historical prologue of Deuteronomy contrasts with other treaties by the nature of its content. It tells what God the Creator did for Israel. This recounting of God's grace provides the ground and motivation for Israel's response of faith and obedience. Hence the *third section*, the *stipulations of the covenant*. Within this section are included the basic call to love and trust God, the Sh'ma (Deuteronomy 6:4 ff), the Ten Commandments (Deuteronomy 5), and the necessity of recalling that God's work for Israel was by grace and because of His faithfulness to the patriarchal promises. Israel was never to think that its inheritance came by its own power or righteousness (Deuteronomy 8-10). Provisions were also given for a central place of worship (Deuteronomy 12) to unite the nation in the worship of one God under the administration of the priests who had charge of the sacrificial system and the teaching of Torah to the nation. The rest of this section of Deuteronomy includes a basic summary of national legislation and moral guidance given through Moses. Provision is also given for testing prophets (Deuteronomy 13, 18) who will call the nation to Torah faithfulness, as well as declare God's leading for the nation's future.

The *fourth section* is the *blessings and cursings* section. Israel's faithfulness and obedience will be richly blessed! Her land will be fruitful, many children will be born, and disease and plagues will be kept from the land. Foreign domination will be prevented. A life with God will produce a nation without fear because of the profound security provided by God. Disobedience, however, will be followed by the very opposite of these blessings: fear, insecurity, plagues, famine, foreign domination, destruction and the scattering of the nation. This section also includes the call for the nation to ratify this treaty—upon entering the land—with specific provisions for a ceremony of ratification which is later recorded in the Book of Joshua.

A most fascinating contrast to other treaties in this section is the paragraph on *witnessing to the treaty*. The ancient king called upon the gods of both nations to witness the treaty and to fulfill the blessings and cursings. The true God, however, has none higher than Himself by which to swear. Hence the treaty calls heaven and earth to witness!

We can see that Deuteronomy is a Mosaic summary given by God as an appropriate recounting of events and instruction before the departure of Moses and Israel's entrance into the land. It thus includes many provisions already given in Exodus through Numbers and is the context in which all previous national legislation is to be understood.

The last section of the treaties includes *succession arrangements*. It provides for covenant continuity by requiring the deposit of the treaty in the Temple and requiring regular public reading. It also includes the passing of leadership from Moses to Joshua.

It should also be noted that in the treaties of the other nations the sin of rebellion is seen as seeking to be free of the lordship of the king or suzerain. This is also the case in Torah; that rebellion is not defined as following another human leader, but as all forms of idolatry—subtle or blatant—

including all occult arts, witchcraft, sorcery, divination and spiritualism, which is consulting with other gods (Deuteronomy 19).

The reason we belabor a summary of the structure of Deuteronomy is to provide a context for truly understanding the Torah. *Since Torah is central to Judaism, a Messianic Jew must gain an accurate understanding of Torah in general if he is to know how to relate his Jewish heritage to Christian theology.* It is essential for integrating the Tenach (Old Testament) and the New Testament into a balanced understanding in which biblical revelation can be properly seen as a whole and in which Torah is not dismissed because of debates which arose from new contexts. This will become clearer as we proceed.

Scholars also point out that Exodus 20 is a covenant treaty document. Our understanding of ancient treaties has greatly improved our understanding of this chapter. To be emphasized most is the opening statement, "I am the Lord thy God, who brought you out of the land of Egypt, out of the house of bondage." The grace of God precedes the commandment and is the motivation for obedience. Blessings and curses are distributed within the document rather than coming at the end. What is of greatest note is the new understanding of the reason for two tablets and for the Sabbath command: Traditionally, it was thought that the commands were divided into two sections, the first having to do with commands in relation to God and the second concerning our relationship to man. This is probably not the case. Rather, our duties to God and man are inseparably related. All of the commands should be thought of as being on one tablet. Indeed, the tablets were probably duplicates! Why? Ancient covenant documents were always made in duplicate. One copy was placed in the temple of the subject nation. Thus the gods of both nations would be called on to witness the covenant and to execute justice if it was violated. The two tablets in Israel were both to be deposited in the Ark in the holiest place in the tabernacle. The Temple of God, the great Suzerain and of Israel, the subject people, was the same. God is the divine witness. One tablet is the copy for the people and one tablet, symbolically, is God's.

The other clarification comes in relation to the Sabbath Command. It is hoped that Messianic Judaism can bring some light to the debate on the Sabbath. It has been thought strange by some that God would place the Sabbath at the center of His lofty commands which deal with the highest dimensions of morality. How is it that there is then this intrusion of a *ritual* command? Christian responses have run the gamut from: (1) those who hold that none of these commands are obligatory for Christians since they are "no longer under law, but grace"; the Spirit produces a parallel morality in Christians called the "law of Christ"—dispensationalists—to (2) adventists who hold that the Sabbath command is as lofty and moral as the other nine and goes back to the creation of the world. Paul King Jewett, in a recent book, argues that although seventh day observance is not necessary, the principle of a day of rest and worship for religious and humanitarian purposes is absolutely necessary, but that it is appropriate that it be on Sunday for Christians. Unfortunately, the whole debate has lost sight of a contextual understanding of the Sabbath command.[6]

The Sabbath reflects the pattern of God's creative work in the beginning; or, in the words of Jewish liturgy, it is a memorial of creation. Secondly, it is the first of the feasts in memorial praise of the exodus from Egypt and the establishment of Israel as a free nation under God. Sabbath, however, is an integral part of God's treaty between Himself and Israel. Although there may be marvelous applications from a humanitarian and religious point of view for Christians, we need first to understand the covenant context.

The Sabbath is called a sign "between me and the people of Israel." In the ancient covenants the center of the treaty would bear a symbol or sign of the king—suzerain—which might have been related to his chief god. However, no representation of God could be made in ancient Israel. Therefore, the respresentation would not be a symbol, a picture, or an idol, but a unique cycle of life. Only Israel had a

seven-day cycle of weeks. We do not sense today how unique
Israel truly was, for the seven-day week has since become
the practice of the world.

This seven-day cycle—with rest and worship on the last
day—was a unique testimony to the covenant relationship
between God and Israel. Hence, the whole of the commands
are part of a *covenant* with Israel, and although we can discern the universal principles of this treaty which apply to all
peoples (as Paul's quoting "Honor your mother and father" to
the Ephesians), the treaty is an indivisible whole as given to
Israel; Sabbath-keeping is just as much a part of this treaty as
"Thou shalt not kill." To spurn the Sabbath as a covenant sign
was to spurn the covenant and the special relationship
between God and the nation Israel. Certainly, huge questions
arise from this discussion. Are the Mosaic covenants still valid
and in effect as a covenant? If not, are there principles that
transcend the Mosaic constitution and apply today? If so,
which ones? Is the Sabbath one of these principles? We shall
address these questions later. Suffice it to say at this point that
the practice of Sabbath celebrates the escape from Egypt, the
establishment and the worship of God as creator of Israel, *all
of which were promised in the Abrahamic Covenant as well
as found in the Mosaic economy.*

Our emphasis heretofore has been on an understanding
of the Mosaic constitution as a gracious constitution offered
by a God of grace. It was to provide Israel with the most
exemplary and humanitarian social system that had been
seen on earth. It was to enable a walk in forgiveness and
fellowship with God through the Temple-sacrificial system.
Israel would thus be a light to the nations, a kingdom of
priests who bring the nations closer to God.

This emphasis might seem strange to Jewish and Christian readers who have hitherto seen Torah in mostly a legalistic framework, although Jewish scholars have pointed out
the error of this common concept. Samuel Schultz, the
Samuel Robinson professor of Old Testament at Wheaton
College, had admirably sought to present the truth to the
Christian layman. In his commentary on Deuteronomy,

Deuteronomy, the Gospel of God's Love, and in the *Gospel of Moses*[7], he has argued convincingly for the gracious nature of the Torah. His thesis is that in every covenant grace is behind the "offer." Faith and love are the primary responses which lead to obedience. So Yeshua taught that our love for Him was proved by our obedience to His commandments. This is repeated in First John and throughout the New Testament. Nor is there any room, argues Schultz, for the idea of a harsh, vindictive God of justice in the Old Testament to be contrasted with a God of love and mercy in the New. Love and mercy are always offered before judgment is rendered. Yeshua's warnings concerning judgment in the New Testament are as severe as anything in the Old, even if we argue that the highest personal revelation of God's love is seen in Yeshua!

This has great implications for our understanding of the New Testament as well. For example, is Paul's argument really with the Law of Moses? Or is Paul's argument with a *system of righteousness before God by works*—a prideful approach to God—which was prevalent in some quarters in first-century Judaism? As George Ladd argues, this system developed in the intertestamental period (300 B.C.E. to 50 C.E.) and was a misunderstanding of the true nature of Torah.[8] Our view is that Paul's argument is with the Law *as a system of merit* and with the forcing of Jewish practice and identity upon non-Jews. This whole question will be addressed in the chapter on Paul, Israel, and the Law.

We must close this section by discussing the sacrificial system. The sacrificial system is a pervasive part of the Torah. As such, it must not be summarily dismissed by moderns. There were several different kinds of sacrifice (see Leviticus 1-7). Some symbolized total dedication in which the whole animal was burned as an offering. Others emphasized expiation for sin. Here, part of the sacrifice was burned—the smoke ascending God-ward—and part was eaten by the priest as mediator. The sin was therefore dissolved through the sacrifice and in the priest's eating. Another sacrifice was eaten by the offerer, the peace offering symbolizing communion with

God through a fellowship meal.

Sometimes combinations of sacrifices were offered, one following another. It is crucial to note the most prominent common aspects of the sacrifices: First is the substitutionary aspect. Because the offerer is willing, by faith, to identify with the animal in repentance, acknowledging his sin as well as sin's destructive nature, he is forgiven. Because God is merciful, He accepts the *identified-with-symbol* in place of the offerer's punishment *if true repentance is present*. All of this has great value for understanding the sacrifice of Yeshua, who is God's greatest love revelation and our *identification-with-symbol*. He alone ties together the central meanings of man, God, repentance, sin-bearing love and forgiveness.

Several feasts in addition to the Sabbath were instituted as part of Israel's national existence. The most prominent is Passover (Pesach), the others are Succot and Shavuot. Yom Kippur is a special day of prayer, fasting and repentance.

Israel as a nation, faithful to God, could rely on His protection. She was not to enter into protective alliances with other nations; for this would not only imply a lack of faith in God, but would, according to the customs of the times, require the sharing of their gods. *All of these stipulations were extraordinary.* They point to the supernatural character of Torah's revelation, and would indeed make Israel a unique light to the nations. It was the breaking of the covenant by attitude and deed that brought the message of the prophets, a message of judgment, mercy and hope.

THE FUNCTION OF THE PROPHETS

The layman assumes that the primary purpose of a prophet is to foretell the future. This is certainly not the case with biblical prophets, although we must not adopt the extreme position of some who neglect the fact that biblical prophets did, at times, foretell future events.

The biblical prophet was primarily a servant of the covenant whose main purpose was *to speak forth the Word of God*. Forthtelling is more primary than foretelling. The Word of God was addressed to the people in an immediate situation, but had relevance to all future generations. Further, the message of the prophets was generally to call the people back to covenant faithfulness—or Torah. If the people repented, God's blessing would follow; but if they did not, punishment was a likely consequence. The message of the prophets was echoed in the Torah. From Amos' lofty messages concerning social justice to Malachi's call for a right heart attitude, the prophets extended the basic principles of the love of God and one's neighbor as set forth in Torah. In the midst of national failure, the prophet looked forward to a New Covenant, enabling greater obedience and faithfulness. The days of the Messiah would bring forth a perfect social order in which love and justice would dominate and war and poverty would cease (Isaiah 2, 11).

Predictions abound, but within a specific context: The predictions foresaw specific judgments, as well as an ensuing Age of Peace. Some predictions were present signs while others related to the distant future beyond this age. The prophet predicted because he heard from God who is the Lord of history. His whole message must come from his gift of hearing God's Word. The work of God's anointed everlasting King, the Messiah, was also described.

A major cause of prophetic concern was Israel's idolatry. Partially the result of accommodation to the spirit of the age, and partially the result of Israel's entering into protective alliances, idolatry threatened to destroy the very reason for Israel's existence. Sharing each other's gods was an ingredient in the alliances of ancient times which was not allowed for faithful Israelites. Hence these alliances were not an option for Israel.

Deuteronomy 13 and 18 give the basic tests for a true prophet. The tests are not exhaustive, but central. One is that the prophet's predictions must come to pass. The other is more central; the prophet's message must be in accord with the teachings of Torah. If his predictions are true but he incites Israel to unfaithfulness to Torah he is stoned; he is a prophet whose powers are not from God but from an evil source.

The Jewish tradition has venerated the Torah above all other revelation. The reason for this is clear: Torah is foundational; all other revelation is to be tested by its consistency to Torah. Therefore, although all Scriptures are inspired by God, Torah is clearly foundational. This has vast implications for our understanding of the New Testament. Any interpretation of the New Covenant Scriptures which is *inconsistent* with the revelation in the Torah cannot be true. Such interpretations lend credence to the Jewish rejection of the New Testament, for there is no revelation that can be accepted if it is inconsistent with Torah; this is the clear implication of Deuteronomy 13. Therefore, Jewish heritage venerates the Torah—Genesis through Deuteronomy—as the foundational Scriptural revelation.[9]

THE PROMISE OF A NEW COVENANT

The promise of a New Covenant was anticipated by the Torah itself. Before Israel had even entered the land, Moses foresaw the nation's faithlessness toward God's Covenant. Indeed, the Book of Deuteronomy called for a circumcision of the heart (Deuteronomy 30:4-6) from which the calloused flesh of the heart would be cut away and an attitude of yielding love and obedience toward God would ensue. But as Israel's history progressed, its continued failure prepared the prophets to receive revelation of something more to come. Israel was depleted by idolatry. First, the nation was split into north and south; then came the captivity of the Northern tribes and an end to their national existence. Finally, in 586 B.C.E., the national life of the Southern Kingdom ended as the King of Babylon conquered the last vestiges of the nation.

The prophets spoke God's Word in the context of these tragic events: Joel foresaw an age in which the power of the Spirit of God would be universally given to all (Joel 2:28-29). Most striking, however, were the parallel promises in Jeremiah and Ezekiel of a New Covenant to be offered to Israel. Jeremiah ministered to the last remnant of people in the land of Israel before their final demise in 586 B.C.E. Meanwhile, Ezekiel ministered simultaneously in Babylon to those taken captive. Despite the seeming hopelessness due to Israel's national demise and the failure of Israel in its call of God, both prophets predicted a resurrection of Israel's national life. The dry bones vision in Ezekiel 37 and Jeremiah's prediction of a limited 70-year exile gave hope. Israel would live (*Am Yisrael Hai*).

Both Ezekiel and Jeremiah predicted a New Covenant (B'rit Hadashah). Messianic Jews believe that B'rit Hadashah has been established by the life, death and resurrection of Yeshua. However, not all the features of this New Covenant have yet been fulfilled. As regards to the presence of the Kingdom, only a partial—but central—part of the New Covenant has come into being; for Jeremiah predicts that all Israelites shall personally know God through and as part of this covenant. It is not our purpose in this section to fully outline the relationship of previous covenants to the New Covenant; this will be a major theme of chapters 2-4 of this book. It is only our purpose now to lay out the structure of this New Covenant in its original context as background material for future exposition. Our outline comes from Jeremiah 31 and Ezekiel 36.

The New Covenant is, first, with the house of Israel and Judah (Jeremiah 31:31). The Messianic Age does indeed include gentiles who have fellowship with God in an age of Israel's full restoration; but an offer of salvation to the gentiles is not in clear view in these passages.

Secondly, the covenant will be *different* from the *Mosaic* Covenant which God offered after the exodus.

Third, this difference is expressed as God's law or Torah being written on the hearts of the people of the nation (Jeremiah 31:33). Ezekiel says "a new heart will I give you; and I will take out of your flesh the heart of stone and give you a heart of flesh. . . ." (36:26-27). After adding the fourth and fifth features, he continues with the promise that God will cause them to walk in "my statutes and be careful to observe my ordinances." The New Covenant is therefore not an abrogation of Torah but an ability to walk *in* Torah! What a contrast to common teachings today! However, is it Torah in the general sense of God's ways (which is reflected in the Books of Moses) or is it the whole Mosaic system? Abraham, in Genesis 26:5, was said to obey God's charge, command-ments, statutes and laws. The rabbis debated whether or not Torah would be altered in the Messianic Age. Some thought that parts of the Torah had a temporary relevance to an imperfect people, but that in the Messianic Age we would be so close to God that Torah would be altered to fit this situa-tion. This problem will be discussed later.

Ezekiel adds a fourth promise: that we would have a new spirit. This is parallel to receiving a new heart. Fifth, God would put His Spirit within us.

Sixth, the New Covenant includes the promise that Israel would dwell in its own land in safety and security (Ezekiel 24-28). *God's name will be glorified/magnified among the nations* through His work in Israel as a nation. What a contrast for those who hold that the New Covenant does away with national Israel!

Seventh, the reception of the New Covenant will bring forgiveness of sin and cleansing from iniquity (Jeremiah 31:34, Ezekiel 36:25), whereby Israel will be God's people and God will be Israel's Lord.

Clearly the prophets, in contrasting this covenant to the Mosaic, knew the extent to which this covenant *would en-able the fulfillment of God's purposes for Israel*. Was for-giveness offered under the Mosaic system? Yes. Was there an ability to love and do God's law? Yes, if we are to believe David's meditation in Psalms 19 and 119. Yet even David had grievously sinned.

The New Covenant would come with a *power* of for-giveness previously unknown. The Spirit would be given in a direct and powerful way to all, never before known. This would enable a real knowledge of God in changed hearts to an *extent* and at a *degree* never before known. This cove-nant would be fully effective in producing the resulting life which the Mosaic Covenant could not. How utterly exciting is the hope of the prophets! This New Covenant is offered in

Yeshua ha Mashiach, Jesus the Messiah!

ISRAEL'S CELEBRATIONS

Israel's year was to be punctuated by marvelous annual celebrations. All of them were occasions of great thanksgiving as well as times for additional sacrifices related to atonement, forgiveness and dedication.

Leviticus 23 gives an outline of these special times. The Sabbath has already been described. Though a weekly feast, Sabbath was considered the most prominent holy day other than Yom Kippur. Pesach (Passover) and the Feast of Unleavened Bread were also prominent. Passover was the great annual commemoration of the events connected to Israel's exodus from Egypt. The feast recalls how the angel of death passed over the homes of the Israelites who had the passover lamb's blood upon their doorposts. The meal of bitter herbs commemorates the bitter life of slavery from which Israel was freed. The lamb is a meal parallel to the Exodus meal and the unleavened bread parallels the unleavened bread eaten when Israel left Egypt. The people left in such haste that the bread had no time to rise.

This is Israel's independence day. Since the exodus was God's means of establishing the nation, Passover as well as the other holy days, were to be celebrated "forever and to all your generation" (l'olam v'ed) by the nation.

It is possible that the "forever" referred to a people under the Mosaic sacrificial system, and that once the sacrificial system was replaced, the "forevers" were of no further legal import, since the Mosaic system was no longer in force. After all, the sacrifices under the Aaronic priesthood were also commanded to be carried on forever. How, then, shall we evaluate the "forever" commands?

Although the "forevers" are all to be taken seriously, there is another dimension for understanding Israel's feasts—which is especially apparent in regard to Passover. *Although the feasts are part of the Mosaic system, they are also indissolubly tied to the Abrahamic Covenant.* The Abrahamic Covenant promised a nation to Abraham and the Exodus was

a means of fulfilling the promise. Passover is the celebration
of the fulfillment of the promise to Abraham! If we take the
Abrahamic Covenant seriously—holding that Israel is promised the land and that Israel is still chosen of God as a
nation—it is then inconsistent to do away with celebrations
of the fulfillment of God's promises to Abraham.

The other feasts are celebrations of Israel's national life
under God in fulfillment of God's promise to Abraham.
They are a unique part of Israel's calling and identity as a
nation called of God.

Assemblies of the people usually begin and end most
feasts. The feast of First Fruits, directly following Passover,
includes an offering of the first products of the earth to God.
By it the whole of Israel's produce is acknowledged as God's,
His gift to the people.

Shavuot is the feast of the first harvest. It is a thanksgiving feast which comes fifty days after Passover. It later
became associated with the time of God's giving of the Torah.
It is no accident that God also gave His Spirit to Yeshua's first
followers on this day, beginning a spiritual harvest through
the Holy Spirit who would enable the Torah to be written
upon our hearts. Shavuot is thus a feast of the Spirit as well.

Succot is the third major feast. Its significance is agricultural as well as historical, for this feast celebrates in thanksgiving the final harvest of the year. Israel is to dwell in tents
or booths during a seven-day period. A great assembly follows. This practice recalls the wilderness wanderings of the
nation. Israel had no material possessions; trust in God was
her only recourse. Wonderfully, Israel was supernaturally
given food (manna) as well as the miracle whereby her clothing did not wear out. God instituted Succot so that Israel
might always remember that "adonai yeera"—God is the
provider. In their own homes and lands, Israel's citizens are
to remember that their existence depends upon God's grace,
not upon their own wealth or efforts. Succot is also a time of
great sacrifices of thanksgiving, a truly joyous and festive
occasion.

Israel's feasts are *all of grace*: God's grace in the Exodus miracle, God's grace in the harvest pro sions and God's grace in providing for all our needs. No taint of legalism is intended. *The feasts are also great didactic lessons for each generation so that Israel's history is given reality in successive generations!*

Other practices concerning specific days and years should also be mentioned. Trumpets is the day of blowing the shofar. This day later became associated with the new year and the creation of the world in the Jewish heritage. As with the Christian celebration of the birth of Yeshua on December 25, we do not know for sure if this day is really the day of the creation's beginning any more than we know if Christmas really is Yeshua's birthday. In the biblical context, blowing the trumpets (shofar) seemed to awaken us to prepare for Yom Kippur.

Yom Kippur is the holiest day of the Jewish year. It is a day of fasting and repentance. On this day, the great sacrifice was offered for the sins of the nation. Another sacrifice functioned as the scapegoat which was sent into the wilderness, symbolically carrying away the sins of the nation. It was on this day that the high priest entered the Holy of Holies in the presence of God, bringing the sacrifical blood. He sprinkled it upon the mercy seat, the top of the Ark containing the tablets of the Covenant. Yom Kippur provides the major levitical background for understanding the work of Yeshua as expressed in the Book of Hebrews. Other biblical writers connect Yeshua's sacrifice to both Yom Kippur and Passover, for He is our paschal lamb whose blood is shed. In John, as the passover lambs are slain, so He is slain (John 19). Therefore, we are to purge the old leaven of malice, replacing it with the unleavened bread of sincerity and truth (I Corinthians 5). It is safe to say that together with Passover, Yom Kippur is the major holy day for understanding the redemptive work of Yeshua.

Special years were also instituted in ancient Israel. First was the Sabbatical Year: Every seventh year Israel was to allow its farm lands to lie fallow. it was a year of even greater rest and sharing. It symbolized the Messianic Age as

well as reflected God's creative work—seven was the number
of distinct creative periods during which God made the
heavens and the earth. Israel was promised a special blessing in the sixth year as well as natural produce in the seventh if it would be faithful to this statute. All slaves would be
freed in the seventh year as well, for God is the Lord who
releases the slaves from their bondage.

Every fiftieth year was to be a Jubilee Year. The requirements of this year were like those set for the Sabbatical year,
with the addition that all land was to be returned to its
ancestral owners. Hence, land could be sold only for 49 years
(or less); its price depended on the time remaining until the
next Jubilee Year. Herein was an incredible balancing of
personal initiative in economic life and the need for a measure of social equality. Wealth was based upon land, and
accumulation of wealth in Israel was to have its limits. So
liberty was proclaimed throughout the land (Leviticus 25);
all slaves were to be freed; all debts were to be cancelled; and
wealth was to be redistributed through the return of ancestral lands. Yeshua connected His ministry to the year of
Jubilee (Luke 4) by proclaiming liberty to the captives.

Despite the limitations of the Mosaic system, we are
indeed astonished at the gracious order of existence that God
proclaimed for ancient Israel. Especially as we look at Israel's
cycle of life through feast, fast and jubilee, grace, love and
mercy shout out to us. We can say as the prophet of old looking
at ancient Israel, "What nation is there that has a God so great
and laws so great as all this Torah which He gave to Israel!"
(Deuteronomy 4).

THE SUCCESS AND FAILURE OF ANCIENT ISRAEL

The obvious failure of ancient Israel was in keeping faithful to her own covenant with God. Her fall into idolatry and
paganism was the major sin of the pre-exilic nation. This was
accompanied with laxity in regard to the feasts as well as
disregard for the claims of social justice. The reestablished
nation (after the Babylonian Captivity) was greatly purified
of external idolatry.

The post-exilic period, saw a gradual movement toward externalism in religion. While Judaism without life or Spirit was never really the case, there was a definite, perceptible fall in which external ritual as well as a prevalent misunderstanding of the Sinai revelation predominated. A great number began to see Torah's instruction not as a guidance for a people who had responded to God's grace, but as a system of works-righteousness by which one could earn merit to obligate God to bless the devotee. That the love of an infinite and holy God could be "earned" is greatly contrary to Torah. A true heartfelt response to God's love and mercy, however, certainly would produce a life of obedience consistent with Torah.

These failures, in addition to a certain fixed interpretation, whereby the new revelation of Yeshua was rejected by the Jewish religious establishment—and hence the majority of the nation—demark Israel's greatest failures and have indeed undercut her role as a light to the nations as well as a kingdom of priests.

We must not simply note the failure; rather, we must understand the extent to which Israel was conditioned to perceive Messiah solely within the context of the *full revelation* of the Days of the Messiah and of a worldwide kingdom of peace. Harsh Roman oppression caused the Israelites to yet further emphasize the political role of the Messiah on earth.

It is also important to note the successes of Israel and question whether Yeshua would have been better received in any other culture. What if He had marched to Rome? Would the Roman religious and political establishment—steeped in polytheism and crude circus entertainment—have accepted the Prince of Peace after His brief three-year ministry? Would the East, whose denial of the law of consistency (in which morality and immorality, truth and error are all part of the incomprehensible "one" in which all the contradictions of life are dissolved) have accepted Him? To the Easterners, life is but an illusion (maya)! Surely Israel, alone surpassed all other cultures in revelation to receive

Yeshua—even to the limited extent that she did.

Scripture teaches that Yeshua's death was foreordained by God and that the sins of the whole world—including Israel's sin—placed Him on the tree. He died for the sake of Israel, that through His sacrifice we might all be redeemed (Romans 5:12).

Israel's successes are also noteworthy. Though all success is a result of God's grace, there was a sufficient response to God's grace in the nation to produce many great achievements.

Israel provided the world with its first true, monotheistic view of God. This faith, in an infinite and personal moral governor of the universe, was ultimately accepted in Israel. Because of this, Israel's history provides us with great lessons of faith—not only of failure. Examples are Joshua, the Psalms of David, the poetry of Isaiah, the hope of Jeremiah, and the amazing deliverance of Israel during the days of Hezekiah when threatened by Assyria.

After the Old Testament period (but before Yeshua), Israel still had its triumphs. The conquering Alexander the Great was so impressed by Israel's unique religion that he sought her prayers rather than her hellenization. Other rulers were not so wise as Alexander. In later times of great oppression, the faith and courage of the Maccabees was a light that still shines to the world. Not only did this period (166-135 B.C.E.) produce great martyrs who would not compromise their faith for a foreign-enforced idolatry, it produced an amazing victory of deliverance from external control by God's mighty power. The "motley" Jewish forces fought with courage and gained Israel's freedom from the Syrian-Greek empire. Why? So that Israel might be true to her covenant with God!

Some years later, Pompey came to conquer Israel for Rome. He thought he would enter the Temple and find treasures of gold and silver, the secret carved images of Israel's gods. So bold was he that he would desecrate God's temple for his own gain. He ordered the priests slain; but line after line of priests took their place to continue the ministrations of the Temple. They all died in martyrdom for God and the Torah. Pompey entered the Temple. He found no gods or treasures of great note in the Holy of Holies. He found to his disgust, instead, scrolls of the Torah. What a crazy people, he thought! But no, these were the people of God—unique in the world—unexplainable without God's revelation—a people without idols but with a scroll from a God who spoke. He failed to realize that he beheld a treasure beyond measure, "More to be desired are they than gold, yea much fine gold, sweeter also than honey and the drippings of the honeycomb" (Psalm 19).

It was to Israel that God's Yeshua (salvation) came. Shall we only mention the rejection, or shall we also mention those who accepted Him, the multitudes who beat their breasts and wept as he walked toward His crucifixion (Luke 23:27)? Shall we not mention the apostles who spread His message beyond Israel, with a zeal to spread His message to the world, *while allowing cultural freedom for non-Jewish believers in one of the most incredible decisions in the history of religion (Acts 15).* And what of Paul, who spread faith in Yeshua and the God of Abraham, Isaac and Jacob to the gentiles? This brilliant rabbi, converted on the road to Damascus, changed the course of history. What of the myriad Jews who believed in Him *and* were zealous for the law, according to Acts 21?

There are lessons to be learned from Israel's early biblical history: her faithfulness to what she perceived as God's call, her continued willingness to be martyred to "sanctify the Name," (Kadush ha shem), her perserverance in pogroms and persecutions—even to the reciting of the Sh'ma (Deuteronomy 6:4 ff) in Hitler's death camps. The sense of community Israel built around the synagogue is a model; and the synagogue was the predecessor of the church.

We do not conclude the matter of the salvation of individual Jews; nor do we blunt the serious words of judgment found in the New Testament, a book written predominantly by Jews. We only say that all these faithful—Peter, Paul, James, Isaiah, Jeremiah and Amos—were of Israel, too.

Israel maintained her identity as a nation and God kept His promise to preserve her as a nation. Could we otherwise believe God today? Praise God for Israel! Her history— which is not yet over—continues. God shall yet demonstrate His victory over all nations through the instrument of Israel (Zechariah 12-14). Israel as a whole will accept Yeshua. Israel will be an example for the building of world-wide faith. As Paul said, her national rejection meant riches for Gentiles, who could thus accept the Gospel without the barrier of taking upon themselves Israel's calling. However, Israel's full inclusion (acceptance of Yeshua) shall yet mean life from the dead—that is the resurrection and days of the Messiah—for God's gifts and call are irrevocable. (All this in Romans 11). God's intent is to preserve a unique nation, even if it is an Israel which has not yet accepted Yeshua.

Such a brief recounting of hope demands that we deal with the issue of Israel's future. What is the future that the Scriptures envision? The reader may not concur with all aspects of the following outline, but the general lines seem biblically clear.

We note that Yeshua foresaw a period during which the Good News would be preached to all nations. During this period, Israel, as a nation-state, would be scattered among the nations. The fall of Jerusalem begins this period, known as the "times of the Gentiles" or nations. In 70 C.E., Titus vividly fulfilled Yeshua's predictions—conquering Jerusalem and ending Israel's national life. Bar Kochba (the false messiah) later sought to reestablish Israel's independence, but his rebellion was an utter failure (130-135 B.C.E.) We read of this period, "they will fall by the edge of the sword and be led captive among the nations; and Jerusalem will be trodden down by the gentiles until the times of the gentiles are fulfilled" (Luke 21:24).

Many have understood the significance of the "times of the Gentiles" to be synonymous with the age of the Church. It is true that during this period, the Gospel "will be preached as . . . a testimony to the nations . . . then shall the end come." Messianic Jews do not distinguish a gospel of the

Kingdom from the Gospel of God's grace, either; for Paul, in the Book of Acts calls the Gospel he preaches, "the Gospel of the Kingdom." Yet it would seem that the "times of the Gentiles" has in view not the Gentile predominance in accepting the Gospel, but relates rather to the relationship of Israel as a nation among nations. Gentile means "nation" as well as non-Jew. The context is "in the times of the Gentiles," Israel ceases to exist as an independent geopolitical entity. Hence, non-Jewish nations dominate world politics.

During this period, the Gospel will indeed by offered so that a pilgrim people of faith might be established within all nations. This period is of limited duration. It is "*until* the times of the Gentiles are fulfilled." In other words Israel again will exist as a geo-political entity, an instrument of God's revelation and judgment which is her irrevocable calling and purpose (Romans 11:29). Many have claimed the word "fulfilled" to mean "until the full number of gentiles accept the gospel and come into the fold of God's people." This seems unlikely since the context speaks of the relationship between Israel as a nation among the nations (Gentiles) and not of individual Gentiles and their relationship to individual Jews.

The Gentiles' time is fulfilled when evil has run its full course under the political domination of the world's principalities. The parallel is God's Word concerning the Amorites (or Canaanites): Israel would be in Egyptian captivity for over 400 years. Then she would be established as a nation, a supernatural instrument for judgment upon the Canaanites. That was not to happen for some centuries: for, as God told Abraham, the iniquity of the Amorites was not yet full (Genesis 15:16).

It is after Luke 21:24 that the apostle recounts God's wonders and judgments upon the nations. As we look down the corridors of history, we indeed see the horrors of wars and the cruelty and injustice in human governments as well as the relations between nations. Though we might be proud of our civility, it was the most "civilized" national of the 20th century that produced Hitler. The wrath of the nations—

even to this day—has always been directed toward Israel, even though she has been scattered among all peoples. God, has said of Abraham's seed, "I will bless them that bless thee and curse them that curse thee" (Genesis 12:3). Surely, the nations have stored up wrath for the Day of Judgment and continue yet to do so. The recent condemnation by the United Nations of Zionism as "racism"—when Zionism is but the Jewish response to racism directed against them—is a most ironic twisting of language and understanding. The "times of the Gentiles" is most certainly close to fulfillment; they have stored up wrath for the Day of Judgment.

Where does history go from this point, now? It is in this context that we see passages of Scripture coming into play which have not yet been fulfilled. Several biblical images come together: There is the image of Israel back in the land, attacked by Gog and Magog—great and godless end-time powers of oppression. We can already see the power of the Soviets and a Europe turned anti-Israel. We desire to be careful not to be overly dogmatic in seeking to linguistically prove the identity of these references.[10]

Scripture seems to foresee several great events during this time, which will usher in tribulation for the whole world. One is that 144,000 faithful Jews will be witnesses for the Good News during this period. Their witness will be a supernatural one (Revelation 14). God once again will use Israel as an instrument of His great revelation: The nations will converge upon Israel in the Battle of Armageddon. All will seem just as hopeless as when Israel stood at the edge of the sea, with Pharaoh's troops approaching. At this great moment, God Himself will fight for Israel through Yeshua. He will supernaturally defeat the nations arrayed against Israel in a victory which will make the exodus seem pale in comparison (Revelation 19:11-21).

This event shall issue in great repentance the whole world over. The nations are said to mourn (Matthew 24:30) and the elect will be gathered together. Furthermore, Israel will mourn (Zechariah 12:10). The world mourns because it has rejected Yeshua. The world did not see Yeshua as a Jew and has rejected the chosen people or nation of Israel as well. Israel mourns as the people discover Yeshua, "whom they have pierced." The one who was thought to be the source of their persecution, thought to be an imposter, is found to be their great champion and savior. What a day that will be! All Israel shall then be saved (Romans 11:26) which will bring about the resurrection of the righteous from the dead (Romans 11:15) and the rapture of living believers.

The Messiah with all his resurrected saints will then set up His rule over all the earth. He shall rule upon the throne of David from Jerusalem. Here is the grain of truth in the anti-Semitic lie. It is not the Jews' plot to rule the world; but Messiah Yeshua, a Jew, will rule the world from Israel. This is the underlying truth that Satan hates and fights, creating anti-semitism to undermine this truth.

We read of many other wonderful images. One is the great brotherhood to be established between Jews and Arabs. Egypt and Assyria (Arab peoples to the northeast of Israel) will all be called God's people. All weapons will be destroyed as Isaiah said, and they shall beat their swords into plowshares. The lion shall lie down with the lamb and peace shall reign (Isaiah 2). The worldwide kingdom shall recognize the feast of Succot (Zecariah 14), sending representatives to Israel. Sabbath will also probably gain worldwide recognition, continuing into the new heavens and the new earth (Isaiah 63:23).

Some argue that the sacrificial system will be reestablished according to their interpretation of Ezekiel 40, ff. If so, these would be memorial sacrifices to Messiah, parallel to the celebration of the Lord's—or Messiah's—Supper (communion). When Messiah reigns, a whole new order will exist, certainly true to the universal principles reflected in the Mosaic constitution. But there will not be a return to the Mosaic constitution which accommodated the needs and limitations of the people in the ancient Near East over three thousand years ago.

God indeed has a great future for Israel as a nation. But what is the role of the universal Church in all of this? Once again, our interpretation relates to Luke 21:24. Some have interpreted "until the times of the Gentiles are fulfilled" to mean that the church age will end and God will now work through Israel—instead of the Church. They see the Church as translated (raptured) out of the earth or removed for the seven-year period of great tribulation. We believe that this doctrine (pre-trib. rapture) is not found in a consistent reading of the Scriptures. The "ecclesia," or congregation, of God world-wide is formed of believing Jews and non-Jews. Yeshua, in teaching His disciples throughout the Gospel accounts, relates all the signs of the end-times to the disciples (Mark 13; Matthew 24; Luke 21), who are obviously His followers and part of the universal people of God—as well as of Israel.

He tells His disciples "when *you* see" the various signs spoken of. When they see the fig tree come out in leaf, summer is near. The fig tree is related to Israel's destiny; but it is also a metaphor for the various signs that will take place in the end. When the disciples see these signs, their redemption draws nigh, "he is near, even at the gates." Followers of Yeshua will not suffer the wrath of God, but are warned to always be ready to endure persecution unto death. The teaching of the New Testament, then, is that the Church will continue until the end in its work of saving, healing, teaching and establishing communities of faith. The sense that the true Church will be taken out of the world, while Israel is left to suffer another great holocaust, might be a comfort to those who believe they will escape. But as Corrie ten Boom stated, it is an utterly foolish doctrine to believers all over the world who already are being tortured unto death. It is a doctrine we do not find in Scripture.

The place of the true Church in the end-times would seem to be that of continuing its witness and supporting Israel as a nation, especially the 144,000 in God's great work of witness and revelation. God's purpose in the universal Church—and in Israel—is not at all mutually exclusive. One purpose need not work against another purpose. No. Through the universal Church, God desires a people among nations through whom He will work. Both purposes are in tandem.

As followers of Yeshua, Jews are part of the universal people of God. Their national identity is still Israel just as a Frenchman's is France. As part of Israel, they participate in God's purposes in the nation. Hence the relationship is not (as diagrammed) what dispensationalists describe: that one is either part of the Church, Israel, or the gentiles.

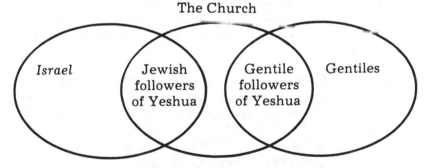

Dispensationalist view

Jews

Church of former Jews & Gentiles

Gentiles

Rather, one is part of either (natural) Israel, the gentiles, the Church, or (redeemed) Israel *and* the Church. Hence:

The Church

Israel

Jewish followers of Yeshua

Gentile followers of Yeshua

Gentiles

The Church is grafted into the true ancient people of God: Israel. When all Israel is saved, they will still continue as a nation but all will be part of Yeshua's congregation too—our diagram is as follows:

The Church

Israel

We do not accept that God's purposes for the Church ever come to an end—even temporarily—so that He might work through Israel. God has a covenant with Abraham's physical seed as well as his spiritual seed and He will always work through both. God does not give the Church up for Israel or Israel for the Church. He will have mercy on all and work both ways that His kingdom might come and His will "be done in earth as it is in heaven" (Matthew 6:10). Praise His Name!

Israel's last great witness in power is crucial when we realize that the world has not responded to the Gospel and that less than ten percent of the world's population has been evangelized. An even greater than the Exodus is coming. No man knows the day or the hour of Yeshua's return. Although it seems to us that His return is imminent, we do not know. It could be 100 years or more. As in the parable of the wise and foolish virgins (Matthew 25) waiting for the bridegroom, we must be prepared for any eventuality. Our outline of the end is not at all to undercut the present responsibility of all to work for peace in the world and justice between and within nations. Neither is there any superiority to Israel's call over that of the Church. Both serve tandem, complementary purposes.

THE TORAH AND THE COVENANTS—REFLECTIONS

An outline of the relationship between the various covenants will provide an understanding of future chapters in the book.

The Adamic Covenant

The first covenant God made is often thought to be one made with Adam. Whether or not there is truly a covenant in Genesis 3, we can say that the Scriptures include God's promise to all mankind. God not only predicts the difficulties that man will experience after the fall, He predicts that the seed of the woman will be bruised in the heel but her offspring will bruise the head of the evil serpent (Genesis 3:15). This has been taken as predictive of the Messiah Yeshua, the seed of the woman, who was indeed wounded by the evil one, but gave a crushing blow to the serpent, the manifestation of Satan. We can immediately see that this promise held true: this testifies to God's faithfulness. The promise is *caught up* with the meaning of its fulfillment and its effect continues.

The Noahic Covenant

The Noahic Covenant following the flood is also a promise from God (Genesis 9): God vows never again to destroy the earth by a flood and gives the rainbow as a sign of His covenant. He also commands man not to eat blood, the sacred symbol of life as well as of sacrifical redemption. The warning against murder is also given, "whosoever sheds man's blood, by man shall his blood be shed" (Genesis 9:6). This covenant certainly continues in effect; for in no way does the covenant God made with mankind and Israel—in Yeshua—invalidate this earlier covenant. The rainbow still continues as a sign; God still will not destroy the earth by flood. Man is still expected to value life as sacred.

The Abrahamic Covenant

We have already described the features of the Abrahamic Covenant. This Covenant is primarily one of promise. We read that "In Yeshua, all the promises of God are yea and Amen" (II Corinthians 1:20). God promises to make a great nation of Abraham's physical seed through whom He is going to bless the world. Furthermore, Israel, Abraham's seed, is promised the land of Israel as its everlasting possession. This Covenant offered to Abraham is sanctified by faith. Furthermore, God promises to bless those who bless Israel and to curse those who curse her. Israel, as a nation, is to be an instrument of God. Circumcision is a sign of this Covenant as well as Sabbath, which was given to Israel in Exodus 20.

There is nothing to indicate that this Covenant has been done away with by God. As a matter of fact, this Covenant foresees a blessing to the nations in Yeshua, so that Abraham is called "the father of many nations." Hence, Paul can

say of the Abrahamic covenant, that God, "preached the
gospel to Abraham" (Galatians 3:8). A careful reading of
Romans 4 gives a wonderful understanding of these truths:
First, the Abrahamic Covenant—so tied up with Messiah's
work—was an offer of salvation to Abraham. "Abraham
believed God and God accounted it to him for righteousness"
(Genesis 15:6). He (Abraham) is the father of all physical
Israelites, but especially of those who are not only of the
physical seed of Abraham but who follow Abraham's faith
example. This is his role as father of the nation, the *circumcised*. However, Abraham was justified (according to Genesis
15) years before he received circumcision as a sign (Genesis
17). Hence, he is the father of those who, although uncircumcised, respond to the Good News in faith, as did
Abraham (Romans 4; Galatians 3).

Thus, Abraham has a spiritual seed in non-Jewish
believers as well. The purposes of God with the nation are
never done away with because of the spiritual seed. Israel is
beloved for the Father's sake in a way that is unique among
the nations; she is still called elect (Romans 11:28-29). The
Scriptures do not blur the distinction between Israel and the
nations. Although there is a universal people of God—
comprised of people drawn from Jewish and gentile ranks—
Scripture maintains the sense of the nation's distinct calling.
(See Romans 11:29, which is crucially important.) A careful
study will reveal that the terms "Jew" and "Israel" are
reserved for the physical nation, also designated by circumcision.[11] Non-Jewish believers are not called spiritual Israel
or spiritual Jews, but Abraham's spiritual seed, or Abraham's offspring (Romans 4; Galatians 3:29).

Why? Because as did Abraham, they, too, have a justification from God—without circumcision. There is neither
Jew nor Greek, male nor female, in the Messiah (Galatians
3:28-29); indeed the wall of partition precluding fellowship
and mutual self-acceptance has been broken down. All followers of Yeshua have spiritual equality. Yet this does not
do away with Israel's calling or election or her distinct purpose in God's economy as a nation among nations.

Neither do the different functions of male and female become blurred in their spiritual equality. Women will still be the child-bearers of the race; men will still perform different functions (note Ephesians 5 on marriage). The Abrahamic covenant is one of unconditional promise. Its validity depends on—and is tied up with—the New Covenant and the sacrificial word of Yeshua. The blessing promised is only realized because of Him; but the Abrahamic Covenant in no way is done away with because of the New Covenant—which is partially envisioned in the Abrahamic Covenant.

The Mosaic Covenant

The next covenant of God was given through Moses. Messianic Jews believe that *there are provisions within the Mosaic Covenant that are so indissolubly tied up with the Abrahamic promises that they are practices as much a part of the Abrahamic Covenant as the Mosaic.*

God promised Abraham a nation. The exodus is the constitutive event which fulfilled that promise. Therefore, all feasts which have the exodus in mind as the inspiration for its celebrations are incorporated in the Abrahamic Covenant; they are celebrations of God's grace. This is true of Passover, Succot and Sabbath, all of which memoralize the distinct national history of Israel and God's fulfillment of His promise of blessing and protection. Sabbath also recalls God's work as Creator. In Yeshua we enter His rest; so we celebrate Sabbath in reference to Him. The seventh-day Sabbath was not given to all nations; it was a blessing and ordinance specifically for Israel. Whenever a Jew celebrates the Sabbath, he testifies to the truth of God's lordship over the universe (which He created in six periods but rested in the seventh). He also testifies to God's victory over the forces of paganism in fulfilling His promise to establish Israel as a distinct nation.

Shavuot is a day of thanksgiving for God's agricultural blessings over the earth. It is also the festival of thanksgiving for the Word of God and the gift of the Holy Spirit (Acts 2).

For a Messianic Jew, the sacrifical dimensions of each of these feasts during this age have been replaced by Yeshua's

sacrifice. He is *the* center of every feast for a Messianic Jew
and we desire to show how each points to Him.

Yom Kippur is tied more to the Mosaic sacrifical system
than other Levitical feasts. Yeshua is described as the high
priest, the sacrifice and the scapegoat. This day, therefore, is
an especially good day of memorial, recalling His work as
well as a day of self-examination, confession and recommitment. It is the day in which we exposit and remember how
all the dimensions of the Temple system find their fulfillment in Yeshua.

A nation was promised to Abraham. A nation has a distinctive language, geographical boundaries and a unique
culture. The Jewish peoples' languge is Hebrew: its land is
Israel; and the feasts connected to the Abrahamic promises
are the centers of its unique cultural inheritance of promise
and blessing. All other cultural identifications are secondary.

The Mosaic Covenant is distinct among covenants. It
was, first, Israel's national constitution and contains instructions for Israel's socio-judicial system as well as personal
moral issues. Great prominence was also given to the religious temple system, the most prominent features being
priesthood and the sacrifices. The New Testament period is
one of transition. As such, we find Paul engaging in sacrifice
to show loyalty to Israel and Torah (Acts 21). Just how far
does this loyalty go under the New Covenant? Let us note
several points in this regard.

As a national constitution, the Mosaic Covenant is not in
effect. The Temple, so central to this covenant, has been
destroyed. The original sacrificial dimension is therefore
impossible to fulfill. The Aaronic identity of the priests who
were essential to this constitution, similarly, can no longer
be fully determined. As a full constitutional system—especially in the dimensions of sacrifice and priesthood—we see
the truth as recorded by the writer to the Hebrews. In chapter nine he states, that in speaking of a New Covenant, the
prophet Jeremiah treats the Old as near vanishing. Even
then, it was growing old and passing away.

Yeshua is now our priest and sacrifice in every sense

that is important. In Torah—He is the reality to which the shadow of the Temple sacrificial system points. Further, Torah applies God's principles to a people living in the Near East over three thousand years ago. They were commanded to build a fence on their roofs—because they used their flat roofs as living space—to protect human life. We must see the principle of love and protection within the command, that is the *spirit* of the law, so we can see its applications for today.

How then shall we respond to Torah? As inspired Scripture it is "profitable for doctrine, reproof, for instruction and for training in righteousness" (II Timothy 3:16). Obviously this is a reference to the Tenach (Old Testament), because the New Testament was not yet written. Hence we must see these truths:

As a constitution bound up with Temple, priesthood and sacrifice, this (Mosaic) covenant is vanishing (Hebrews 8). Yet we can still study these aspects of Torah to enlighten us concerning the *spiritual* meaning involved in this system, as well as for a deeper understanding of Messiah's work.

The Torah reflects God's universal and eternal moral standards. Once we recognize Torah's accommodations to its age (as well as keeping in mind New Testament truth) we can still be instructed by Torah as inspired Scripture. We are inspired by its commands of love toward one's neighbor, the poor and the needy. We rejoice at its command to aid our enemy when his ox has fallen under its load: a true anticipation of Yeshua's command to love our enemies. We also recite the Sh'ma as the greatest command of all, since Yeshua taught that it and the admonition to love our neighbor as ourselves (Leviticus 19:18) were the foundational commands of the whole Tenach revelation. Therefore, with the Psalmist we will say, "O how I love thy law, it is my meditation all the day long" (Psalm 119:97).

Nations, as well, can be instructed by the principles of business, honesty, judicial wisdom and social equality found in Torah. This is the universal dimension of Torah which shall never pass away. Yeshua taught, "Think not that I am come to destroy the law. I am not come to destroy but to fulfill. Till heaven and earth pass away, not a jot or a tittle shall pass from the Torah until all is fulfilled. Whosoever shall teach another to break one of the least of these commands shall be called least in the kingdom of heaven, but whosoever teaches and practices them shall be called great in the kingdom of heaven" (Matthew 5:17-19).

We do not fulfill Torah to gain merit before God, but as those who are led by the Spirit to do God's will in response to His grace. We are guided by the whole counsel of the Word of God.

There is also the dimension of Torah which relates specifically to Israel's calling as a nation and its identity. As already stated, this aspect of Torah transcends the limitations of the constitution as a covenant. The feasts and other practices connected to Israel's national heritage are maintained as part of a Jewish identity and calling. Some laws (such as the food lists, etc.) will be difficult to interpret as regards their present application. Are they mainly for health reasons? Are they part of the old sacrificial system (uncleanliness precluded one from Temple participation)? Are they a significant part of Jewish identity today? These questions will be addressed later. People of good intentions may disagree on these points and our freedom in Messiah should prevail. We can say, however, that rightly understood and applied by the above criteria, Jews—including followers of Yeshua—are called to maintain Torah. This is not done because of legalistic bondage; it is motivated by love and the calling to be part of Israel's national identity and is laid upon hearts by God's Spirit.

What is so exciting about the perspective we are developing is that the Scriptures are herein seen as a unified revelation; as a whole, the Scriptures are God's Word to all the people of God.

The Davidic Covenant

The last Old Testament covenant is the Davidic Covenant, found in II Samuel 7. This is also an unconditional covenant of promise which remains in effect and is fulfilled in Yeshua. David is promised an everlasting throne through his descendants as well as worldwide dominion. All the Messianic prophecies concerning the everlasting rule of the Messiah are extensions of this covenant.

For Those Familiar with
Dispensational and Covenant Theology

Two great theologies have predominated in the interpretation of Scripture in the believing Church over the past seventy-five years. One has been called "covenant theology," the other "dispensationalism." We agree with the dispensationalist view of the literal fulfillment of God's promises to Israel, including the Messiah's 1,000 year reign on earth. We find it misleading, however, to speak of the Old Testament period as the dispensation of law and to *contrast* *it* with the present age as an age of grace. We certainly agree that there is a distinction between the Mosaic covenantal government and the New Covenant. Both, however, are covenants of grace, even though the Mosaic (as a national constitution) is much more concerned with judicial matters. We must not confuse the Mosaic Covenant as understood by its later Judaic interpretation as a system of works-righteousness. God never sought to convey, under any age, any concept other than that of salvation by grace through faith.

We might speak of the Mosaic dispensation with its system of Temple and sacrifice as a means of grace anticipating Yeshua, and contrast it with the New Covenant in Yeshua which is our primary and sole means of entrance into God's presence. Salvation is always offered by grace in Yeshua whether explicitly as in the New Covenant Scriptures or implicitly, by anticipation in the sacrificial system. We agree with the dispensationalists that each covenant should be seen as distinctive, even if intertwined with and anticipating others.

Contrary to some dispensationalists, Messianic Jews do not see a complete distinction between redeemed Israel and the Church; rather, we see redeemed Israel as a distinct part of the universal people of God from all ages. Furthermore, we do not perceive that Yeshua ever offered Israel the literal

earthly kingdom, but then postponed it. John 6 shows that the
people were only too ready to receive this literal "kingdom."
Yeshua offered Israel the *spiritual* Kingdom that all might
have an opportunity throughout the years to come under
God's rule. Matthew 13 summarizes the nature of the Kingdom that Yeshua intended to offer. The worldwide earthly
Kingdom of God will yet come as the fruition of the Spiritual
Kingdom when Yeshua returns. We do not find the tribulation period to be one in which the Church is removed from
the earth, while Israel alone is used for God's purposes on
earth. Hence, we may see a Jewish believer as both part of
Israel and the universal people of God.

Covenant theologians also emphasize the universal
dimensions of the moral law in Torah. They, too, emphasize
the oneness of all God's people from all times, even seeing the
saved of Israel as the "Church" in the Old Testament. Noting
the graciousness of all the covenants the covenant theologian
unifies all covenants as reflections of one universal covenant
of grace. However, he sometimes goes so far in this that he
misses some of the distinctions between the covenants which
are all covenants of grace. The promises to Israel are spiritual-
ized as symbolic, and are applied to the Church. God's purpose through a nation among the nations is lost. There is no
biblical reason to think that God's purpose in the Church
excludes His purpose in Israel.

Covenant theology also denies the literal reign of the
Messiah on earth, which is consistently taught in Scripture
(Revelation 20, i.e., the Millenium). This loss of place for
Israel caused the older covenant theologians of years past to
think that a "Christian nation" where all citizens professed
faith could be enforced. The Church is a pilgrim people
within all nations but is not itself to directly rule the state. A
state church brings oppression, for God did not call the
church to civil rule, but to be an influence as salt and light in
society. Yet the Puritans of 17th century America were correct to seek to base civil law and government on biblical law.
The covenant theologian lost the place for Israel in God's
purposes and falsely thought of the Church as a new, spiritual

Israel replacing forever the old physical Israel which no longer had any spiritual purpose, despite Paul's strong words concerning the gift and call of God as being irrevocable (Romans 11).

However, the people of God do seek to influence society toward a social consensus in which biblical law has a great sway in our legal system (e.g., law based on the Judeo-Christian ethic).

We have great respect for the truths discovered by both dispensational and covenant theologians. We believe, however, that Messianic Judaism offers the opportunity of a fresh perspective which is more comprehensive than either and maintains the best discoveries of both.

Israel's purpose remains as a test to all nations in which Jews reside.

CHAPTER TWO

Israel's Call and the New Testament

Israel's Call and Yeshua

One of the most wonderful studies that can be undertaken is that of the relationship of Yeshua to the Nation of Israel. As the true representative of Israel, His life and teaching are integral to the life and heritage of the Children of Jacob.

In the beginning of His ministry, Yeshua chose twelve disciples. To most observers, the twelve represent the Nation of Israel with its twelve tribes. They are, therefore, representatives of Israel as well as the foundational teachers for a new universal and ingrafted people of God (Ephesians 2:20; Romans 11:17-24).

Yeshua taught that he was sent only to the lost sheep of the house of Israel. When a Canaanite woman sought His ministry, it was only given after an amazing demonstration of tenacious faith on her part (Matthew 10:5-8; 15:24). This was not because Yeshua lacked concern for the rest of the world, but rather because Israel was called to be a nation of priests. As a light to the world, the Israelites were to be given the opportunity to be a light in responding first to Him Who was the light of the world. Indeed, as representative Israel, Yeshua is the light to the nations as predicted (Isaiah 42:1-7); but Jews who responded to Him brought that light to the

Gentiles and were themselves light.

As representative Israel, Yeshua fulfills Israel's role by recapitulating its life within Himself. This is especially seen in the early chapters of Matthew's Gospel. Many have puzzled over Matthew's Old Testament quotations, i.e., "That it might be fulfilled . . ." Fulfillment has meant to many that a prediction comes to pass. But this is not the meaning of "fulfill" in Matthew. When one looks up some of Matthew's quotes there is no prediction to be seen. Others might indeed include a prediction come to pass, but with much more. If we reverse the word—"fill-full"—we get a more adequate sense of Matthew's meaning. Matthew's sense was to bring history's redemptive meaning to its climax. To Matthew, Yeshua brought Israel's meaning to its fullest depth. He was Israel's climactic focus.

We know that fulfillment had also a broader sense than completing a clear prediction for Matthew's readers. The Qumran community which produced the Dead Sea Scrolls also sought to find a fullness of meaning in present events according to their parallels in history. Scholars called this type of interpretation "peshar."[1] Yeshua really is the climactic fullness of Israel's history as Israel's representative; the parallels of His life to Israel's illustrate the connection.

Yeshua, like Israel, is born in dangerous straits. As Pharaoh of old, Herod orders a mass annihilation of Jewish children. Like Moses, Yeshua is spared. He goes with his family to Egypt. In the words of Matthew 2:15, this was to fulfill what was spoken by the prophet: "Out of Egypt have I called my son." The quote from Hosea 11:1, however, is not a prediction of the Messiah, but speaks of Israel's call from Egyptian bondage—Israel being God's son. The passage goes on to mention Israel's faithlessness. The more that God called, the less faithful was Israel. Yeshua, in contrast, is called from Egypt; He is fully faithful. He fulfills Israel's meaning as her representative. As representative Israel, Yeshua goes through the water of baptism by John. He can then bear Israel's sins, and the sins of the world. Israel went through the Red Sea. In the wilderness, Yeshua is tested by Satan for 40 days, a parallel to

Israel's 40-year wilderness wanderings. (See Matthew 2-4 for the full accounts.) Yeshua then goes up the mountain to give the authoritative discussion and interpretation of the Law, a direct revelation, not as the argued out interpretations of the scribes (Matthew 7:28). He taught with amazing authority. So also, as Moses provided manna, Yeshua provided supernatural bread paralleled in the feeding of the 5,000 (John 6). Many people expected the Messiah to be a prophet-king like Moses, who would duplicate his miracles. Hence, some sought to make Him king when they recognized the significance of His works.[2] Even beyond these great passages, Yeshua identified with Israel through its feasts, in His illustrations and practices.

Yeshua, the Law and the New Covenant

Yeshua indeed preached the coming New Covenant. He also taught on the Law. Understanding Yeshua's teaching in these two areas is crucial to Messianic Judaism.

In Matthew 5-7 we have a wonderful summary of Yeshua's teaching, which centers on major aspects of the Law. It is also interesting that Matthew 5-7 has covenant features reminiscent of the Mosaic revelation.

Instead of beginning with a specific act of God's grace (e.g. the Exodus) which should cause us to respond according to the covenant teachings, Yeshua begins by promising blessing to people who demonstrate certain behaviors and attitudes (the Beatitudes). This is because Yeshua Himself—His life, death and resurrection—is God's act of grace which leads to a new response of faith and obedience under the New Covenant. The Beatitudes are those basic moral qualities which bring a rich life: the poor in spirit (who recognize their need of grace); those who mourn (especially over spiritual corruption); the meek; those who hunger and thirst for righteousness; the peacemakers; the pure in heart; and those who are persecuted for righteousness' sake. These are the truly blessed ones!

There then follows an exposition of Torah and a discussion of true piety and prayer. Instructions on trusting God for all our human needs are given (not laying up treasures for

ourselves) as well as the example of true prayer. The section
ends appropriately with *blessings and cursings* (7:21-27). The
wise man who hears and responds obediently to Yeshua's
teaching is like the man who builds his house on a rock. He
will be able to withstand the storms and trials of life. The
foolish man (who does not respond) will be like the man who
builds his life on sand. In the storms of life, he will be swept
away.

These chapters are central for an understanding response
to the Torah. Yeshua never confutes the intended meaning
and purpose of Torah if properly understood. When Yeshua,
says, "It has been said . . . but I say unto you," His argument is
with the interpretation of the Law, not the Law itself. Hence
Yeshua seeks to bring out the inner implications of the Law in
terms of its deepest intent. His emphasis is on our inner
attitude or motive and not just on our external actions.

We are still looking for those who will take with utter
seriousness the background statement for Yeshua's teaching
in Matthew 5, that is verses 17-19, (parallel is in Luke 16:16-17),
"Think not that I am come to destroy the law and the
prophets, I am not come to destroy but to fulfill. Till heaven
and earth pass, not a jot, not a tittle shall in any wise pass from
the law until all is accomplished. Whosoever then relaxes one
of the least of these commandments, shall be called least in
the kingdom of heaven, but he who does them and teaches
them shall be called great in the kingdom."

Though it seems incredible, some have actually read this
passage ignoring v. 19 and have said that "fulfill" means to do
away with because we now just have to obey the Spirit.

Others have taught that Yeshua here was speaking to
Jews still under the Old Testament; that Matthew 5-7 is law,
not grace, but that New Covenant life is under the Spirit and
not the rigidities of Law.

Still others have taught that Matthew 5-7 is a kingdom
ethic for the Millenium. Yet one wonders if, in the Kingdom,
when Yeshua reigns, Jews will still be constrained by Roman
soldiers to carry their load a mile as in the first century
(Matthew 5:41). Should they then respond by going the extra

mile in the light of Yeshua's teaching! Injustice will not exist in the Millenium. Yeshua's teaching is for the present unjust age. The law Yeshua gave applied to His day directly.

Matthew 5-7 seeks to distill the essence of Torah insofar as it reflects God's eternal standards of love and truth. It is not the Old Testament dispensation exposited nor the millenial ethic; it is God's eternal law made clear and applied to human life in this unjust world. It is clear that no one can live up to the standard Yeshua taught. Yet we only recognize our need for grace when we realize how far short we fall from God's requirement. Relaxing the Law produces the illusion of thinking we have attained righteousness by our self-effort. We would then cease to depend on God's grace in Yeshua.

Yeshua teaches that Torah is God's Word; He is not teaching the eternality of the Temple system whose demise He predicted. But *so far as the Books of Moses reflect God's eternal law*, they will never pass away. Until heaven and earth pass away is a way of saying until there is no human society, or never. Hence, rather than relaxing Torah, Yeshua exposits it to show the heights and depths of God's requirements in deeds, attitudes and love so that no man will hold himself as righteous in himself.

Only the fruits of the Spirit can produce a likeness to the Messiah in us from "glory to glory" (II Corinthians 3) whereby we live increasingly as Matthew 5-7 teaches and as Yeshua lived. Furthermore, it is in light of the high standard here that we confess our sins and forever depend on the power of Yeshua's atonement and the Holy Spirit to produce righteousness, knowing that we are accounted righteous in Yeshua alone. Matthew 5-7 then becomes our guide under the New Covenant by the power of the Spirit.

Let us now look more closely at Yeshua's exposition, remembering that His quarrel was not with the Law but with the misinterpretations of the Law—God's standard.

In His exposition of "You shall not kill" (Matthew 5:21), He goes to the issue of heart attitude: The source of murder is hate in one's heart. Therefore Yeshua teaches that anger and insult are from the same source and also bring judgment

upon a person. We must not think ourselves to be pure simply
because we have refrained from committing an external
deed. Hence, before we bring an offering, we are to seek to be
reconciled to our brother. True worship only flows from the
heart that bears no bitterness and seeks reconciliation.

His exposition of the command against adultery is similar. The external act flows from a lustful heart attitude.
Therefore, "everyone who looks at a woman lustfully has
already committed adultery with her in his heart" (vv. 27-28).
It is that heart attitude to which we must give our attention.

Rather than allow a commitment to sin to keep us from
eternal life, it would be better to do away with the eye or arm
which is the organ executing the sin and hence our idolatry of
the sin (vv. 29-30).

On the command to write a bill of divorce, given as an
accommodation for the protection of woman and the hard-
ness of man's heart, Yeshua reasserts God's original (Torah)
standard of the lifetime commitment of marriage: "Everyone
who divorces his wife, except on the ground of unchastity,
makes her an adulteress; and whoever marries a divorced
woman commits adultery" (vv. 31-32).

In regard to the command against swearing falsely—but
performing our oaths to the Lord—Yeshua goes beyond the
command to the ultimate standard of God behind it. This
ultimate standard is the sacredness of giving our word, the
standard of honesty and truth. Hence, a man's word is to be
his bond of commitment without the need to swear.

Yeshua says, "But I say to you, do not swear at all either
by heaven, for it is the throne of God, or by the earth for it is
his footstool, or by Jerusalem for it is the city of the great king.
And do not swear by your head for you cannot make one hair
white or black. Let what you say be simply yes or no; anything
more than this comes from evil" (vv. 34-37).

Why? Because the godly man says "yes" and his word is
honest. Any need to invoke heaven or earth is extraneous to
the truly righteous man.

The command of an "eye for an eye and a tooth for a
tooth" was a judicial principle to guide the judges of Israel: A

punishment was to fit the crime. In the ancient near East, this limitation of vengeance respected the dignity of man. Unfortunately, some took this principle limiting revenge to be a vendetta *allowing* personal revenge. To this Yeshua responds by commanding a loving response to the enemy that reflects God's love and mercy—to turn the other cheek. Even when the hated Roman occupation troops under the law of conscription forced Jews to carry a load for one mile, their response was to take that burden an extra mile. The Torah had already taught that if your enemy's ox falls under his load, you are to go and help your enemy (Deuteronomy 21). This is all summed up in the command, "You have heard that it was said, you shall love your neighbor and hate your enemies, but I say to you love your enemies and pray for those who persecute you so that you may be the sons of your father who is in heaven; for he makes his sun to rise on the evil and the good and sends rain on the just and unjust" (5:43-45).

Some have thought that this was a command against all self-defense. That is not the issue; the issue, rather, is to have love as a motive in all situations. Love may defend another or prevent evil; but the motive must be love, not selfishness. The illustrations given—turning the cheek and going the extra mile—are examples of love. Yeshua said, "You must be perfect as your heavenly father is perfect" (6:48). This can only be accomplished in Him!

Yeshua also teaches on a piety that is truly godly, not an outward display for the praise of men. This involved almsgiving, fasting and prayer, the latter exemplified by the wonderful model of prayer he taught: "Our Father who art in heaven . . ." The first two lines of this prayer are parallel to the Kaddish (sanctification) prayer still recited in many parts of the synagogue service. Compare the first two lines of each:

"Our Father who art in heaven, hallowed be thy Name. Thy kingdom come, thy will be done on earth as it is in heaven" (Matthew 6:9).

"Glorified and sanctified be God's great name in the

world which He created according to His will. May he
establish His kingdom during your days and during the
life of all the house of Israel" (Kaddish).

Yeshua taught the avoidance of bondage to material
things—not laying up treasures on earth—and trusting God
to provide for all our needs.

"Seek (ye) first the kingdom of God and His righteousness and all these things will be added unto you" (6:33).

Yeshua was the greatest upholder of the true nature of
Torah that the world has known. He lived it! He fulfilled the
Law in living it and providing a way by His sacrifice and
resurrection that we might be empowered by God to live it as
well!

Yeshua did have controversies with the religious leadership. Perhaps the most famous controversy was in regard to
the Sabbath. Yeshua intensifies the meaning of law by bringing out its deeper intention as opposed to the rabbinic understanding of the Law by multiplying its external requirements. Yeshua never invalidated the Sabbath. He taught that
He was Lord of the Sabbath and that the Sabbath was made
for man, not man for the Sabbath. This is clearly the implication of all the teachings in Torah about the Sabbath. Hence,
Yeshua rejected the multiplication of rabbinical laws defin-
ing what was and was not permitted on the Sabbath. To go
through a field on Sabbath and to pick and eat the grain on the
way was not harvesting to Yeshua nor work in the biblically
intended sense (Matthew 12). He invoked the example of
David, who even ate the holy Temple bread in circumstances
of need.

Nor was it a violation of the Sabbath to provide healing
when compassion spontaneously welled up within, for this
would enable another to experience Sabbath rest through the
miraculous power of God's love. If circumcision was performed on the Sabbath to make a minor member of the body
whole before God—it being a covenant sign—He who had
miraculous power could as well make the body whole. This
was argued on the rabbinical principle "From the minor case

to the major" (John 7).

One of the other great controversies regarded the rabbinical extensions of the law relating to clean and unclean foods (Leviticus 11). It was held that unless one washed before meals according to ritual prescriptions, he was unclean. Galilean commoners uninformed of such procedures were considered unclean and their food unclean. Some members of the religious establishment thus despised all the *am-har-aretz*, the people of the land.

Yeshua's teaching was rejected because he was not a graduate of rabbinical training. Yeshua taught a Torah-true spirituality which applied not only to rabbinical scholars but to artisans, farmers, craftsmen and fishermen. His response was to first call into question the rabbinical tradition as a standard of cleanliness (Mark 7:14-23; Matthew 15). What defiles a man is not what goes into him but what comes out. It is our corruption of heart attitude that is most serious; we must not be diverted from this main issue by questions of external cleanliness. The important issues flowing from an evil heart are, "evil thoughts, fornication, theft, murder, adultery, coveting, wickedness, deceit, envy, slander, pride and foolishness. All these things come from within and they defile a man." Either Mark or an early scribe added the phrase "Thus he declared all foods clean" (Mark 7:21-22).

What constitutes a food? Does this mean we can now eat blood (forbidden in the Noahic covenant) or even vermin?[3] No, *food* is defined by the scriptural lists in Torah. To any Jew in Israel, the meaning of food was therein defined. There was no thought among any Jews of eating non-Biblical substances. Hence, in Mark 7, what God calls food is clean, whether or not rabbinical ritual and washing has been followed.

Matthew 15 states the clear conclusion, "to eat with unwashed hands does not make a man unclean." The tradition of the elders was questioned to show how this tradition contradicted Torah itself. Yeshua quoted Isaiah, who stated that they "taught as doctrines the precepts of men" (Mark 7:6; cf. Isaiah 29:13). Indeed, they rejected the intent of the command of God to maintain their tradition. The Scripture com-

mands us to honor our father and our mother, but the tradition taught that the means that would be used to honor them
could be kept back from them if it was declared "korban,"
dedicated to God. Thus the Word of God was voided by
tradition (7:6-13).

Yeshua's most biting criticism appears in the 23rd chapter of Matthew, amazingly prefaced by this statement: "The
scribes and the Pharisees sit on Moses' seat, so practice and
observe whatever they tell you *but not what they do*"
(emphasis added).

They are then denounced for binding heavy burdens on
men's shoulders, motivated by the desire for external show
and the praise of men. The inconsistency of parts of the tradition is again demonstrated. The tradition said that if one
swore by the Temple or the altar it was worthless; but to
swear by the gold of the Temple or the altar, that was serious
and binding.

Yeshua said, "You blind fools! For which is greater, the
gold or the temple that has made the gold sacred? . . . For
which is greater, the gift or the altar that makes the gift
sacred? So he who swears by the altar swears by it and everything on it; and he who swears by the temple swears by it and
by him who dwells in it" (vv. 17-22).

This is not to cast aside the whole rabbinic tradition, but
simply to question its tradition (as when He took the position
of Shammai or Hillel in the debates on divorce or the resurrection, respectively). However, when tradition went against
God's Word and when religious leaders missed the true
essence of Torah, Yeshua was severe in His criticism.

Yeshua never hinted that the Torah, in its role as a reflection of God's eternal standard of righteousness, would be
invalidated. He himself wore the fringes (of Numbers 15:37-
39) and it was this religious part of the garment that the sick
woman sought to touch for healing (Matthew 9:20).

In John 5 we read of Yeshua and the Sabbath. Yeshua is
the Lord of the Sabbath. He does not identify Himself as Lord
of that which he seeks to abolish. In John 6, we read of Yeshua
and Passover (Leviticus 23:5). The miracle of the feeding of

the 5,000 recalls the Passover feast of unl .vened bread and the manna in the wilderness. Of course all of the Gospels record Yeshua's last Passover seder with his disciples. We read that Yeshua blessed the bread, probably the afikomen or sacred dessert portion of the meal, and broke it as a symbol of His body broken for sin. The third cup of wine in the meal, the cup of redemption, was then made to stand for His blood, shed for the remission of sin. The Talmud enjoins that wine should be red in sacred contexts to remind us of sacrificial blood. In John's gospel, Yeshua is the Passover lamb who takes away the sins of the world—just as the Passover lambs are slain in the temple. And, like the Passover lamb, not one of His bones is broken (John 19:36).

In John 7-9, the context is the feast of Succot (Leviticus 23:34). On this occasion Yeshua uses the impressive ceremonies of Succot recorded in the Talmud tractate Succot to illustrate the truths that He gives to the water of life and that He is "the light of the world." The procession carrying water from the pool of Siloam would circle the Temple and pour their libations on the altar. This was done seven times on the last day of the feast. Yeshua said "If any man thirst let him come to me and drink. He who believes in me, as the Scripture has said, out of his belly will flow rivers of living water. Now this He said about the Spirit" (John 7:37-39).

The evening witnessed the impressive sight of the lamps being lit in the Court of the Women. Light streamed forth, illuminating the Temple with great brightness. In this context Yeshua said, "I am the light of the world, he who believes in me will not walk in darkness but will have the light of life" (John 8:12). Yeshua is the light which illumines our path indicating the way to go. He is our image of what God is like and what man should be.

John 10 mentions the feast of dedication (or Chanukah), a post-biblical feast which celebrated the great victory over the Syrio-Greek oppressors who desecrated the Temple in 165 B.C.E. Chanukah at this time was a minor feast. In the days of the Maccabees, evil shepherds sought to compromise their religious practices with the culture of Greece in its pagan idolatry. This provided a context for Yeshua's discussion of his role as the Shepherd of His sheep.

Yeshua established the New Covenant. This is clear in Matthew 5-7 where He recapitulates the life of Moses and gives the stipulations of a new covenant. The nature of this covenant only becomes clear in His death, resurrection and ascension, and the interpretation of these events by the rest of the New Testament writings. However we see aspects of this New Covenant in other Gospel teachings. Key chapters are Matthew 13, 16, and John 17.

Matthew 16 records the great confession of Peter that Yeshua is the Messiah, the Son of the living God. We recall that "son of God" was *a title for Israel* (Hosea 11:1), *Israel's king representative*, and hence especially of the Messiah. At this point Yeshua makes His great statement concerning a new worldwide movement of faith, although its extent outside of Israel may not at that time have been clear to the disciples. He says, "Upon this rock I will build my congregation (Kahillah—original language of speech) and the gates of hell shall not prevail against it" (Matthew 16:18).

This new movement of God worldwide must have a covenantal basis. That covenant is the New Covenant; entrance into it is through the confession of the Messiahship of Yeshua. Its foundation is the death and resurrection of Yeshua. As seen from the rest of Matthew 16, his Messiahship entails not only the kingly crown, but His suffering death as a prelude to the reign of resurrection power. The New Covenant includes the way of entrance into the presence of God through Yeshua's atonement, the reception of the Holy Spirit and a newly recreated human spirit (Ezekiel 36:26-27), and incorporation to the universal body of Messiah.

John 17 makes it clear that Yeshua seeks the salvation of the world. He prays for His disciples to love one another—to be one as He and the Father are one—and that those who believe in His name through their witness might be one in love in the same way. Then *shall the world* know that He was in the Father and the Father in Him. Jochaim Jeremias brings out the universal scope of the ministry of Yeshua in his fine little book, *Jesus' Promise to the Nations.*

Yeshua's goal is not to do away with Israel's purpose as a nation, but to establish a worldwide spiritual kingdom. In Matthew 13, we find that Yeshua's intention was not to set up the worldwide (earthly) Messianic kingdom at that point in history, but a spiritual kingdom under the rule of God that would spread among all peoples. It would be a grain of mustard seed, starting from the tiniest beginnings but growing into a large bush. It would be as wheat among tares or weeds. Both grow together until harvest. Any attempt to root out all the weeds before harvest would also destroy the wheat. So, too, Yeshua's Kingdom would grow in the midst of an evil society. It would itself be contaminated by it. However, at the harvest, the Messiah's return, the Kingdom would be fully separated from evil.

Yeshua's words after His resurrection were to, "Go ye therefore and make disciples of all nations, baptizing them in the name of the Father, of the Son and of the Holy Spirit: teaching them to observe all that I have commanded you: and, lo, I am with you always, to the close of the age" (Matthew 28.19-20). We note that obedience to a command is not contrary to the spirit of the Gospel!

The covenantal nature of Yeshua's work is brought out especially in the accounts of His crucifixion. When He died, the curtain of the Temple was torn in two, from top to bottom (Matthew 27:51). The curtain separated the Holy of Holies from the rest of the Temple. Only the High Priest entered this holiest place annually, with the blood of atonement for Israel on Yom Kippur. The separation was an ever present reminder of our transgressions separating us from God's presence. The torn curtain indicated that through Yeshua's atonement we now had entrance into God's presence. As we were in Him, the separation from God was removed.

The Temple system was central to the Mosaic Covenant. The torn Temple curtain demonstrated the reality of a new covenant and a new sacrifice superior to the old system (Hebrews 7-9). So, too, Yeshua's promise of the coming of the Spirit (in all of the Gospels as well as in Acts 1:8) is clear reference to a fulfillment of the promise of the New Covenant which includes the promise of the Spirit in Ezekiel 36. In the midst of all this, the crucial place of the call on the nation of Israel is not lost. Luke 22:28-30 promises the disciples a place in the Kingdom, judging the twelve tribes of Israel. Judges are rulers. However, the passage in Acts 1:6-7 is even more significant. At the end of his forty-day period of post-resurrection teaching, before His ascension, the disciples ask: "Lord will you at this time restore the kingdom to Israel?"

Yeshua replied, "It is not for you to know the times or seasons which the Father has fixed by his own authority" (1:7). The disciples were clearly concerned about the literal establishment of the Kingdom of the Messiah on earth during which Yeshua would reign on the throne of David over the nation of Israel, and from Israel, over the whole world. The disciples saw themselves as part of this restoration even though they were followers of Yeshua during the *age of the universal body of the Messiah.* Hence, Jewish believers do not lose their calling to maintain their part in the call of the nation Israel.

It would have been so easy for Yeshua to correct His disciples' misperception, *if it was a misperception.* For forty days after His resurrection—and especially at that moment—He could have conveyed to them that this hope was a mistake of their too literal understanding of the Scriptures; and that the kingdom would never be restored to Israel. But no, He indicated that this hope would come to fruition some day; but only the Father knows the times and the seasons during when these things would take place. Yes, the gift and call of God remain for Israel, as well as the fact that Yeshua truly established a New Covenant which would include Gentiles who responded in faith.

THE NATURE OF MESSIANIC PROPHECY

Before leaving the topic under discussion—Yeshua and the call of Israel—it would be wise to state our viewpoints concerning the nature of Messianic prophecy or those passages from the Old Testament which are usually used to "prove" that Yeshua is the Messiah.

At times, followers of Yeshua have been zealous to quote passage after passage as predicting the details of His life. Unfortunately, thoughtful people who have checked out some of these references claim that some do not speak of the Messiah at all, but of Israel or King David. If what we have written heretofore is correct, the problem is not that Yeshua doesn't fulfill many predictions, but that the word "fulfill" does not always mean to resolve a prediction. It oftentimes means to fill up the meaning of Israel's history and to bring it to its epitome of meaning.[5]

We believe in Yeshua because of the reality of the faith walk with God we experience through Him; answered prayer, supernatural healing and peace. We not only believe in Yeshua because He fulfills the predictions, but because of the evidence that He is the representative of Israel and Israel's meaning as focused in one individual. Further, we believe because of the nature of the Gospel reports of His wonderful teaching, His amazing healing ministry and the excellent testimony of His resurrection.

We have already looked at those passages which speak of His solidarity with Israel. They are not predictions, strictly speaking, but tell of events which fill up the meaning of Israel's history in the Messiah-representative. We have looked as well at His marvelous teaching, incisive and with authority; not as the Scribes. His resurrection is the best attested fact of ancient history.[6] There are several sources: the Gospels and the writings of Paul, James, Peter and Jude. They all assert a real resurrection and an empty tomb. The disciples of the disciples—the fathers of the Church—in their writings, verify the testimony of the disciples as well as the fact that most of them died for this testimony of truth. These are not the stories of liars or deluded men. The disciples testified that Yeshua appeared publicly, taught, ate and fellowshipped with them over a period of forty days before His ascension.

Those who opposed the movement only had to produce His body to end the movement. Yet, as the great scholar Merril Tenney said, "only the reality of the resurrection can

explain the establishment of this movement among thousands of Jews in Jerusalem and its spread to the uttermost
part of the earth."[7] No other theory does justice to all of the
facts. After years of personal skepticism and searching out
every angle, I can testify that this evidence now speaks more
strongly than ever. Read the Gospels in an unbiased way.
Who but Yeshua died as a sacrifice in love and even as He
hung on the cross said, "Father forgive them for they know
not what they do"? Here the depths of the love of God touched
the human race.

Since my earlier days of skepticism I have witnessed
miracles of healed lives through the mighty name of Yeshua,
bodies healed, the healing of inner hurts, families restored,
addicts healed without withdrawal, and schizophrenia
healed—all through the ministry of prayer in Yeshua's name.
In the light of the whole context of Israel's purpose to be light,
in the light of the fact that through Yeshua the Scriptures
have spread to the non-Jewish world, in the light of the
foregoing, I can only ask, how can you not believe in Yeshua?

Too, there are those real predictions. Only Yeshua ties
together the meaning of the Scriptures and human history in
a coherent way: His birth in Bethlehem was predicted (Micah
5:2). It was predicted (Daniel 9:25) that the Messiah would be
cut off before the destruction of the second Temple and then
confirm a covenant to the nation. It was predicted that the
New Covenant would be established and the Holy Spirit
would be poured out on all flesh. This occurred as recounted
in Acts 2 (see Joel 2 and Ezekiel 36). People from all over the
Mediterranean world—Jews who spoke different languages
of the countries of their habitation—came to Jerusalem for
the feast of Shavout. All heard the Good News of Yeshua
preached in their own tongues by people who didn't even
know these languages.

Isaiah 53 refers to Yeshua, His sacrifice and resurrection
for us. I remember a brilliant biology professor in Chicago
who came to our congregation. He had become interested in
the Bible and began to teach the Tenach as he learned it to
Jewish people from all over the city. He had five evening

classes with several rabbis in attendance. When he came to the Messianic prophecies which have been taken to refer to Yeshua, he avoided the conclusion that Yeshua is the Messiah and convinced himself of other interpretations. However, when he came to Isaiah 53, no other interpretation but that this passage referred to Yeshua could be made to fit the chapter. In turmoil he cancelled all his classes. Later he became a follower of Yeshua. What was so convincing to the professor? It was a description that fits Yeshua perfectly and no one else. We do not deny the fact that Israel, also, has played a role as the suffering servant. However, as the servant songs of Isaiah progress (there are four major songs from Isaiah 40-53) the image becomes more and more focused on an individual who works in representation of Israel. A simple reading of the chapter shows us that the Scripture cannot be fully applied to Israel! "He is despised and rejected of men, a man of sorrows and acquainted with grief and *we* (Israel) esteemed Him not. He was wounded for our transgressions and bruised for our iniquities." Could it be said of Israel that "He made his grave with the wicked and with a rich man in his death"? Yet Yeshua died between the wicked and the rich man, Joseph of Aramathea, was with Him in death and buried His body. Yeshua returned from the dead, fitting the sense of this chapter also.

The Scriptures teach that Yeshua died as an atonement for our sins. This teaching grates upon modern sensibilities and pride but is a perfectly consistent doctrine, though of great depth. How is this so? Scripture teaches the truth of our own individual responsibility for our own acts. However, it does *not* teach that we can atone for our own sins. In fact, Scripture does not see men and women as separate individuals, but sees them rather in terms of their identity within the family, the nation and the human race.

In Scripture, we are *a fallen race*. Adam died because of his sin; the whole human race dies because it is also under the power of sin through its connection to Adam. Our connection with a fallen race is part of our identity. We are considered dead to God. The Bible teaches that we are to be perfect, just

as God is perfect. God is perfectly holy and cannot look upon
sin without judgment. What then is the solution?

We can accept Yeshua's death for us and His resurrection
and be accounted as having died in Him and been raised to
new life in Him. In other words, we may change our spiritual
racial descent from the fallen race of Adam by identifying
with the perfect man: Yeshua. We are accepted by God in
Him. We are considered as having paid the price, in Him.
Biblical scholars have long known of this truth about the idea
of man's connection to the human race and to its representatives. They have called this the concept of "corporate solidarity." When we identify with God's work in Yeshua for us and
receive Him as Savior, we are recreated in the depths of the
inner man. We are not fully perfect, but are given a recreated
spirit (II Corinthians 5:17). His life is in our lives and we are
bound up with Him.

Let us note that the biblical idea of atonement is not just a
concept of another person dying for our sins so we go free no
matter what we do or no matter what kind of people we are.
This is a common misperception. Yeshua, rather, is represen-
tative-God and representative-man. As representative God,
He demonstrates the love of God and the suffering that God
Himself experiences for the human race. God suffers our
every sin and pain and yet desires to forgive. This is manifested most fully at the cross. As representative man, Yeshua,
in His loving identity with us, suffers what we would not
suffer. He shows fully the destructive nature of sin, which
seeks to destroy Him, the perfect man. When we believe in
Him, we repent of our sins and identify with Him in such a
way that He lifts our burden. To be under His atonement we
must be part of Him.

Yeshua is not just a separate being (from us) who dies in
our stead. God expects us to *respond* to this great act of mercy;
and if we do, we are under His representative's cover; racially
and spiritually in him. Just as Adam's sin corrupted the
whole race, so the righteousness of Yeshua is now in us. In the
resurrection, He will bring us to complete sinlessness. Therefore, both because He paid the price representatively and we

are judged as part of Him by God (as some have said, when God looks to us He sees the righteousness of Yeshua) and because we are now children of God headed toward perfection, God can fully accept and forgive us while yet maintaining the absolute holiness and inviolability of His law.

Certainly this does not even plumb the depths of the atonement. Yet it fits the nature of life itself. We find that children do participate in the life of their parents, but are not totally bound by their inherited tendencies. We find that people who love us suffer terribly when we sin; yet they are willing to bear the cost of our sin and forgive us when we repent. We find that when another cries and suffers with us, the burden of shame and grief is lifted.

In Yeshua, God brought these realities to bear upon the whole human race that we might have our burden lifted, that we might be forgiven and be made new creatures in Him. It is to this that the (Old Testament) sacrificial system of substitution points. Praise God for these wonderful truths and the power of goodness that comes into our lives by faith when we truly believe.

THE COVENANT STRUCTURE OF
THE OLD AND NEW TESTAMENTS

Meridith Kline, from his studies of the covenant documents of the Torah, perceived that the whole Bible takes on the character of covenant documents. The parallel structure and coherence between the Tenach (Old) and the New Covenant Scriptures is amazing! The present arrangement of the Scriptures is not accidental; it reflects that covenant structure. Even if placed in different orders, the general structure of the Bible shows a very coherent character which yields a deep sense of inspiration by the same covenant-making God.

The Tenach (or the Old Testament) begins with the Torah, the five Books of Moses. These books are the covenant foundations for all of Scripture. They record the creation, the fall, the Noahic Covenant, the Abrahamic Covenant, the lives of the patriarchs (who were the recipients of the Abrahamic Covenant) and the Mosaic Covenant.

Actually, four of these books are devoted to the history of
the Exodus period and to the covenants and legislation, which
became the foundation of life in ancient Israel. We have
called this covenant material the Mosaic Covenant. Israel is
the recipient of the Abrahamic and Mosaic Covenants. These
documents are foundational for all future revelation; for
God's character and law are revealed in them. Furthermore,
prophets are to be judged by their consistency to these Covenant documents. (Deuteronomy 13, 18).

Prophetic-historical books follow the Torah: Joshua,
Judges, Ruth, I and II Samuel, I and II Kings, Ezra, Nehe-
miah, Esther, etc. These books are not mere history, but
inspired accounts that interpret the meaning of Israel's history in the light of her responses to the Torah. As such, the
books are based squarely upon Torah, as well as serving to
inspire fidelity to the Torah as the covenant foundation of
Israel's life.

Even the Book of Ruth shows us life among the covenant
people in a personal vein. And the Book of Esther shows us
the preservation of God's covenant people, as promised to
Abraham. All is built squarely upon Torah.

The poetical books then follow, which describe the
expressions of faith by a covenant people in literature, worship and proverb. After poetry, the prophetic books follow.
The role of the prophets was consistently to call Israel back to
Torah. Their predictions of judgment and blessing followed
from the promises and curses laid down by God in Torah
(Leviticus 26). At times their predictions were amazing as in
the detailed fulfillments of judgment.

It was in the light of Israel's national failure that the
prophets looked forward to the coming of the New Covenant.
This hope was also based upon Torah truth; for the prophets
looked for a way that man could both be accounted as righteous before God and empowered to perform His Law by the
power of the Spirit (Ezekiel 36). Even the Messianic prophecies fit the implications of the Torah. This includes the promise of worldwide blessing given through Abraham, to be fulfilled finally and most fully in the Messianic Days or the

Millenial Kingdom. It also includes the need of Messiah to suffer, die and rise again, for the whole Temple sacrificial system pointed to Him. Yeshua could well say that Moses wrote of Him and His ministry.

The New Covenant Scriptures, built upon God's revelation in the Tanach, exhibit an amazing similarity of structure. The four gospels, parallel to Torah, are the primary covenant documents. They record the history of the One who made the Covenant, as well as the foundation event of the Covenant in His life, death and resurrection. They record His words instituting the people of the New Covenant (Matthew 16, etc.) as well as the promise of the Spirit, which is central to the New Covenant.

Yeshua Himself, in a sense, is our New Covenant with God; and the Gospels are the portraits of Yeshua. The Book of Acts is also a prophetic-historical book, telling us what happened among the people who accepted the New Covenant. It also interprets the implications of this New Covenant. The twenty-one letters to the various New Covenant congregations parallel the writings of the prophets. They call the people to fidelity to the New Covenant in the midst of their straying. They apply the New Covenant and its implications to the specific situations which arise. They also have material which is predictive and looks forward to the return of Messiah and His reign through Israel over all the earth.

At the end of all this material is one great book of prophecy which ties together all the material of Scripture concerning the dangers of the last days, as well as the coming of the Messiah to rule and reign upon earth. This book strengthens believers in the midst of persecution by showing the ultimate Lordship of Yeshua over all the forces of evil.

The Bible is a marvelous unified and coherent revelation. Truly "men spake from God as they were moved by the Holy Spirit" (II Peter 1:21). Their personalities were not violated, but they conveyed the very words God intended to communicate—whether through the dictation to Jeremiah of a "Thus saith the Lord" and, "write these words," to the letters of Paul to Timothy. The Scriptures are uniquely the inspired Word of

God, revealing a God who acts in history and speaks in history and who seeks to redeem history as it progresses to the Age of Messiah. Indeed, the Bible is "His-story," which has no parallel in any of the quasi-religious literature of the world.

THE BOOK OF ACTS AND MESSIANIC JUDAISM

It is only in recent years that the Book of Acts has been given its due as a most significant book for our understanding of holistic New Testament teaching. In years past, the Book of Acts was read as an exciting history of what happened during the forty or so years after Yeshua's ascension. However, when issues of doctrine were at stake, the Book of Acts was passed over and people turned intead to the epistles for answers. This was unfortunate, for the Book of Acts provides the *context* for understanding the epistles.

Furthermore, a deeper reading of the Book of Acts—the sequel to the Gospel of Luke—exhibits a selection of material and an organization that is clearly intended to bring out a more complete understanding of the movements of the followers of Yeshua. Central to this purpose is the clarification of the relationship between Jews and Gentiles in the "kaheelah," or church of the Messiah. It is now commonly recognized among biblical scholars that Luke is a writer who seeks to convey theological understandings.[8] Luke, the travel companion of Paul, researched his material well and wrote his work after most of Paul's epistles. The Epistles of Paul are written for very specific situations, and a lack of understanding of those situations can cause us to generalize from the epistles in ways that illustrate poor interpretation. However, Luke's perspective is general: a summary made after the epistles were written. The perspective of his work on the issues that involve Messianic Jews will therefore be less misleading.

The Book of Acts begins with the record of Yeshua's ascension. As previously noted, the disciples are concerned about the establishment of the Kingdom on earth through Israel. Yeshua, however, reminds them to be patient and to do God's work; the times and seasons are in the hands of the

Father (Acts 1). As we concluded earlier, this passage foresees a continued purpose for the nation of Israel, as well as an eventual coming to the world of the earthly reign of the Messiah as presaged by the prophets. However, the disciples are told to wait for the outpouring of the "Ruach Ha-Kodesh," the Holy Spirit, after which they will be mighty witnesses of all that God has done through Yeshua (Acts 1:8). Their ministry is to have worldwide dimensions according to this passage. Yet the disciples believed that this worldwide dimension was to come by witnessing to Jews scattered all over the world. They believed that gentiles would also respond, but they thought they would do so by becoming Jews at the return of the Messiah once Israel had accepted His Good News.

The account of the coming of the Spirit on the day of Shavuot (Pentecost) is one of the most wonderful in all of Scripture. Remember that the 120 who were gathered in the upper room in prayer on this day were all Jews. We read that there appeared tongues of fire on each one of them and they began to speak other languages as the Spirit gave them utterance.

We should recall that the feast of Shavuot is one of the three major feasts of Israel, for which men were to travel to Jerusalem. Hence we read that devout men from every nation under heaven were dwelling in Jerusalem for the feast. This fact is incredibly overlooked: the men at the feast from all these nations were Jews, Jews who spoke the languages of the countries from which they resided. This miracle of languages points to the truth that the Good News was for every nation and tongue. Yet at that time it was only the Jews from those nations who were hearing the Good News. We read of the crowd who gathered that "they were bewildered, because each one heard them speaking in his own language." They were amazed and asked, "Are not all these who are speaking Galileans? And how is it that we hear, each of us in his own native language, Parthians and Medes and Elamites and residents of Mesopotamia, Judea, Cappadocia, Pontus, Asia, Phrygia and Pamphylia, Egypt . . . and the parts of Libya . . . and visitors from Rome . . . we hear them telling in our own tongues the mighty works of God?" (Acts 2:5-11).

It is true that proselytes were present on this occasion; but proselytes were converts to Judaism or would-be converts. It was Peter who stood up and gave the great interpretation of the event. His message is a ringing affirmation of the truths of the Messiah's life, death, resurrection, ascension and return. He calls upon the people gathered to repent: The miracles were undeniable; Yeshua was resurrected. Many signs and wonders were done and those who were added to this young congregation of believers numbered about 3,000. A significant congregation of Jewish believers in Yeshua thus was established at Jerusalem. Their lives were changed and there was a demonstration of love and an unparalleled sharing. They sold their possessions to meet each other's needs, broke bread in one another's homes and enjoyed a deep fellowship and praise toward God.

The disciples—most prominently Peter and John—continued their miracle works and teaching under the power of God. Although the Jewish religious establishment sought to prohibit them, and whipped them for doing so, they continued the work under obedience to the Spirit. This they considered a privilege—to suffer for Yeshua and righteousness' sake.

There are a few things to note in these chapters for our discussion: First, the number of followers swelled to over 5,000 (4:4). Second, we note that Peter still addressed the people as "sons of the prophets and of the covenant which God gave to your fathers, to Abraham . . ." (3:25). The covenant with Abraham is still perfectly valid and is fulfilled and will be fulfilled in Yeshua's ministry according to 3:26 and Acts 4. The story of Acts continues with the death of Ananias and Sapphira for lying to the Spirit of God about their contribution, the arrest and beating of disciples, great miracles of healing, the famous speech of Gamaliel to let the movement be, "for if it is not of God it will come to naught . . ." (5:37-39).

In Chapter six we read of the appointment of deacons to serve the congregation, thus freeing the apostles for teaching and prayer. This was occasioned by the fact that Hellenistic

Jews (Greek-speaking) complained of unfair treatment toward their widows and needy in the distribution of community funds. One of the deacons appointed was Stephen.

Stephen had a powerful preaching and teaching ministry. Others hated his teaching and conspired to have Stephen arrested on (trumped-up) charges of blasphemy. Acts 7 records Stephen's great defense in a sermon that recounts the whole of Israel's history. At the end of his speech, Stephen made a strong accusation against his accusers, calling them stiff-necked, uncircumcised in heart and ears, resisting the Holy Spirit and following in the tradition of those who killed the prophets. They were enraged and stoned Stephen (illegally) on the spot; but Stephen saw a vision of Yeshua and prayed for Him to receive his Spirit.

In all of this, the Good News still has not really spread beyong geographic Israel. The struggle is between Jews who follow Yeshua and a Jewish religious establishment that seeks to destroy the movement. It is the persecution which follows (in Acts 8) which finally becomes the means of forcing the Good News out of its confinement.

As already stated, there was no sense yet that the Gospel was to be offered freely to gentiles; the Good News was for Jews only! Chapter 8 begins the story of God's preparation for a change of understanding by: spreading the Gospel to the Samaritans, the amazing conversion of Saul to the movement, and the wonderful story of Peter and the conversion of the Gentile-proselyte Cornelius. This prepared the apostles to accept a ministry to the Gentiles. The most prominent ministry was the work of Saul, the former great persecutor of the "followers of the Way," the earliest name for believers in Yeshua (see Acts 7:58 and 8:1).

Chapter 8 records Philip's preaching to the Samaritans. The response was tremendous. Many believed and many were cleansed from unclean spirits; many were healed. Philip baptized in the name of Yeshua, but strangely, the Holy Spirit did not come upon them. The story of Acts 8 is not an example of the way the Spirit must come to indwell a person, but is rather exceptional because these people were

Samaritans. In general, people could receive the Spirit without the apostles' laying on of hands. Unless the apostles
became the source of their receiving the Spirit, however, the
conversion of the Samaritans would be suspect, for the Samaritans were not accepted as Jews. They were considered "half-
breeds," who no longer followed the truth.

Over 700 hundred years earlier, when the Assyrians took
the northern tribes captive and scattered most of them to
various parts of the empire, non-Jews were settled in the
region of Samaria and intermarried with the few remaining
clans. Some hundred years later, when the Jews returned
from the Babylonian captivity to reestablish the nation and
Temple, the Samaritans, fearing loss of their own political
position, opposed them. Great hatred grew between the Jews
and Samaritans. The latter worshipped at Mt. Gerizim, not
Jerusalem. They accepted the Torah (namely, the Books of
Moses), but not the prophets and were accommodated to
pagan elements. Many Jewish "followers of the Way" would
certainly have held that Samaritans could not accept Yeshua
unless they renounced their Samaritan religion and converted to full-fledged Judaism. Peter and John laid hands
upon the Samaritans and they received the Holy Spirit with
supernatural manifestations. We are not told what these
manifestations were. It might have been prophecy, tongues,
etc. However, it was a clear manifestation of the Spirit and
there would be no dispute from the Jerusalem Congregation
as to its veracity. Yet to accept the Samaritans, who, despite
their errors had a Jewish ancestry and accepted the Torah,
was quite different than accepting gentiles who were foreign
and pagan.

How providential was the conversion of Saul (Acts 9)! He
was a student of Gamaliel, the greatest rabbi of his day; he
was a Roman citizen from Tarsus; he was a Pharisee of the
Pharisees (Philippians 3:5, 6). He journeyed to Damascus
with letters of authority from the Jerusalem establishment to
bring the followers of "the Way" to Jerusalem to be beaten
and imprisoned. It was while on the road to Damascus that he
saw his great vision of Yeshua, was blinded and told to enter

Damascus.

This event was truly one of the great miracles of history. Those who seek natural explanations of this event by such theories as "Paul's malaria" or "epilepsy" or "propensity to visions" are to be pitied. They ignore the rest of the story. For a disciple at Damascus named Ananias also had a vision and was told to go to the house of Judas in Damascus to find the blinded Saul. God also gave Paul another vision: to expect Ananias to come and lay hands on him to receive back his sight. Ananias was not acting out any "wish fulfillment." He didn't even know that Paul was there; but when told of his misson, he argued with God, for he had heard of Saul's great record of persecution. Then we read of the great revelation that salvation is to be offered also to the gentiles, for God says to Ananias, "Go, for he is a chosen instrument of mine to carry my name before the Gentiles and kings and the sons of Israel, for I will show him how much he must suffer for the sake of my name" (9:15).

And so Ananias obeys, Saul receives his sight and is baptized, accepting his commission.

Saul now preaches the Good News in the synagogues; he escapes an attempt to kill him and seeks to join the disciples at Jerusalem who cannot believe that he, too, is a disciple. Through the intervention of Barnabas, who recounts the story of Paul's conversion, they accept him. In danger again, Saul is sent to Tarsus. As yet, we still have only a Jewish movement for Yeshua! Acts chapter 10 is the great turning point. It is crucial for us to realize at this point that we are still reading Jewish history. Against all the prejudice of the ages, we must shout that Yeshua is the Messiah and Savior of Jewish people.

Once again it was the supernatural work of the Spirit of God which brought the progress of the next chapters. No human intention was behind it, but the Spirit worked against the intentions and proclivities of the apostles to bring the Gospel to the gentiles, without the restrictions of having first to become part of the call of Israel! Who was to be chosen for this work of the Spirit? None other than the burly Peter himself.

Once again, God's method of communication was by
supernatural visions: A vision was given to Cornelius, a man
who feared the God of Israel. He was told to send for Peter in
Joppa. While his messengers journeyed, Peter had his great
vision of a sheet descending from heaven containing all kinds
of non-kosher or unclean food. Yet Peter was told to kill and
eat. Peter refused, protesting that he had never eaten anything unclean. God's response is, "What God has cleansed,
you must not call common."

To make its full import, this vision occurred three times.
Some hold that God hereby signified an end of the applicabil-
ity of the food lists in Torah for Jewish people. Yet we never
read that Peter ate the food or thought that the vision implied
anything about food laws. Instead, we read, "Peter was
inwardly perplexed as to what the vision he had seen might
mean." As Peter reflected, the messengers arrived from Cornelius in the perfect timing of God. Peter was told by the
Spirit to accompany them. *The significance of the vision was
that gentiles who turn to the God of Israel in Yeshua are not
to be considered unclean.*

This then is the issue of Acts: are gentiles fully accepted
by God in Yeshua without adopting the call of the nation of
Israel? *It is never an issue that Jews might be called to give up
their calling as part of the nation of Israel along with their
practice of the Jewish-biblical-national heritage. It is assumed
that they will maintain their heritage in a biblically consistent way as Jews.*

So Peter preaches the Good News to Cornelius and makes
the marvelous statement, "Truly, I perceive that God shows
no partiality, but in every nation anyone who fears him and
does what is right is acceptable to him" (10:34-35). While Peter
preached, the Spirit fell upon the listeners. The believers
from among the circumcised were amazed because the gentiles were given the gift of the Spirit! They spoke in tongues
and extolled God, yet they had not become Jews! Further, the
usual order of Acts 2 (repent, believe, be baptized and receive
the gift of the Holy Spirit) is reversed: Here they believe and

receive the Spirit *before* baptism. Peter says, "Can anyone forbid water for baptizing these people who have received the Holy Spirit just as we have?" (10:47).

We also note the supernatural manifestation of the Spirit in this case as in Acts 8. It is completely unprompted. Again, this manifestation and the apostolic presence would be used to enable the Jerusalem disciples to accept these events. Many people in the Book of Acts believe the Gospel, but it was only in three incidents after Pentecost that the supernatural accompaniments were emphasized. In each case, it was for the purpose of enabling the disciples to overcome barriers to the acceptance of others as one in faith with them. In Acts 8 it was the Samaritans; in Acts 10 it was the Gentiles, a designation covering everyone else. Late in Acts 19, it was the exceptional group known as disciples of John the Baptist, who still existed years after the beginnings of the movement for Yeshua.

In Acts 11, Peter was questioned concerning his actions by the Jerusalem community. They asked, "Why did you go in to uncircumcised men to eat with them?" All Peter had to do was recall the supernatural work of God's Spirit, which he could not resist. Their response is recorded in verse 18.

"When they heard this they were silenced. And they glorified God saying, Then to the Gentiles also God has granted repentance unto life."

The work of God's Spirit perfectly prepared the Jerusalem leadership for a new situation which arose in Antioch: There the Good News was preached to Greeks. Previously, even those who were scattered spoke "the word to none except Jews." Hence Barnabas was sent to Antioch, a mixed congregation of Jews and non-Jews. Barnabas then went to Tarsus and, upon finding Saul, brought him to Antioch. For one year they taught this congregation. They also sought to exhibit unity with the Jerusalem leadership by sending aid (v. 30) to them.

All of this led to the greatest endeavor to spread the Good News among gentiles. It was the ministry of Saul of Tarsus. Saul and Barnabas were called out by prophecy from the

Antioch congregation in which they faithfully ministered. They embarked under the guidance of the Holy Spirit.

The ministry of Saul will be the primary focus of the Book of Acts. Who was this man, vilified by some as the adulterator of the simple truths of Yeshua's teaching, criticized as a renegade Jew, and hailed as the founder of Christianity?[10]

In Saul we find a zealous Jew, educated in the best tradition of Pharisaical (later Rabbinic) Judaism (Philippians 3). We find a man who used the Jewish methods of reasoning in which he was so steeped.[11] Yet we also find one who was a Roman citizen who could quote the philosophical views of his day (Acts 17). Here was a man who could tell the Corinthians that he did not come with words of human wisdom in great oratorical power, for it was necessary that his message gain adherence by the power of the Spirit and not by human ingenuity. Perhaps the problem in seeking to understand Saul is ours, not his: a man too great for our limited understanding, with a perspective so vast that we distort it by our ability to only see certain facets of it.

Barnabas and Saul believed in a big God, big enough to reach out to the gentiles with the Good News of Yeshua. Yet they never forgot God's chosen people of whom they were. In every town, a pattern was repeated. As they traveled from country to country, they went first to the synagogue. The synagogue had the "Torah and the prophets" which were the source for conveying the truth of the Gospel. The response varied from town to town. Many Jews believed; many did not. However, perhaps in ways unexpected, gentiles responded in droves:

"The next Sabbath almost the whole city gathered together to hear the word of God. But when the Jews saw the multitudes they were filled with jealously and contradicted what was spoken by Paul and reviled him" (Acts 13:44-45).

We must note that in those days, Judaism was a proselytizing religion. Many gentiles sensed the bankruptcy of pagan religion and attached themselves to the synagogue and its high view of one great God and the ethics of the Bible. Some converted; but many could not take the final step. The barrier was circumcision. This sign was looked upon as barbaric by Greeks, even a scandal, especially for adults. So there were the so-called "proselytes of the gate," who remained close to the synagogue but did not become Jews.

The preaching of Paul enabled the gentiles to be blessed by a life and fellowship with God on a high spiritual and moral plain without requiring their conversion to Judaism. This truly incited the Jewish synagogal leadership to jealousy, for they lost many of the "proselytes of the gate" for whom they had labored so long and hard. The movement of the Gospel among the gentiles thus dampened the prospects of adding converts to Judaism. Although the disciples in Jerusalem had rejoiced at Peter's explanation of Cornelius' conversion, the influx of gentiles would soon require a clear and definitive decision regarding the relationship between Jewish and gentile "followers of the Way" as well as the requirements vis-a-vis Judaism for the gentiles.

Acts 15 presents the controversy which was the catalyst for a discussion on these issues. We read, "But some men came down from Judea and were teaching the brethren, unless you are circumcised according to the custom of Moses, you cannot be saved. And when Paul and Barnabas had no small dissension and debate with them, Paul and Barnabas and some of the others were appointed to go up to Jerusalem to the apostles and elders about this question. . . . But some believers who belonged to the party of the Pharisees rose up, and said, it is necessary to circumcise them and to charge them to keep the law of Moses" (15:1-5).

This is the story of what became known as the "Judaizing" controversy. The term "Judaizing" is easily bandied about today by many who do not truly understand what the controversy was all about. This is a sad example of human carelessness in handling the holy Word of God. What is Judaizing? Let us begin with a negative and then a positive. Negatively, *it is not* a term to be applied to believing Jews who maintain their practice and heritage in their call to be part of the nation of Israel. Neither does Judaizing refer to non-Jews who have a love and appreciation for Jewish things. As the Scriptures define it, Judaizing is the view that unless you are circumcised according to the custom of Moses you cannot be saved, i.e., "it is necessary to charge them to keep the law of Moses . . . (15:1).

Judaizing is also any position which holds that circumcision and following the call to be a Jew places an individual on a "higher plain of spirituality" with God which is otherwise unobtainable.

The Book of Acts and Galatians are the primary sources for understanding this controversy. The former provides the broader context; the latter, a specific situation. It is the writer's view that the Book of Galatians not only was written before the Book of Acts (this being universally acknowledged), but that the book was written before the events described in Acts 15. The bases of this view are beyond the scope of this book, but can be found in several books on the date, authorship and purpose of Galatians.[12] If this is so, the Book of Galatians reflects the situation when the Judaizing controversy was as yet not settled by the apostolic authorities over the church. Acts 15 would then be the definite statement of authority in regard to that controversy.

The problem in Galatians is essentially the same as the problem in Acts 14 and 15: Congregations had been terribly troubled by the teaching that circumcision (a human work) was necessary for salvation. The response of Saul of Tarsus to this controversy was multi-faceted.

First, there was his verbal chastisement of those who would fall away from the Gospel. The Gospel is a message of salvation by grace through faith. No human work can be an ingredient in that salvation; nor can it be said that any human work is necessary to fulfill that salvation. Paul then went on to assert his apostleship as of equal authority to the Jerusalem apostles, and dependent upon a direct call of God. This apostleship and the validity of the Gospel he preached were clearly recognized by the Jerusalem apostles (Galatians 1:11; 2:10).

If the Acts 15 decision had already transpired it would

have been strange indeed that Paul did not quote the decision, which had the backing of all the apostles in Jerusalem, to silence the Judaizers. He did not quote it because the decision had not yet been reached. Paul then recounted some history to show the truth of his position that gentiles are saved by grace through faith, without adopting the call and life of Israel. The example from history related to Peter: For "James and Cephas and John, who were reputed to be pillars, gave to me and Barnabas the right hand of fellowship, that we should go to the gentiles and they to the circumcised" (Galatians 2:9-10).

The great "but" comes in v. 11, for Peter came to visit the Antioch congregation. In an incident unrecorded in the rest of Scripture, Paul discusses a controversy he had with Peter. Peter had been willing to eat with gentile believers but, in fear of the Judaizers, he drew back and separated himself. Paul publicly rebuked Cephas (Peter) "before them all" (v. 14). The issue is that Peter was not sincere about the Gospel. The chapter continues with Paul's rebuke,

"If you, though a Jew, live like a Gentile and not like a Jew, how can you compel the Gentiles to live like Jews! We ourselves, who are Jews by birth and not Gentile sinners, yet who know that a man is not justified by works of the law, but through faith in Yeshua ha Masiach, even we have believed in Messiah Yeshua in order to be justified by faith in Messiah, and not by works of the law, because by works of the law shall no one be justified" (Galatians 2:14-16).

A full exposition of Paul's view on the relationship of law, grace and the covenants awaits the next chapter. Here it is clear that Paul was saying that the Judaizer's position implied that a man was righteous in the sight of God by his works according to the Law, rather than by faith in the atonement and resurrection of Yeshua. This was heresy.

Peter was called insincere about the Gospel because he *refused to eat with gentile* believers. It is crucial to understand the implications of this: To the practicing Orthodox Jew, the gentile was unclean. In Acts 11 Peter was first questioned as to why he would stoop to eat with unclean gentiles.

The uncleanness stemmed from the fact that they engaged in
all sorts of practices forbidden in the (clean-unclean) lists of
Leviticus and Deuteronomy. To touch a dead body, to eat
blood, to eat pork or shellfish, to not be purified from bodily
emissions, all made a person ritually unclean and not privileged to engage in Temple worship or service. To maintain
cleanliness, Jews would distance themselves from gentiles.

However, if a gentile had accepted Yeshua, he was clean
in Him. This was the import of Peter's vision in Acts 10,
accompanied by the words, that "what God has cleansed, do
not call it unclean." If gentiles were clean in Yeshua, then the
truth was to be reflected by eating with them. In the culture
of the Near East, table fellowship was *the* symbol of mutual
acceptance and spiritual unity. Peter's withdrawal under the
pressure of the fear of man undercut the whole sense of the
truth of salvation by grace and the spiritual unity of Jews and
gentiles in Yeshua.[13] Table fellowship was therefore a key
issue in Galatians.

Paul's words to Peter were biting. For he called Peter a
Jew who lived like a gentile, but who by his actions, was
hypocritically requiring gentiles to live like Jews. The only
explanation for Paul saying that Peter lived like a gentile is by
comparison to his very strict Pharisee standards.[14] To a
trained Pharisee, a Galilean fisherman would be living like a
gentile. All of the evidence of early church history justifies
the view that Peter continued his Jewish practice in a general
sense. Paul then goes on to say, "we who are Jews by birth
and not Gentile sinners" (Galatians 2:15). That is, we are
people under God's covenant with the opportunity to live
accordingly. We *are* Jews; we still have the covenant call as
Jews; but we also understand justification by faith *and must
not do anything to undercut it.*

There is great humor and irony in the greatly trained
Pharisee taking a Galilean fisherman to task for trying to
appear so Jewishly kosher, when he, the trained Pharisee,
undercuts Peter's whole attitude of withdrawal as contrary to
the very Gospel he seeks to profess.

Paul's whole point in retelling this event is that Peter

accepted the rebuke. The story provides an incident whereby all would know the Judaizing teaching was wrong, as proved by Paul's correction of Peter. If Paul had the decision of Acts 15 to go by—which he later enthusiastically communicated as an emissary of the apostles (Acts 15:27, 30, 31)—he would have simply quoted it at this time.

Therefore it is of utmost importance to understand the implications of Acts 15 and all later passages in the Book of Acts connected with it. In Luke's account of the Acts 15 council on Judaizing, Peter is first to speak. He recalls the supernatural work of the Spirit leading to his preaching to the gentiles in Acts 10. They were given the Spirit even though they were not Jews (15:8). God did not distinguish the Jew and non-Jew in regard to the gift of His Spirit. Hence, Peter speaks against any Jewish yoke for gentile believers. Barnabas and Paul speak next. They point to God's great work among the gentiles through their ministry. However, it is ultimately James who gives the viewpoint which becomes the definitive view of the council.

Who was this James? He was none other than the brother of Yeshua, the author of the epistle bearing his name. The testimony of history is that James became a firm believer after the resurrection of Yeshua and was soon accepted into the apostolic circle. Eventually, he became leader of the Jerusalem community of Yeshua. According to Josephus and Eusebius, James' piety and loyalty to the Jewish biblical heritage were absolutely steadfast.[15] So much was this case that when James was murdered by the plot of the wicked high priest (a Sadducean), the Pharisees were incensed. They proceeded to agitate the people against the priest and through their efforts he was deposed.

James' speech first recalls those scriptures which point to the salvation of the gentiles by the Messiah's work. James clearly has great leadership sway over the whole council, for his judgment becomes the position of the gathered council.

He says, "Therefore my judgment is that we should not trouble those of the Gentiles who turn to God, but should write to them to abstain from the pollutions of idols and from

unchastity and from what is strangled and from blood. For
from early generations Moses has had in every city those who
preach him, for he is read every sabbath in the synagogues"
(15:19-21).

The gathered elders then sent Paul and Barnabas, along
with Judas and Silas, as witnesses from their own community
with a letter recording the decision for all the churches. The
letter indicates that those who troubled them were not sent
by the Jerusalem eldership. Next, the letter conveys that the
decision is from the gathered assembly of elders and apostles
(v. 25). The decision is said to be the decision of the Holy Spirit
(v. 28).

What exactly is the meaning of this decision? Of great
note is that not a word of the decision or the discussion leading
up to it questioned the propriety of Jews maintaining their
call and heritage. This was never at issue in the new Testament period but was assumed to be the natural stance of
Jews.[16]

The only reason we do not find much New Testament
material specifically teaching this is that it was so obviously
assumed. The New Testament books were written to settle
problems and controversies as they arose. All of church history testifies that Jewish believers maintained their heritage.[17] This was so obviously accepted by all the apostles that it
was never addressed as an issue until after their death! Scholars today are beginning to perceive that the apostolic position
was that Jews should maintain their biblical calling and
heritage.[18]

In his First Letter to the Corinthians Paul makes his
position clear.

"Only let every one lead the life which the Lord has
assigned to him and to which God has called him. This is my
rule in the churches. Was anyone at the time of his call circumcised? Let him not seek to remove the marks of his circumcision" (I Corinthians 7:17-18). Acts 21 is Luke's key chapter for applying the decision to Jews.

As for gentile believers, they are given the direction to
"abstain from the pollutions of idols and from unchastity and

from what is strangled and from blood" (Acts 15:29). We recognize here one of the historic Jewish positions: A gentile who is to be accepted as righteous must follow the Noahic Covenant. That covenant (in Genesis 9), universal for all mankind, was interpreted as forbidding idolatry, immorality and the eating of blood. Hence, James is affirming the fact that gentiles can be in Messiah without becoming Jews and are spiritually one with the community of faith. Yet those basic Noahic stipulations would be certainly followed by anyone in the Messiah. Hence, they affirmed the basic moral dimensions of the Law as universally applicable as well as the sanctity of blood.

It is also of note that this is the minimum standard for Jews and gentiles to achieve table fellowship, that great symbol of spiritual unity. Table fellowship in the early communities of Yeshua was celebrated with the Messiah's Supper, thus making mutual acceptance through a common meal crucially significant.

Jews, by implication, would have to lower their standards of rigorous ritual cleanliness to maintain such fellowship, whereas gentiles would avoid grossly offensive practices in regard to eating things forbidden in Leviticus 11. (See Romans 14 on the principle of mutual love in non-biblically binding standards.) The interesting statement of Acts 15:21 is also significant: "For from early generations Moses has had in every city those who preach him, for he is read every Sabbath in the synagogue." James here is saying that the testimony to a fully Jewish lifestyle is already present in the synagogues of the Diaspora. Moses is read weekly in the synagogue and if gentiles are interested, they have ample opportunity to respond. The job of the apostles, however, is to spread the Good News of Yeshua without any barriers of culture or national calling standing in the way of its acceptance.

Acts 21 is commentary on this decision. It is the most crucially important passage in the New Testament for gaining an understanding of the apostolic position on the practice of Jewish believers. *It reflects what was the assumed stance of the apostles and makes what was only implicit in the New*

Testament explicit.

In Acts 21, Paul travels to Jerusalem. He goes under prophetic warnings of danger to his life, but is constrained in spirit to go.

When Paul arrives in Jerusalem, we read that the brethren "received him gladly" (21:17). The next day Paul meets with James (who has formulated the Acts 15 statement regarding Judaizing) and all the elders. After Paul testified of God's mighty work among the gentiles, those gathered "glorified God." However, a problem had arisen:

"And they said to him, 'You see brother how many thousands there are among the Jews of those who have believed; they are all zealous for the law, and they have been told about you that you teach all the Jews who are among the Gentiles to forsake Moses, telling them not to circumcise their children or observe the customs' " (vv. 20-21).

The Good News had truly spread within the Jerusalem community. The Greek word is that there were myriads who believed. They were all zealous for the Law.

Paul, at this point, had an opportunity to admit that he did teach Jews to forsake Moses and to not circumcise. Luke's purpose in this passage is clearly to show that Paul was loyal to his heritage and that his later arrest was unfair in the light of this loyalty. The advice Paul is given is to purify himself with four men under a Nazarite vow. This was a special vow taken for service to God during which the person neither drank wine nor cut his hair. Paul was to take the men, purify himself with them, and pay their expenses for offerings. In the words of the chapter, the purpose is, "Thus all will know that there is nothing in what they have been told about you, but that you yourself live in observance of the law" (v. 24).

Clearly, the facts as the elders knew them testified that Paul lived in observance of the Law. That he taught Jews to forsake their observance was considered a vicious rumor. ". . . there is *nothing* in what has been told about you . . ." (v. 24).

There is no argument; Paul does exactly as advised. However, he is later arrested due to the force of the rumor anyway.

It has been argued that Paul compromised under pressure. Did James also compromise? He gave us the Book of James and maintained his observance until his death. If Paul compromised, why is there no hint of it in the text? Why is Luke so misleading? Did the same Paul who was stoned and whipped for the Gospel—who went up to Jerusalem knowing that he would be arrested—compromise at this point? It is so out of character that it is unacceptable. Further, Luke, in the same passage, notes that the elders recalled their decision in regard to gentile freedom. "But as for the Gentiles who have believed, we have sent a letter with our judgment that they should abstain from what has been sacrificed to idols, and from blood, and from what is strangled, and from unchastity" (v. 25).

Why is this passage included? It is so we will understand that Paul's maintaining his heritage was no compromise of the principal freedom in the Gospel, laid down in Acts 15. *No!* Paul did not compromise! Luke is clearly revealing the difference of call in one universal body of faith: Jews are part of the call and identity of the nation Israel, whereas gentiles are free from this call. The view that Paul compromised at this point in his life is given its death sentence in Acts 18:18 where we read, "At Cenchreae he cut his hair, for he had a vow." The vow related to cutting the hair was a Nazarite vow based on the Torah (Numbers 6). It was the same vow that was taken by the four men in Acts 21!

Here, Paul observes the Law with no external pressure! Furthermore, we find indications of such observance throughout Paul's whole life. Clearly his epistles must be interpreted in this context:

● In Acts 15:22, Paul agrees to carry out the decision of the apostles which allows full Torah identity for Jews.

● In Acts 16:3, we find Paul in the synagogue on the Sabbath *as was his practice.*

● In Acts 20:16, we see Paul hastening to be at Jerusalem for Shavuot. This was one of three major feasts wherein Jewish people were commanded to appear before God in

Jerusalem.

● In Acts 22:3, 12 Paul defends himself as having done nothing against the Law.

● In Acts 23:1-5, he quotes the Law in response to his own necessity of respecting rulers—even the high priest.

● In Acts 24:11-17, Paul argues that his accusers are angry with him due to his belief in the resurrection. He recounts his Acts 21 action as part of maintaining a clear conscience of witness before men (24:17).

● In Acts 25:8, he says, "Neither against the law of the Jews, nor against the temple have I offended at all."

● In Acts 26:5-8, Paul testifies that he has lived as a strict Pharisee with no qualification stated in regard to recent practice. In Acts 26:19-20, Paul said he called for deeds worthy of repentance. This is strictly Jewish phrasing.

Acts 28:17 is a real clincher. Paul says to the Jews in Rome, "Brethren, though *I had done nothing against the people or the customs of our fathers*, yet I was delivered prisoner."

The conclusion becomes inescapable: the evaluation of the elders concerning Paul was absolutely correct; there was nothing to the rumor that had been spread about him.

There are many biblical scholars who have recognized this truth. H.L. Ellison states that to be part of his nation, Paul would have worn the fringes of Judaism,[20] which were memory aids to recall our responsibility to live according to Torah. So also J.H. Yoder states that Paul's concern *was not* with Jewish loyalty to the Law for he himself conformed to the Law.[21] The most stirring statement comes in the classic work of W.D. Davies, *Paul and Rabbinic Judaism.*

"We begin with the significant fact that throughout his life Paul was a practicing Jew who never ceased to insist that his Gospel was first to the Jews, who also expected Jewish Christians to persist in their loyalty to the Torah of Judaism, and who assigned to the Jews in the Christian no less than in the pre-Christian dispensation a place of peculiar importance."[22]

The conclusion of this chapter on the Book of Acts is

clearly to support the thesis of this book as a whole, namely that Jews under the New Covenant are still called to maintain their historic national identity as part of Israel. Being part of the universal body does not remove the specific expression of that salvation in a way that befits the call to be a part of the nation of Israel in its distinctive task of witness. Many believers have diverse calls to different nations and cultures. The call to Israel is valid.

In addition, we must express our belief that the apostles are our authorities in doctrine by their teaching *and example*. We cannot, as Karl Barth said, look over their shoulders and correct their notebooks. If they—including Paul—maintained their Jewish practice and identity, that settles the issue for us. They did! Even Paul, the apostle to the gentiles as a Jew, maintained his practice and identity as did the disciples of the disciples, the Nazarenes. Praise God for the revelation of His truth.

We then continue our practice, knowing that Yeshua is the One to whom all things point. All is done with an eye to its fulfillment in Him. And ours is a rich heritage of the acts of God, rooted in history, exemplified by the apostles and full of God's grace, a witness to the world of God's faithfulness to Israel and all the children of God.

CHAPTER THREE

Paul, Israel and the Law

In all of Scripture, there is no greater theological depth and glorious truth than is revealed in Paul's teaching on the Law. This teaching is central to the meaning of the Good News itself. Yet, how tragically this teaching is misunderstood, both by Yeshua's followers and those who do not follow Him. The error is usually one of carelessness. A verse is taken out of context and false conclusions are drawn, when the true meaning of the verse can be seen only in the light of Paul's *whole* connected presentation. Further, various meanings of the word "law" or "nomos" are not distinguished; all are lumped together. Yet, in everyday speech, we know one word may carry several meanings—according to the context of usage. In addition, there are plays on words, so loved by Jewish thinkers, but totally missed by the modern reader. We believe that Paul's teaching is thoroughly in line with his profession and example in the Book of Acts and fully in accord with Messianic Judaism.

Any teaching on Paul and the Law must take note of his key foundational statements in relation to Torah as God's revelation, as well as a reflection of His eternal standard of right and wrong. So far as the Law reflects this eternal standard of God, it is irrevocable. As such we should note these verses:

• Romans 3:31—faith established the Law. "Do we then overthrow the law by this faith? By no means! On the contrary, we uphold the law."

• Romans 3:2 states that the Law is a gift of God.

• Romans 3:7 teaches that the Law defines what sin is, while Romans 6:1-2 says we are not to continue to sin.

• Romans 7:12 states the the Law is holy. "The commandment is holy and just and good."

• Romans 7:14 states that the Law is spiritual; 7:16, that the Law is good.

In the Law the great wisdom of God's standards is revealed. Only the Bible reveals an infinite, personal, *ethical* God!

Paul certainly had the Law in mind when he said, "*All Scripture* is given by inspiration of God and is profitable for correction, for instruction and for training in righteousness that the man of God may be complete, equipped for every good work" (II Timothy 3:16-17).

This verse was written before the New Testament came into being. The Torah is to be a source of our correction and training. As Paul said, the Law is good if one uses it rightly (I Timothy 1:8-11).

Paul also quoted the Law to give ethical direction to congregations under the Spirit: In Ephesians 6:1-3, "Children obey your parents in the Lord, for this is right. Honor your father and mother; this is the first commandment with a promise, that it may be well with you and that you may live long on the earth." Paul takes it that *the promise of Torah will apply to them who obey*.

Paul also maintained the validity of the Law as uniquely related to Israel's continuing religious national identity and special witness as a people.

Then what is the problem? Is it that there are passages in Paul addressed to the misuse of the Law which are interpreted to invalidate the Law itself? Is it that there are uses of the word "law" that do not refer to the revelation in Torah, but are, instead, false applications of it?

The major assault in Paul's writings is in regard to the use of the Law as part of a system of works-righteousness. According to this system, man stores up merits before God by keeping the Law, i.e., earning God's acceptance and salvation. Such a view produces hypocrisy, since the person with such a view does not see how much he breaks the Law, though professing to keep it. It also produces self-righteous pride. The exposure of the wrongness of this view is central. We must first see that God's standard is absolute holiness and perfection. Falling short of this, we stand condemned by the Law before a holy God. Paul quotes a medley of passages from the Psalms and Prophets to show God's view of *our self-righteousness*—from Psalm 53, "There is none that doeth good, no not one, they are *all* fallen away . . . all alike depraved." Paul's conclusion is, "All have sinned and come short of the glory of God" (Romans 3:23), and "the wages of sin is death," spiritual separation from God (Romans 6:23).

We think we can earn God's righteousness because we tend to compare our achievements with others, not God's absolute holy perfection and standard of total love and self-lessness (Deuteronomy 6:4; Leviticus 19:18). We may seem miles ahead of others, but are still light-years away from real perfection when we examine our heart attitudes and motives. Our self-righteousness further calls into question whether we are really ahead of others at all. Before God's Law, we all stand condemned; not justified.

There is within us a nature that desires to break the Law, to sin; it is called a sin nature. The rabbis perceived this in their doctrine of the "Yetzer ha ra," the evil impulse. This sin nature is such that the Law may even inspire it to desire to sin more since sin finds the forbidden fruits sweeter. This is a principle that Paul also calls a law, making a play on words with "nomos" or "law." It is a "law" within me ("law" used in a different sense than Torah) that when I want to do right evil lies close at hand. To eliminate misunderstanding, Paul, in this same chapter, calls *the law* (Torah) "holy, just, good" and "spiritual," which of course is not the case with the law (principle) "that evil lies close at hand."

These facts evoke two other principles also called "law"

in a play on words; *again, they are not Torah.* They are the
laws of sin and death. The law of sin is the principle that God's
holy righteous Law is more a source of temptation to fallen
man than a source of righteous motivation. This is not
because of any fault in the Law, but because of sin's nature.

"But sin, finding opportunity in the commandment
wrought in me all kids of covetousness" (Romans 7:8). The
weakness of the Law is not its high standard, but that it is
powerless to cause the sinful man to fulfill it. "For we know
that the law is spiritual: but I am carnal, sold under sin (7:14).
The law is "weakened by the flesh" (8:3). So Paul says, "I see
in my members another law at war with the law of my mind
and making me captive to the law of sin which dwells in my
members" (7:23).

Breaking the Law leads to greater bondage, to more law-
breaking and sin. The pervert, for example, holds that one
more indulgence of curiosity will assuage his desires. This is
so, but only temporarily. Later temptations are stronger and
even grosser. The liar, the drunkard, the thief and the glutton
all find a similar operation of sin in their lives!

This law of sin leads to death, in all its ramifications. The
law of death is the law of the wages of law-breaking, separation from fellowship with God, physical death and, finally,
eternal death.

What an incredible tragedy that some think the law of
"sin and death" is the Torah! How unfortunate is this false
interpretation.

As John said, "Sin is the transgression of Law"; in Paul's
words, "where there is no law there is no transgression." All
therefore stand "guilty."

Paul's central question is: How then shall we stand as
righteous—not guilty—or justified before God? He finds his
solution in Abraham: "Abraham," says Genesis 3:15, "believed
God and God accounted it to him for righteousness." Abraham was justified by faith! Only years later did he receive the
sign of circumcision as the sign of his covenant relationship
with God (Romans 4:12).

In Galatians, Paul argues that any interpretation of the

Mosaic revelation must be based on the foundational revelation of the Abrahamic Covenant. The Mosaic Law, which came 430 years later, "cannot annul a covenant previously ratified by God, so as to make the promise void" (Galatians 3:17). Paul is not, as some think pitting the Mosaic revelation against the Abrahamic. They have different but complementary purposes. "Is the law against the promises of God? Certainly *not!*" (Galatians 3:21).

It is then that Paul goes on to delineate that we can be accepted as righteous before God by faith; by believing in Yeshua's life, death and resurrection. Combining the truths of the old sacrificial images and of the teaching on Abraham, Paul argues as follows:

As Adam (and all humanity) fell and became *a fallen, sinful race*, so there is a new humanity in Yeshua. We, by faith, must recognize that He died for our sin. He is the representative of the race and the race is tied together into one human family. Our reality is not only our separate, individual selfhood, but the reality of the whole interconnectedness of the race.[1] In identity with us, the sinless One pays our penalty. He also exhibits the suffering love and mercy of God and reveals the destructive nature of sin which seeks to annihilate the one righteous and perfect man. His sacrifice was accepted and He arose from death. By faith we accept these truths. By faith we are accounted as "In Messiah." These words, "in Messiah," are perhaps the two most significant words in the New Testament. We are part of His reality now. By faith we are given a new nature of righteousness (II Corinthians 5:7) and are given the Spirit of God to dwell within as promised in Jeremiah 31 and Ezekiel 36. We are not guilty but are justified in Him by faith.

So Paul can quote David, who was not justified by the Law but by God's mercy and grace:

"Blessed is the man to whom the Lord reckons no sin" (Psalm 32:2).

"Wash me thoroughly from my iniquity and cleanse me from my sin" (Psalm 51:2).

The believer now has supernatural power in identifying

with His atonement which puts sin to death as he prayerfully applies its power, and in the new nature or spirit he is given, and lastly by the power of the Spirit which motivates him and enables him to do God's will. His eternal fate is sealed; he is righteous *in Messiah* and has eternal life. Progressively, this life works itself out into daily growth so he becomes more like the Messiah.

Now, what is the relationship of the Law to all of this? First, we no longer turn to the Law seeking to find intrinsic righteousness. To the whole legalistic preoccupation with the Law we have died in the Messiah. Paul gives the example of a woman whose spouse's death has freed her from the legal bondage of the marriage. We have died to the Law (Romans 7:4) in the sense that there is no more penalty to be paid or legal bondage. Our primary focus now is on the power of the Spirit and His love working in a life lived according to the law of love.

If this love is real, however, then the Law makes its reappearance as a guide and teacher under the power of the Spirit. Without the power of the Spirit and the power of the atonement of Yeshua as our focus of dependence, our old nature shall reassert itself. This is also the case with the mistaken focus on the over 1,000 commands in the New Testament which can also become a focus—of works-righteousness.[2]

The Law will now be kept progressively in Spirit and truth in response to God's mercy and grace. The whole Bible—including the Mosaic Law rightly applied—will be our guide, "profitable for doctrine, reproof and training in righteousness" (II Timothy 3:16). The reformers rightly perceived the wonderful use of the Law as a guide, as well as a standard by which we are convicted by the Spirit, "to continually confess our sins and find forgiveness." They call this the third use of the Law.[3] The Law is a mirror for seeing the blemishes of your life; Yeshua is the living Torah. Hence, the Christian reformers found no conflict parallel to the conflict of today's misinformed Christians in reciting, "Oh how I love thy law" (Psalm 119:97).

This view of Law and grace may seem paradoxical, but
when understood, it is certainly consistent and full of the
depth of truth. Even psychologists have learned that on a
human level, acceptance and forgiveness must precede obedience. Forgiveness and acceptance by grace thereby become
the motive for obedience.[4] This is our focus; this is the emphasis of all Scripture; "I am the Lord thy God which brought you
out of the land of Egypt" (by grace, Exodus 20:2). Therefore,
"you shall have no other gods before me" (Exodus 20:3). To
think we can earn God's love and salvation is an affront to his
holiness.

The confusion comes also from those who say that salvation by grace through faith will lead to a moral laxity. This
shows a superficial understanding of grace, indeed. For the
acceptance of God's grace is the acceptance of a new nature
which wants to obey God, and the acceptance of God's own
Spirit, who Ezekiel said would dwell in our new spirit, caus-
ing us "to walk in" God's "statutes" (Ezekiel 36:27). Paul also
had to answer the foolish arguments of those who did not
understand, of those who said we could "continue to sin that
grace might abound." If we have living faith and love for God
we can respond as did Paul: "How can we who died to sin still
live in it?" (Romans 6:2). There are a few phrases which tend
to cause confusion; but with a little prayerful thought they
are quite clear. One we shall cover here: "For sin will have no
dominion over you, since you are not under the law but under
grace. What then? Are we to sin because we are not under law
but under grace? By no means!" (Romans 6:14-15).

Again, some take the phrase "not under law but under
grace" to imply that we have no relationship to "Law" or
Torah. This cannot be in the light of II Timothy 3:16, 17 and all
the other verses we have previously recorded. The context
makes this verse clear. The key word is *under*. The Law is no
longer a tyrant of condemnation to us. We are not *under* the
condemnation of the Law. We are not in bondage and fear,
seeking to obey the Law through our own power as a way to
please God, which is impossible. This becomes wonderfully
clear if we substitute Paul's own definition of sin, since the

Law defines sin—"therefore by the deeds of the law there shall no flesh be justified in his sight: for by the law is the knowledge of sin" (Romans 3:20)—or, as John and James say, "sin is the transgression of law," or "law breaking" (I John 3:4; James 2:8-10).

Let us then paraphrase: "For law-breaking will no longer have dominion over you since you are not under the condemnation of the law or a system of works righteousness, but under grace. What then? Are we to 'break the Law' because we are not *under* law but under grace? By no means!" (Romans 6:14, 15).

It is the same teaching as in Ephesians 2:8-10. "For by grace you are saved through faith, and not that of yourselves. It is a gift of God, not of works lest any man should boast. For we are his workmanship, created in Messiah Yeshua, for good works, which God prepared beforehand that we should walk in them."

And in Titus 3:5, "Not by works of righteousness which we have done, but *according to his mercy he saved us*, by the washing of regeneration and the renewal of the Holy Ghost."

Often we hear Romans 10:4 quoted out of context as well. "For Messiah is the end of the law . . . ." The word here is *telos*, which is "end" in the sense of goal or purpose. Many have pointed out that the word *telos* does not in this context mean the end in the sense of the finish or abolition of something.

What does it mean to say that Yeshua is the "telos" of the Law?

In Romans 9:31, Paul says the problem is not that Israel pursued the Law, but that "they did not pursue it through faith, but as if it were based on works." Israel's problem was not that they pursued the Law, but *the way* they pursued the Law. In context, Messiah is *telos* in these senses:

He is the personal embodiment of a human life lived in spirit and truth according to Torah standards. He is the living Torah. He is the goal of Torah, the perfect life to which holy standard and sacrificial sytem had pointed. He is the finisher of the misuse of Torah as a system of works-righteousness. When we believe in His sacrifice, we understand the true purpose of the Law was never to be a system of merits by works.

The "telos" of the Law, however, can never mean doing away with the Law since the cardinal rule for interpreting Scripture is that the true meaning of a passage must always be understood in the light of the whole of the Bible! *Scripture is a consistent revelation* from the infinite personal God of the universe.

I believe that we shall find Scripture to bear out this exposition. Salvation is "by grace through faith" indeed! Yet God is a God of Law, of principle upon which basis the universe rests. God himself could save us and yet be righteous according to His own standard of justice only by the righteousness of the Messiah and His death for our sins. We are counted as righteous in Him (Romans 3:26).

So we also hope with the prophet, "for out of Zion shall go forth the law and the word of the Lord from Jerusalem" (Isaiah 2:3).

PAUL AND ISRAEL

The preoccupation of much religious preaching today is personal peace and happiness. The desire for God is really part of a desire that He might make us happy. Fellowship with God is the greatest joy and treasure to be enjoyed by human beings. However, God desires us to lose our self preoccupation and be enveloped in prayerful intercession for the salvation of the world. Every person won by the Good News or by the coming of God's Kingdom to earth through the reign of the Messiah Yeshua in us is a fulfillment of God's real goal and burden on our hearts. Therefore, God seeks to have us fulfill this burden in our own witness and prayer for our immediate contacts—neighborhood and city. If our hearts are knit with him we shall *hear* the Word, "God so loved the world" (John 3:16).

Great saints have at times understood that the full coming of God's Kingdom and the hope of every creature hearing the Good News are tied up with God's purpose of manifesting Himself through Israel. Thus, Rees Howells interceded and

prevailed after years of prayer for the state of Israel to be
formed. So Messianic Judaism believes in a crucial future for
Israel. Furthermore, Messianic Judaism itself may somehow
be significantly related to the future. One of the keys to
understanding all of this is Paul's teaching on Israel.

Romans 9-11 are the central chapters in the Pauline writings on a theology of Israel. The ninth chapter begins with
Paul's statement of his great burden of sorrow and anguish
for Israel. Surely this was a prayer burden. He even says that
he could wish himself cut off for their sakes. Furthermore,
Paul fully recognizes Israel's national calling and in the present continuous tense says that they have "the sonship, the
glory, the covenants, the giving of the law, the worship and
the promises; to them belong the patriarchs, and of their race,
according to the flesh, is the Messiah" (Romans 9:4-5).

Paul then goes on to state, however, that not all who are
descended from Israel are spiritually considered to be Israel.
This is the doctrine of the remnant, an important concept
which we must unpack. Then he responds to those who would
accuse God of injustice in the matter of Israel's failure as a
nation to embrace Yeshua as Messiah.

Romans 9 seems like a very "harsh" chapter; it concerns
itself with Israel as a nation. It is not speaking of the opportunity for individual salvation. In the affairs of nations, God's
wisdom goes far beyond our intellectual capacity. We cannot
accuse God, for "who are you, a man, to answer back to God?"
(9:20). Then Paul gives a lesson in pottery, a lesson greatly
misunderstood. He names several vessels: wrath, mercy,
honor and dishonor. Honor was a beautiful vessel, chosen to
be displayed for pouring water to drink, etc. Dishonor was a
vessel which did not come up to such a high standard of
beauty; it was used to wash feet or for other menial uses. The
potter makes the choice as to which vessel he will make, but
both are needed. Mercy is a vessel which breaks in baking, but
is repaired and rebaked. If it stays together it will be used, a
vessel of mercy. If it does not, it is a vessel of wrath or destruction. Note that Romans says that "God endured with much
patience the vessels of wrath made for destruction" (9:22).

Any judgment by God took place after much long suffering.

The mercy of God to Jews and gentiles is even more pronounced in the light of this; and despite our sin, we are vessels of mercy made for His glory. All of the decision, however, must be left up to God's sovereignty. Now that Paul has boldly asserted this sovereignty, he can delineate some considerations in the Spirit which reveal God's continued purposes in Israel.

First are prophetic intimations. In Hosea, we see that God's relationship to different groups changes: "Those who were not my people I will call my people" (Hosea 2:23). Isaiah in his day (10:22-23) says that only a remnant would be saved from war's destruction.

There are other reasons, too. One is that Israel pursued the Law in the wrong way, as a system of works-righteousness. Israel did not succeed because they did not "pursue it through faith, but as if it were based on works" (Romans 9:32). This produced an attitude of self-righteousness whereby Israel, "being ignorant of the righteousness that comes from God, sought to establish their own" and did not "submit to God's righteousness" in Yeshua (10:3). Hence the gentile, who did not have the pride of the Law, was more capable of seeing his need and submitting to God's righteousness than was Israel which, in a self-righteous pursuit of the Law, did not see their need!

In addition, the Gospels clearly show that Israel expected the Messianic king to defeat their enemies and set up His worldwide reign of righteousness from Jerusalem. This is certainly one of His roles. However, so preoccupied were the Israelites with this image of the exalted King Messiah, that there was little room for another Messianic visitation in which the Messiah's role would be a suffering servant who bears the sin, grief and sickness of the world as a dispensational step toward His reign. The Messiah king would die a shameful death on a cross of wood: "cursed is he that dieth on a tree" (Deuteronomy 21:23; Galatians 3:13), which was more than many Israelites could accept. Yes, that curse was in identity with us, for us, and in our place. Yet only God's Spirit could open up hearts to this truth, for this message was a "stumbling block" to Jews, a scandal! (I Corinthians 1:23). To the reasons for the Jewish non-acceptance of Yeshua, we can add the importation of pagan elements into institutional Christianity—even if such elements were rebaptized and changed. In addition, there is the almost unbroken persecution by the institutional Church for 1,900 years, despite the fact the non-Jewish followers of Yeshua were counseled in Romans 11 to make Israel jealous for their own Messiah by great acts of love (Romans 11:13, 30-31).

The incredible capstone to Paul's argument is found in Romans 11:1. Has God rejected his people? By no means! Paul points to himself as proof that God has not rejected Israel. What meaning this must have in the light of Paul's own recollection of his past as a persecutor of "the Way!" Indeed, there were 7,000 more than Elijah realized who were true to God in his day (I Kings 19:18)! "So, too, at the present time there is a remnant chosen by grace" (11:15). This remnant should not be thought of as excluding the rest of the nation as God's elect, but as a first fruit pointing to the eventual salvation of the nation as a whole.

Paul quotes the prophets and David to show that the lack of response on Israel's part was foreordained. The whole situation of Israel and its pursuit of righteousness by works (in Chapter 10) now brings God's judgment. For now, Paul states that Israel's unbelief is an act of God as well. "But have they stumbled so as to fall? By no means" (11:11). The Greek here implies, "is their stumbling fatal, an irretrievable fall?" Paul's answer is an emphatic "No!" Israel shall yet have its day! However, their trespass in not recognizing the righteous way of God in the Messiah is the means by which "salvation had come to the Gentiles" and "riches to the world" (vv. 11-12).

What could Paul mean by this? Why would Israel's unbelief have anything to do with gentile salvation? The historical context of the Book of Acts makes this clear. Whenever posssible, in each town to which Paul traveled, he went first to the local synagogue. Some Jewish people accepted the

Good News of Messiah, but the majority usually rejected the Gospel. However, Gentiles came in large numbers *when they were given the opportunity to know the God of Israel without the barriers of circumcision and the Jewish national lifestyle* being required of them.

Let us note Paul's controversy with the Judaizers. These Jewish followers of Yeshua taught that gentiles could not be saved unless they were circumcised and kept the Law of Moses. With great difficulty, the apostles prevailed (Acts 15) and refuted this view. Many Jews did accept the Gospel—myriads according to Acts 21—as well as numerous Gentiles; yet these believers were still greatly a minority in Israel. Part of this minority doggedly hounded Paul and the gentile converts. The problems they brought about are addressed in Paul's epistles.

What if instead of a minority, the majority of Jews had accepted? The percentage of Judaizers was not small. In every major city there was a large Jewish presence, not to mention the powerful Jews of the land of Israel. One to two million it is estimated were in the land, four to five million in the Diaspora. Imagine the pressure for the Judaizing viewpoint from three to five million Jews "all zealous for the law" (Acts 21). This would have been a huge barrier to the Gospel among the gentiles who were not called to be part of the nation Israel. Now we see the sense of Paul's words; but once the purpose of hardening has been accomplished, "how much more will their full inclusion mean." Jewish rejection also caused an intensified effort in preaching to non-Jews.

Paul would see Israel made jealous for their own Messiah through the riches gentiles had received by the grace of God; so he "magnifies" his ministry. Here comes a semi-climax in the argument:

"For if their rejection means the reconciliation of the world, what will their acceptance mean but life from the dead? If the dough offered as first fruits is holy, so is the whole lump, and if the root is holy, so are the branches" (Romans 11:15-16). As the first fruits sanctify the whole harvest, so Israel as a whole is sanctified and will some day be accepted, as evidenced by Jewish believers who are first fruits.

In other words, Paul foresees the acceptance of Israel by God, and this event will mean the resurrection of the dead and the establishment of the Kingdom of God over all the earth. Paul breaks off his argument for a moment and now anticipates the possible response of gentile converts.

He likens the community of salvation to an olive tree. Some natural branches were broken off, not all (v. 17), and wild branches were grafted in, that is, non-Jews who had no "cultivation" as a covenant people. Paul warns them not to boast, but to stand in awe, for the root of salvation history in Israel supports them, not they, the root. They are to stand in awe, for if God did not spare natural branches, He will not spare them unless they stand in humble faith. Now Paul begins an argument again in relation to Israel. In v. 23 we read that, "God has the power to graft them in again . . . how much more will these natural branches be grafted back into their own olive tree?" And this is exactly what will happen:

"Lest you be wise in your own conceits, I want you to understand this mystery, brethren, a hardening has come upon *part of Israel, until* the (fullness) of the Gentiles and so *all Israel will be saved*" (vv. 25-26).

Again we are amazed to learn that some take "all *Israel* to be saved" as meaning the Church! How would this destroy non-Jewish conceit? Indeed, such an interpretation makes the whole argument of the chapter superfluous. Certainly the salvation of the Church is not at issue here, but the nation of Israel. Could Paul quickly change terminology here and, after speaking of Israel, all of a sudden be speaking of "spiritual" Israel, the equivalent of the Church? Incredible! The rest of the chapter looks toward things which totally refute this false view. Paul quotes Isaiah 59:20-21, that "the Deliverer will come to Zion; he will banish ungodliness from Jacob and this will be my covenant with them when I take away their sins." (Romans 11:26-27).

To Paul this will still yet happen; for the New Covenant we are under shall be confirmed to all of Israel.

"As regards the gospel they are enemies of God, for your

sake, but as regards election they are beloved for the sake of their forefathers. For the gifts and call of God are irrevocable" (Romans 11:28-29).

Israel is still elect of God. Elect for what? To witness that God is creator and the One who established them as a nation. Sabbath and Passover reflect the call of Israel. In Israel's preservation, the world sees the faithfulness of God. As a nation, Israel shall yet be God's instrument in gaining His rule over all nations. There will yet be a large minority in Israel which will witness to the truth of the Good News.

Mention should be made here of the phrase "fullness of the Gentiles." It could mean until all of the Gentiles are saved who will be saved. Or it could parallel the phrase "fullness of Amorites" in Genesis 15:16. This implied the fullness of the stored up iniquity of the Amorites, whereby it would be the right time for Israel to be used as God's instrument of judgment in history. This phrase could parallel the one in Luke 21:24.

The iniquity would consist of all godless wars, killing, murder and rebellion against God. Even more, God said, "I will bless those who bless thee and curse those who curse thee" (Genesis 12).

Surely, the period of Auschwitz when 6,000,000 of our people were slaughtered while nations watched in apathy has brought God's judgment. Israel's history in the Diaspora, although a severe discipline, has also been a test for the nations; and we can discern in the historical maltreatment of Israel a corresponding correlation in the decline of the nations and people who acted unjustly. Israel's prophetic purpose thus continues even in the age of Diaspora; but now that Israel is in her own land, as predicted in Scripture, one can even now hear the steps of Messiah approaching.

Paul concludes his chapter by reviewing the course of history. First, Israel is obedient, then disobedient while gentiles are obedient; then Israel is again obedient. The reason for all this? That God may have mercy on all! Only words of praise can now leave the apostle's lips. "O the depth of the riches and wisdom and knowledge of God" (11:33).

Nothing in Paul's teaching here blunts the truth of Messianic Judaism—or that Jewish followers of Yeshua may still maintain a glorious call as part of their people in their witness to the world and in a personal witness to Israel of salvation in Yeshua.

One other issue must be briefly discussed: Does Paul use the term "Israel" to refer to the Church, including non-Jews who are in Yeshua? Is the Church "the new, true spiritual Israel," as one person put it?

Many who hold that Paul might have used the term "Israel" of the Church, argue that the Scriptures retain a definite place for national Israel.

It is this author's view that the terms "spiritual Jew" and "spiritual Israel" are never used by Scripture to refer to non-Jewish believers in Yeshua. This has been thoroughly argued in many articles.[6]

We have already concluded that Romans 11 does not use these terms in this sense. Romans contains an often quoted verse, though, which is thought by some to refer to non-Jewish believers as spiritual Jews.

"For he is not a real Jew who is one outwardly, nor is true circumcision something external and physical. He is a Jew who is one inwardly and real circumcision is a matter of the heart, spiritual not literal. Its praise is not from men but from God" (Romans 2:28-29).

There is no reason to think that the "real Jew" within the verses is a gentile who has a circumcised heart toward God. The word "Jew" is related etymologically to the word "praise." Paul is saying that if a Jew is to be a praise to God and is to truly fulfill his destiny, he must not only have external circumcision but the circumcision of the heart. This is what Moses told the people in Deuteronomy 10:16-17: "Circumcise, therefore, the foreskin of your heart and be no longer stubborn."

Indeed, the uncircumcised externally (the non-Jew) who keeps the Law will condemn the circumcised who do not. The true Jew, however, is one who has *both* circumcisions.

Romans 4 is a key to making the proper distinction. Here,

gentiles who accept the Gospel are called the children of Abraham by faith. They are not called the children of Jacob or Israel. There is a reason for this. The gentile has a glorious place in God's eyes when he turns to God. Like Abraham, he is not descended physically from a people under God's primary covenant. He is justified by faith without being first circumcised. His life parallels Abraham's more than Jewish people who are simply physically descended from Jacob. The promise of blessing through Abraham rests on *faith*—both for the adherents of the Jewish Laws (Israel) and for those whose lives parallel Abraham's (Romans 4:16). As we study further, we find that non-Jewish believers are the spiritual seed of Abraham or children of Abraham by faith! Spiritually, the gentile convert is no longer a gentile, especially in any sense of the word "pagan"; but neither is he a Jew, although *his spiritual* status before God is equal to the Jewish follower of the Gospel.

Galatians 6:16 states, "Peace and mercy be upon all who walk by this rule, upon the Israel of God." However, it could as well be translated *and* upon the Israel of God, distinguishing those Jews who did not follow the false teachings of the Judaizers.[6] Enough has been said to establish our view that calling the Church "spiritual Israel" is not biblical terminology. "Commonwealth Israel" would be a more accurate term (see Ephesians 2:12, R.S.V.). It reflects that gentiles have been grafted in but do not replace Israel proper. Yet they have become part of the commonwealth under the Messiah's rule. Besides these few passages, the whole of the New Testament is silent on any such use for the term "Israel." This silence should cause us to forego the use of the term "Israel" to refer to the church.

CHAPTER FOUR

Messianic Judaism—Difficult Passages

Messianic Jews establish congregations of Jewish and non-Jewish followers of Yeshua whose worship style is Jewish and Hebraic. In addition, we teach that the Jewish follower of Yeshua is still a part of Israel as well as the universal people of God. Therefore, Jewish members of these congregations are encouraged to maintain appropriate biblically grounded Jewish practices and identity.

Jewish life is a glorious call that witnesses to great truths about God. By being loyal to his heritage a Jew maximizes the opportunity to share his faith with other loyal Jews who would otherwise dismiss it out of hand. As I Corinthians 9 states, "To the Jews I become as a Jew, in order to win Jews, to those under the law I became as one under the law . . . that I might win those under the law" (v. 20).

However there are several passages which are used by some to refute this position. It is to these passages that we turn now.

I CORINTHIANS 9:19-21

At first glance, these verses would seem to support Messianic Jewish conclusions. However, there are interpreters who find in these verses two phrases which are a source of anti-Messianic Jewish viewpoints. We quote the passage in its entirety.[1]

"To the Jews I become as a Jew, in order to win the Jews,
to those under the law I become as one under the law—
though not being myself under the law—that I might win
those under the law. To those outside the law I became as one
outside the law—not being without law toward God, but
under the law of Christ—that I might win those outside the
law."

We should first note that Paul here establishes a valid
principle for sharing the Good News. That is, we are to have a
loving indentification with those whom we seek to win.
Clearly, the Messianic Jew is heartened by the **clear statement** that one may practice the Law, "I become as one under
the law." One reason for the practice of the heritage, but
certainly not the sole reason, is loving identification with
those we seek to win. Two other phrases bring various interpretations: "though not being myself under the law"—by
some is taken to mean that the Mosaic revelation with its
standards and practices no longer has any meaning to the life
of the believer. Rather, the believer is now under the "law of
Christ," not the Law of Moses. The "law of Christ" is variously explained as loving God and our neighbor or as all of
the New Testament commands.

However, there are problems with this view. First, the
command to love God and our neighbor (in Mark 12 and the
other Gospels) is a quotation from Torah. Some say that when
the New Testament quotes Torah, it becomes part of the "law
of Christ" but otherwise has no force over us. This view is
certainly "forced." When the New Testament quotes Torah, it
does so because it is Scripture. This settles the issue. (Note
Ephesians 6:1 ff.) I Corinthians 9:8 says, "Do I say this on
human authority; does not the law say the same?"

It is clear that Paul, by example and other teaching (II
Timothy 3:16) taught the valid inspiration and authority of
the Torah. The law against incest is not in the New Testament. Therefore, can we say that since incest is not quoted in
the "law of Christ" it is permissible? No, of course not! The
same is the case with just weights and measures.

The author believes that the phrase "law of Christ" is a

synonym for "law of the Spirit" found in Romans 8:1. When
we are in the Spirit, we are no longer under the **Law as a
fearful taskmaster**, hoping to gain eternal life by our works.
Our essential and central content of faith is the love of God,
the atonement in Yeshua and the power of the Spirit. This
produces a new approach to Scripture whereby the Spirit
places God's desires upon our hearts as well as empowers us
to perform God's will. The reading of Scripture is a primary
means for the Spirit to give us a depth of conviction and
power. This all occurs on the basis of an intimate fellowship
with God rather than a rote maintenance of a code which
seems external to us. Yet it is the very Torah which the Spirit
will use to "instruct" in God's ways and to "train in righteousness' (2 Timothy 3:16; Ezekiel 36; Jeremiah 31).

However, none of God's eternal standards are invalidated; all are made part of the Covenant relationship of walking in the Spirit.

Furthermore, Paul seeks to present himself and the Gospel in such a way that there will be no stumbling blocks to his
listeners' acceptance of the Good News. Gentiles were not
required to take on the call of national Israel. This does not
mean that Paul ceased to be a Jew in Gentile settings, but he
certainly did not make his Jewishness so prominent that it
would blunt the Gospel. When Paul says in v. 22, "to the weak
I became weak," he does not mean that he literally gave up
his courage, faith and strength. It means he identified with
the weak in such a way that his presentation of the Gospel
would meet them where they were.

The "law of Christ" does not replace Torah, but is a principle of approach to all of Scripture in the power of the
atonement and the Spirit. This is the meaning of not to be
under the Law as a system of righteousness. This passage is
perfectly exemplified by Paul's life and practice in the Book
of Acts.

Of special significance is the fact that the Apostle to the
Gentiles, because of his Jewish identity, never ceased to care
for his people and his heritage. Though called to Gentile
ministry, he lived as a Jew. If this be the case, how can Jewish

followers of Yeshua, who believe themselves called to Israel,
live in ways that befit non-Jews? We do not seek to bring
anyone into bondage; all must be done in the Spirit. However,
the example of all the apostles, even Paul the Apostle to the
Gentiles, properly causes us to believe that those who are
negative to the Jewish biblical heritage have not heard the
Spirit in regard to these questions.

PASSAGES IN GALATIANS

We will not repeat the basic discussion of passages in
Galatians already covered in the Section on the Judaizers in
the chapters on the "Books of Acts and Messianic Judaism"
and "Paul, Israel and the Law." The reader should turn to
these chapters for more information on Law and grace and
the Judaizing controversy. We do recall for the reader that:
(1) Galatians was written before the Acts 15 decision on Gentile freedom in the Gospel; and (2) the Judaizers were a
group which taught that a person who is uncircumcised must
follow the law of Moses to be saved. Their view thoroughly
invalidated the Gospel of salvation by grace through faith.
(3) Furthermore, to the Judaizer, the Gentile was unclean
and could not be eaten with unless he was circumcised and
followed the Law. Table fellowship, the proof of the spiritual
equality of Jew and Gentile, in the Messiah was to them
impossible.

We should note that the Book of Galatians does *not*
address the issue of Jewish followers of Yeshua maintaining
their Jewish practice and identity. This is not even in view;
Alan Cole states that Galatians does not at all preclude such
Jewish practice and identity but that its principle of freedom
in Messiah fully allows for the possibility.[2] *The question of
Jewish practice in Yeshua must be settled by those passages
which speak to it*; the Book of Acts, etc; the testimony of
history concerning Apostolic practice and identity, and the
whole drift of Scriptural teaching on Israel.

Once again, in all of the discussion on the Law in Galatians, we must remember that Paul does not demean the Law
as a standard of God. Rather, with the advent of the Messiah,

all is done in His power and under the inspiration of His Spirit. We approach the Law as "adults," not as children who have rules set over them due to their immaturity, hence, the analogy of the schoolmaster and the Law before Messiah. In Messiah, we are sons of God's kingdom and not under the Law as a custodian, but under the power of the Spirit as sons who follow by inspiration and reason, not rote. Having given these general comments we turn to these specifics:

GALATIANS 3:28

"There is neither Jew nor Greek . . . for you are all one in Christ Jesus." (Colossians 3:11—parallel). It is sad that we even have to respond to the use of this verse as a proof-text against Messianic Judaism. Incredibly, the answer would be obvious if the *whole* verse was quoted. The left out portion is "there is neither slave nor free, there is neither male nor female." Paul is not saying that all distinctions between men and women have been obliterated! This would lead to the end of marriages and families. In what sense is there neither male nor female, then? It is defined in vv. 26, and 29-"In the Messiah, Yeshua, you are all children of God, through faith And if you are Messiah's, then you are Abraham's offspring, heirs according to promise." Men and women are exactly one in this, that they are equally children of God and spiritually of equal significance. In no way does God envision men bearing children or an end to all the wonderful joys that the male-female distinction brings to life as a result of His creation-order. Men and women have different callings in life, though they are one in Messiah.

It is precisely the same with Jew and non-Jew in the Messiah. Both may be called to different styles of life and witness, to different fields of service, yet they are spiritually one in the Messiah. The oneness spoken of does not lead to a dullness of all peoples, nations and races becoming the same in speech, manner, dress, mission and style. What a horribly boring world that would be! It would be like a symphony orchestra composed of all violins! God's unity is a symphonic unity, blending all together under the head conductor, the

Messiah. Oneness in the Messiah leaves ample room for varieties of life and calling, especially in regards to Jew and non-Jew. Note as well, non-Jews are called (in v. 29) not spiritual Israel, but the offspring of Abraham by faith.[3]

EPHESIANS 2:14

"For he himself is our peace, who has made the two one and has destroyed the barrier, the dividing wall of hostility." Messianic Jews, on the basis of this passage, are often accused of re-erecting the "wall of partition" between Jew and Gentile. It is charged that because Jews maintain their Jewish-biblical heritage, they become distinct from other believers, hence re-erecting the wall.

The wall of partition does not refer to a difference of practice and lifestyle by which Jews and non-Jews may be distinguished. It rather refers to practices which precluded table-fellowship between Jew and Gentile and produced hostility.[4] Gentiles were then pagans, idolators. According to biblical Law, contact with unclean meats precluded on the food lists of Leviticus and Deuteronomy, contact with blood and with death made a person unclean. Uncleanness precluded visiting the Temple for a specified period of time, one to seven days. Since it was impossible to know if a Gentile had such contact, the oral tradition of Judaism concluded that contact with Gentiles made one unclean. The solution for the religious was to avoid all contact with Gentiles.

In Yeshua, however, the Gentile is no longer a pagan or unclean (Acts 10). Both Jew and the non-Jew are spiritually one in Yeshua. The non-Jewish believers are given a charge to avoid those things which would be especially abhorrent to Jewish believers (Acts 15). Now in Yeshua, Jew and Gentile accept one another and have table fellowship, prayer and praise together! This does not imply, however, that they are to have *identical calling and lifestyles*. As J.H. Yoder argues, the wall has to do with acceptance and table fellowship which was such a crucial demonstration of acceptance. The rejection of fellowship implied that the other person was not spiritually acceptable. The wall of partition is not a wall of distinctions, but a *wall of hostility* as Ephesians 2:14 clearly states. Now in the light of this, let's quote the whole of the passage from 2:13-16, "But now in Messiah Yeshua you who were once far off have been brought near in the blood of Messiah. For he is our peace, who has made us both one, and has broken down the dividing wall of hostility, by abolishing in his flesh the law of commandments and ordinances, that he might create in himself one new man in place of the two, so making peace, and might reconcile us both to God in one body through the cross, thereby bringing the hostility to an end."

The commands and ordinances are not necessarily intrinsically Torah, but the oral extensions of these laws made Gentiles unclean and contact with Gentiles something to avoid. As well, it would abolish commands precluding a Jew worshiping in the most intimate way with a Gentile since the Gentile, in Yeshua, is no longer an idolatrous sinner, but has been cleansed by the cross. In the Messiah, a universal body of believers of Jew and Gentile is formed. This does not preclude a Jew's special calling—for he is both part of the universal body and the nation of Israel. It does not preclude the instruction of Torah (II Timothy 3.10-17).

It is crucial here to note that a Messianic Jewish congregation is a *New Covenant congregation* in which Jews and non-Jews fellowship together in oneness. Each have equal privilege in Yeshua. However, the style of worship is Jewish and Jewish members are encouraged in their identity and calling. Because there is mutual acceptance rather than seeking to press one another into preconceived molds, true love can flourish. The greatest proof of an end to the wall of hostility is the Messianic congregation where Jews and non-Jews— in significant proportions—worship together. In a non-Jewish congregational setting where a lone Jew has lost his practice and identity there is little testimony of this truth. However, there is a place for Jewish segments of predominantly non-Jewish congregations which maintain their Jewish involvement in the present and future through *their children*. A Messianic Jewish congregation is just one kind of expression of the universal body of the Messiah!

GALATIANS 4:8-10

Verses 9-10, in particular, speak of this—"You observe days, and months and seasons and years! I am afraid I have labored over you in vain."

The obvious conclusion drawn by the foe of Messianic Judaism is that Paul here is against anyone observing Jewish holidays. However, what were the *special months* and *years referred to in Judaism*? They are not found in Scripture, except for the seventh sabbatical year when slaves were freed and the land was given beneficial rest. Once again, the context of preceding verses is essential. According to what we know of the region of Galatia historically, Paul is writing to predominantly non-Jewish people.

He says, "Formerly, when you did not know God, you were in bondage to beings that by nature are no gods; but now that you have come to know God, or rather to be known by God, how can you turn back again to the weak and beggarly elemental spirits, whose slaves you want to be once more. You observe days, and months and seasons and years; I am afraid I have labored over you in vain" Galatians 4:10-11.

The full context has prompted many commentators to hold that Paul here is not speaking of Jewish biblical celebrations. There must have been another problem in Galatia, it is thought. This problem is acknowledged to be connected with astrology. It is also known that heretical groups existed which *connected some of the Jewish holidays to astrology* and superstition.[5] Paul could not be speaking of celebrations given by God as putting people under the bondage of evil spirits! Nor could he be speaking of Jewish holidays in saying that they, a non-Jewish group, are *turning back* to weak and beggardly elemental spirits.

Apparently, what Paul refers to is a drift into superstition connected to special years, days and seasons—akin to astrology. This is a bondage, for during such days, some actions are safe and others are unsafe, some endeavors are to be undertaken and will be especially fruitful, while others are especially dangerous. This actually brings bondage to evil spirits. There may have been a perverted Jewish content added to some of this. Certainly, in the light of this background, this passage has nothing to say against Jewish people celebrating God's grace in their history through feasts of Israel. There is no superstition connected to this and no bondage to evil spirits! Again, Paul's example in life shows the critics of Messianic Judaism to be misinterpreting this passage, ignoring not only the historical context, but the very words of the whole passage itself. We might also note that Derek Prince in a taped message quotes this passage in regard to astrology. He notes that the wording recalls Deuteronomy 18:10-14 in speaking against astrology as "observing seasons." II Kings also says in a context of astrology that Manasseh "observed times" or seasons (II Kings 21:6).

SARAH AND HAGAR—GALATIANS 4:21-31

There is a very unusual allegory given whereby Paul states that Hagar and her son, Ishmael, parallel the Covenant from Mount Sinai representing children who are slaves. This, says Paul, stands for the present city of Jerusalem. However, there is a Jerusalem above that is free. It is this Jerusalem who is our mother. We are like Isaac, children of the promise and like Isaac—who was born by the Spirit—we are persecuted by the son born of the flesh.

Sarah's words are then quoted: "Get rid of the slave woman and her son, for the slave woman's son will never share in the inheritance with the free woman's son" (Galatians 4:30) The conclusion is that we, as followers of Yeshua, are not children of the slave woman, but of the free woman. The whole allegory is given to enlighten those who desire to be under the law of works righteousness—that is, those who have accepted the *theology of the Judaizers*. This is a very difficult passage of Scripture to interpret. We do not know the exact nature of the situation in which Paul would respond with such an unparalled analogy. This passage should definitely be understood in the light of the clearer, straightforward passages, such as those in the books of Romans and Acts.

A quick reading of this passage has caused some to con-

clude that Jews who follow their calling are under bondage
and are slaves; they should therefore give up all Jewish practice and identity. This, however, *cannot* be the meaning of
this text, for several reasons. It was not the example of Paul in
the Book of Acts, nor the import of his teaching in the Book of
Romans on the value of being a Jew. Next, *Isaac is the son of
promise* according to the analogy. He was the one given the
promise of blessing, land and nationhood from his father
Abraham. Because Isaac is the son of promise and the product
of miraculous birth, Jews exist today. Paul, therefore, cannot
be saying that being a Jew is a slave-type bondage.

The contrast is not at all about being called to Jewishness,
but is rather a contrast between flesh and spirit. Paul is contrasting the spirit, promise, and faith to the flesh and a *fleshly
understanding* of the Law.

Abraham was given the promise of many descendants, a
great nation through which all the world would be blessed.
He believed God, but Sarah was barren. Hence he sought to
bring about God's promise by human fleshly (ordinary)
means. In the ancient Near East, if a man's wife was barren,
she could give him her maidservant. The children born to the
servant would count as their own.[6] Hence, Abraham would
have descendants; human means would be used to secure the
promise of God. However, this was contrary to God's way of
working. Abraham was to have the son of promise miraculously—by his own wife—by the power of the Spirit.

The Judaizers also sought to use human means to fulfill
God's divine purposes. Keeping the Law by human effort,
they contended, would bring salvation. Indeed, they taught
that Gentiles must accept circumcision (become Jews) and
keep the Law of Moses to be saved. Human works would
produce the salvation of God. How similar to Abraham's use
of human work in producing Ishmael by Hagar.

The approach of the Judaizers to the Sinai covenant is
tantamount to slavery and parallel to the slave woman and
her child. Those who seek justification before God by their
own good works will find only greater condemnation, and
even bondage to sin (Romans 7:8). Only dependence on the

grace and promise of God will bring true freedom and deliverance. Hence, although the Judaizers in the flesh are sons of Isaac, they act more like sons of the slave woman, Hagar. They are acting in the flesh and do not give a true testimony to the meaning of God's promises to Abraham's descendants. In fact, they are like the then-present state of Jerusalem—in bondage to Roman occupation—rather than the future Jerusalem of promise to be brought about by the power of God's Spirit. The slave does not inherit the promises of God, but remains in bondage to the way of human works.

There is nothing in this passage to suggest that fulfilling the God-given call to be part of the nation of Israel is, itself, bondage. Both Jew and Gentile are children of promise—like Isaac—when they approach God by faith unto salvaton. However, in the leading of the Spirit, both may indeed have a difference of calling and lifestyle. The Jew who follows the way of the Spirit may sense a love for his nation and a call to witness to God's purposes in it. The non-Jew may take a different path. Paul had no arugment with a Jew expressing his faith by identity with the calling of Israel, and he expected both Jew and Gentile to reflect the moral dimensions of the Law in the life of faith. His quarrel was with legalists who sought to bring non-Jews forcibly into the role of Israel by their teaching that no salvation was otherwise possible. They showed themselves to have completely misunderstood the "Good News."

Why would Paul use such a difficult analogy to make this point? We cannot know for sure; but we are comfortable in that the above exposition is acceptable to the evidence of Scripture. Perhaps the best suggestion was given by R.N. Longnecker,[7] who held that Paul was probably responding to an analogy that the Judaizers used. They would have been teaching that non-Jews must become Jews and adopt the whole of the Sinai revelation and Jewish practice in order to be children of the promise. Otherwise, they would be castoffs, like Hagar and her child, Ishmael. Paul thus uses this argument to turn the tables on his opponents, holding that they show themselves to be akin to the slave status of Hagar and

Ishmael by their legalistic *bondage*-producing teaching.

THE BOOK OF HEBREWS—CENTRAL CHAPTERS

For Messianic Jews, the Book of Hebrews is a truly wonderful book. It presents the greatness of God's revelation in Yeshua in an unparalleled way, revealing Him as Prophet, King and—most of all—High Priest. The middle chapters of the book bring out the dimensions of the work of Yeshua as priest and sacrifice, primarily by contrasting His work with the priesthood and sacrificial system which foreshadowed and pointed toward His redeeming work. Yom Kippur, the Day of Atonement, in which the High Priest entered the holiest part of the Tabernacle and sprinkled blood upon the ark for the nation's sin, is the central Holy Day emphasized here. In its sacrificial dimensions, Yom Kippur is the great pointer to Yeshua's work.

Why then is Hebrews listed among difficult passages? It is because there exists an interpretation of the book which is anti-Messianic Jewish. This interpretation is not in accord with the biblical context or history, yet it has gained popularity. The view teaches that Hebrews precludes following the calendar of Judaism and any identity with Israel's feasts and festivals, because all of these things have been replaced by a New Covenant that does away with the Law. Chapter eight is the central chapter for this discussion. For we read,

"The ministry Yeshua has received is as superior to theirs as the covenant of which he is a mediator is superior to the old one, and it is founded on better promises. For if there had been nothing wrong with the first covenant, no place would have been sought for another" (8:6-7).

The writer then goes on to quote Jeremiah 31:31-34, which gives the promise of the new Covenant and says, "By calling this covenant 'new,' he has made the first one obsolete and what is obsolete and aging will soon disappear" (8:13).

A critic of Messianic Judaism thus draws the conclusion that all dimensions of Jewish identity and practice are part of what is obsolete and should be forsaken. Furthermore, we are even accused of making the blood of Messiah of no effect and spurning His sacrifice when we remember our national origins in the Exodus by celebrating Passover!

"It is impossible for those who have been once enlightened, who have tasted the heavenly gift, who have shared in the Holy Spirit, who have tasted the goodness of the Word of God and the powers of this coming age, if they fall away, to be brought back to repentance, because to their loss they are crucifying the Son of God all over again and subjecting him to public disgrace" (Hebrews 6:4-6).

How this interpretation can be *fairly* gleaned from these passages without great violence to the context is paradoxical.

Let us respond as follows. If this is the true interpretation of Hebrews, all first-century Jewish believers (including Paul and the other apostles) would have been guilty of these horrible sins. Yet these apostles are our examples. The problem of Hebrews for Messianic Judaism dissolves when we take the time to carefully read just what is being said to whom!

Recent studies have shown—by language parallels and emphases—that the Book of Hebrews was probably written to a group of Essene Jewish followers of Yeshua.[10] The book emphasizes the Tabernacle in the wilderness instead of the fixed Temple which was built later. All its imagery and teaching on sacrifices is related to the Tabernacle. The Qumran community (an Essene-like community) held the Temple and its present priesthood to be greatly corrupt. They therefore expounded the sacrificial system dimension of Scripture in relation to the Tabernacle, even though the Temple was then the scene of these rituals . . . and the Tabernacle did not exist.

Qumran also emphasized the Melchizedekian Priesthood in their teachings. Moreover, Qumran rejected the then present priesthood as illegitimate since they were not descended from Zadok. Hence it is now becoming a generally accepted view that the Book of Hebrews was addressed to a group of Essene-like Jewish followers of Yeshua, of which there were probably many in the first century.

They were in danger of giving up their faith in the work

of Yeshua and returning to the hopes of the Essenes who did
not follow Him. They would hence be depending upon Essene
ritual for salvation and the hope of the reestablishment of a
true priesthood which parelleled the purity of the period
when Israel worshipped and sacrificed at the ancient Tabernacle which anteceded the Temple. The emphasis was then
on the Mosaic sacrificial system purified,[12] as the way of
bringing the power of God to Israel and deliverance from the
hands of oppressors. It is thought that in this time of national
crisis—perhaps during the Roman invasion of Israel to quell
the rebellion of 66-70 CE—that the Jewish believers in
Yeshua here addressed were forsaking their faith and in
danger of returning completely to Essenean-type beliefs. By
doing this, they would spurn the Gospel and crucify the Son
of God afresh. It was not by remaining Jewish that they did
this. This is why there is such exhortation in the face of
grevious trial (12:7-13).

The essence of argument of the book is to not place our
hopes in ritual or in a purified human priesthood because in
Yeshua we have *a better sacrifice, a better priesthood* and *a
better Covenant. There is no statement to the effect that we
have a better Law,* for, as we have seen, *the New Covenant
promise is to write God's Law, statutes, and ordinances upon
our hearts (Ezekiel 36:27).* Further attention to the Book of
Hebrews shows that what is referred to as being "obsolete" is
the whole Temple-priestly, sacrificial system. Indeed the
word *obsolete* is literally in "process of vanishing" in the
original. Paragraph after paragraph emphasizes the limitations of the blood of bulls and goats and the repeated ministrations of the priesthood.

The writer to the Hebrews emphasizes that the *Mosaic
Covenant*, as a Covenant, is essentially connected to this
system—which is vanishing. The New Covenant replaces this
Covenant because of the weaknesses inherent in that old
system which was given only for a time to point to the
sacrificial-priestly work of Yeshua.

We have stated clearly that we believe the Abrahamic
Covenant with Israel is still in effect (Romans 11:29). We have

also argued that the Mosaic Covenant, as a Covenant, is no longer in full effect and that God has sovereignly removed the possibility of following this Covenant by allowing the Temple to be destroyed. Hence, *as a Covenant by which we gain entrance into the presence of God, this Covenant is superseded.* Note that the writer of Hebrews is clearly referring to the Mosaic Covenant and *emphasizing its priestly-sacrificial dimensions when he states that it, as a Covenant, is vanishing* (see all of Chapter 8). (The reader should note that "obsolete" is not the correct translation from the Greek.)

The suspension of the sacrifical system is thought by many to have reference only to this age of the Temple's suspension and that a re-establishment of the Temple system will occur in the Millenium, under the Messiah. However, as the Temple system in ancient times pointed forward in anticipation of Messiah's work, so it will point back in the future. The sacrifices also exemplified dedication and thanksgiving (see J. Walvoord, *The Millenial Kingdom*). However, this would not be the *same* Temple system as before (see Ezekiel 40-48.)

This does not mean that the Mosaic writings are not Scripture, profitable for doctrine, reproof, correction and training in righteousness (see II Timothy 3:16). Nor does it mean that these documents (Torah) cannot give guidance to a Jewish calling and identity which transcends the sacrificial-priestly system. The feasts, for example, are the national celebrations of Israel and exist because of God's promise to make of Abraham a great nation. They celebrate God's acts of grace to Israel. Although recorded in Mosaic writings, they are essentially connected to the Abrahamic Covenant, a Covenant of faith and promise still in effect. Nowhere does Hebrews even hint that the writer is opposed to the celebration of God's faithfulness in Jewish history when Yeshua—not the sacrifices—is the center of every feast.

The Books of Hebrews is one of the most "Jewish" books ever written! By its specific emphasis, it shows the meaning of Yeshua in a most Jewish way. Because it only emphasizes the obsolescence of the Temple-sacrificial system and not of

Israel and its national life, and because it appeals to the great
heroes of Jewish history as the major example and spur to
faith, it is a book which certainly supports a Messianic Jewish
calling.

II CORINTHIANS 3:7-18

"Now if the dispensation of death, carved in letters on
stone, came with such splendor that the Israelites could not
look at the face of Moses for the glory of his countenance;
which glory was to fade away, should not the dispensation of
the Spirit be attended with greater splendor? For if there was
splendor in the dispensation of comdemnation, the dispensation of righteousness must far exceed it in splendor. Indeed,
in this case, what once had splendor has come to have no
splendor at all, because of the splendor that surpasses it. For if
what faded away came with splendor, what is permanent
must have much more splendor.

"Since we have such a hope, we are very bold, not like
Moses, who put a veil over his face so that the Israelites might
not see the end of the fading splendor. But their minds were
hardened; for to this day, when they read the old covenant,
that same veil remains unlifted, because only through Messiah is it taken away. Yes, to this day whenever Moses is read a
veil lies over their minds; but when a man turns to the Lord
the veil is removed. Now the Lord is the Spirit, and where the
Spirit of the Lord is, there is freedom. And we all, with
unveiled face, beholding the glory of the Lord, are being
changed into his likeness from one degree of glory to another;
for this comes from the Lord who is the Spirit."

This chapter provides us with several unusual statements. Here a contrast is made between the New and Old
Covenants. We should note that the references contrasting
the New Covenant relate not to the Tenach or the Old Covenant Scriptures as a whole, nor even the Torah (Genesis—
Deuteronomy), but only the Covenant which Moses received
from God. There is no contrast with the Abrahamic Covenant, for example, in Genesis 12-17. Of this Mosaic Covenant
received from Sinai we read these descriptive words: "The

written code kills," "the dispensation of death," "dispensation of condemnation." In contrast the New Covenant is called the "dispensation of the spirit" and the "dispensation of righteousness." Indeed, the New Covenant is compared to the old as one which has greater splendor and permanence while the old is fading away.

A superficial reading of this passage causes some to reach very popular untenable conclusions. A reading in the light of the whole context of Pauline theology, however, gives an understanding that is both rich and consistent. Among the untenable conclusions reached by some are that: (1) We should have nothing to do with the content of Torah, since its content produces spiritual death; (2) A Jew who accepts Yeshua, but practices his heritage of feast and nationhood, seeks to remain under a dispenstion of death rather than fully embracing the new dispensation of life in the spirit.

The first conclusion is utterly false. Need we again quote II Timothy 3:16-17, "*All Scripture* is inspired by God and is profitable for doctrine, reproof, correction, etc." The psalmist says "the law of the Lord is perfect, giving life to the soul" (Psalm 19:7). Is Scripture contradictory? Does what brings life in Psalm 19 bring death in II Corinthians 3? Obviously not. Paul clearly says of the Law that God gave as part of His revelation, "So the law is holy and the commandment is holy and just and good. Did that which is good, then, bring death to me? By no means! It was sin, working death in me through what is good, in order that sin might be shown to be sin and through the commandment might become sinful beyond measure! We know that the law is spiritual; but I am carnal, sold under sin" (Romans 7:12-13).

This passage gives the solution to false interpretations which despise Torah. When Paul called the Mosaic Covenant the dispensation of death, it was not because of its inherent nature. It was rather because of what people made of the Torah by their approach to it. Because humans are sinful, they approached Torah as a system of works-righteousness and falsely sought to earn God's favor by their own merits. Although the Law is a guide under the leading of the Spirit of

God, when used as a written code to be followed in our own
fleshly power, it condemns. For by the Law's high standard,
we all stand condemned (Romans 3:23). So as to not face this
condemnation, a person becomes a rationalizer of his faults
and becomes self-righteous. Yet Scripture says God dwells
with those who are of a contrite and humble heart (Isaiah
57:15). Hence, an approach to the Law with this self-righteous
attitude served to separate people from God, producing a
dispensation of death.

The Mosaic revelation itself was not a dispensation of
death; but man's approach to it produced this legalistic
period. Even the foremost 16th century Christian theologian,
John Calvin, said of this passage, "there are some rash
teachers who hold we should throw out the tablets of the law
calling the law a dispensation of death." He responded "Perish this wicked thought from our minds."[13]

The issue is not whether the Torah is used for guidance,
teaching and correction (II Timothy 3:16, 17) but, rather, the
attitude of approach. Approached with dependence upon
God's mercy, the Law, as Psalm 19 says, gives life to the soul.

What of the contrast between the Mosaic Covenant and
the New Covenant in terms of glory?

The Mosaic Covenant of Exodus 20 and Deuteronomy
was glorious. However, the New Covenant—which outstrips
it in power—has much greater glory! It is by the light of the
New Covenant that we see, once and for all, the end of all
self-righteousness. As man gazes at Yeshua hanging on the
tree, all pretensions to merit-by-works are utterly stripped
away.

The New Covenant replaces the Mosaic as the way of
entrance into the presence of God and providing a new way of
approach to God by the sacrifice of Yeshua, which replaces
the sacrifices of the Mosaic revelation central to it. The
splendor of Yeshua's personal revelation makes the other
revelation fade in comparison. It does not provide a new Law,
but rather the power to do the Law in Him. In that covenant
we are accepted as perfectly righteous before God and are
privileged to enter boldy unto the throne of Grace. Hence, the

Mosaic mediation system of priest and sacrifice is superseded.

Nothing in this passage, however, removes the gift and call of God to Jewish followers of Yeshua, which Paul calls (in Romans 11:29) "irrevocable." The apostles' example in maintaining their heritage is clear. Some years *after this passage was written,*[14] Paul testified that he lived in observance of the Laws and customs (Acts 27). He was not contradicting his own writing. The call of a Jew to the purposes of Israel is a result of God's everlasting covenant with Abraham. Jewish national practices rooted in Torah primarily celebrate the fulfillment by God of those promises. In every practice we see Yeshua's meaning and light over all. The message of this passage is parallel to that of *Hebrews*, as delineated above. For it is now by the Spirit and His conviction that we are guided to do God's will and follow His call with the Scriptures as our resource. This is freedom indeed. In this walk we are transformed step-by-step into the likeness of the Messiah (II Corinthians 3:18).

ALL FOODS DECLARED CLEAN—MARK 7:19 (ACTS 10)

This passage is usually quoted to imply the end of any relevance for the food laws of Leviticus 11, and to give evidence that all practices rooted in Torah (Genesis—Deuteronomy) are also to be eliminated.

Messianic Jews have various interpretations of the food lists contained in Leviticus 11. Their approaches seek an understanding of the purposes of the lists. Some hold that these laws are related to the symbolic meaning of animals as not fitting a concept of wholeness, or because they feed on carrion, and are thus too tied to the death and decay (symbols) resulting from sin for proper usage. Others hold that these laws have definite health value and are still valid today. Some hold that such laws of clean and unclean only penalized a person by precluding them from Temple worship for a day or a week, etc. Hence, without a Temple system, these laws lose direct relevance for those who are in Yeshua. Others hold that these laws have continuing validity in keeping Jews a distinctly-called people through being unique in what they

eat.[15] Chapter VII will give this writer's perspective on these
laws. However, the issue of food laws must be settled in the
light of their purpose. We must also take into consideration
the elimination of the Temple system by the work of Yeshua.
The phrase in Mark has little bearing on the issue.

A careful reading of the passage in context proves that
the passage does not eliminate the distinctions of Leviticus. *In
chapter seven, Yeshua was criticized because His disciples
ate without following the prescribed hand washing ritual by the
tradition of the Pharisees.* According to tradition, this made
the food unclean. Yeshua's response was first a criticism of
the tradition which set aside the commands of God by interpreting them in such a way that the actual command in its
intent is disobeyed!

Yeshua taught that the more important issue of clean and
unclean is not foods or rituals of washing, but the nature of
one's heart attitude. Real spiritual defilement does not depend
upon what goes into a man and passes out, but relates to the
spiritual heart of the person, which, when corrupt, is the
source of sin (evil) thoughts, sexual immorality, theft, murder,
adultery, greed, malice, deceit, etc.

Yeshua did not directly teach at this time that the food
laws or the Biblical heritage of Jews was then at an end.
Indeed the statement, "Jesus declared all foods clean" may be
a scribal addition, as noted in English versions by brackets.
We cannot be sure that it comes from Mark himself. Let us
assume that it does. If so, it does not say, as often misquoted,
that "all things are clean" but that all *foods* are clean. A
"food" would be defined as that which was listed as acceptable in Leviticus 11 and Deuteronomy. Hence the passage may
only mean that foods not ritually treated according to the
non-biblical Pharisaic tradition are yet acceptable for eating.
When we turn to the parallel of Matthew 15, this becomes
almost certain—for Yeshua there concludes, "Eating with
unwashed hands does not make a man unclean."

The issue clearly is the clean and unclean nature of foods
in regard to ceremonial washing. Pork would not be considered a food. Certainly, poisonous plants are not options for

our eating. "You shall not test the Lord your God" would apply to the foolishness of eating poisonous foods knowingly and expecting God's protection. Some hold that the unclean foods of Leviticus 11 possess such dangers in more limited degrees.

However we may interpret the above Scripture, an application of the biblical kosher laws is not determinable on the basis of this passage alone. The passage gives no weight to a generalized conclusion that all celebrations of the Jewish biblical heritage are now to be eliminated.

MATTHEW 6:7

"And in praying do not heap up empty phrases (vain repetitions) as the Gentiles do; for they think that they will be heard for their many words."

Jewish worship, even in the time of Yeshua, was liturgical in part. The word *liturgy* does not connote a dangerous practice to avoid. Liturgy simply is an order of prayers and readings that are written or orally memorized and repeated as part of worship. The Psalms, for example, are liturgical. Jewish prayers—some of which go back to the time of Yeshua—primarily weave Biblical verses, promises, and teachings together and put them into prayer form so that Scripture will be prayed into one's life and the life of the community. Spontaneous prayer, memorized prayers and Biblical passages are all integral to worship that is pleasing to our Father in Spirit and truth (John 4:24).

The problem, as indicated, is simply this: Messianic Jews have adopted some of the great prayers of Judaism which are biblical in content. Despite the fact that such material *is* biblical, Messianic Jews are accused of engaging in vain repetition which is contrary to the Spirit. To such accusers, only worship that is made up "on the spot," spontaneously is of the Spirit. These folks do not recognize that such a view would actually *eliminate* their choruses and hymns as well. But since music makes these forms more enjoyable to them, they are accepted.

A hymn is a prayer sung to God; and there is no reason

why a spoken prayer may not be as spiritual as a hymn sung.
The accusation of *"vain repetition"* comes because the prayer
may be *repeated* daily or weekly, as well as from the allega-
tion that such prayers are not as *emotionally* moving to some
people as musically-sung choruses and hymns. The interpretation of this passage in some quarters arises from a contemporary cultural prejudice against form, and is, itself, fraught
with difficulties.

What is Yeshua saying in Matthew 6? He was first teaching His disciples not to pray like *Gentiles or pagans.* The
characteristic of pagan religion He probably had in mind was
its magical-legalistic character. Pagans envisioned that if
they said a phrase over and over it would produce certain
definite results. The prayer could be babbled over and over
without *any meaning* or thought, but as a magical way of
manipulating the gods or nature. This was thought to be of
value.

Yeshua's point is that when we pray, we are coming
before our personal heavenly Father. Hence our prayer must
be given consciously as a *heart-intended* offering to Him of
praise, or a *heart-intended* request of intercession. If the
prayer is written or memorized, it should be said with
thought so that we will mean it! We must make it *our own*
through our heart attitude. If the prayer is spontaneous, the
same holds true. How vain are the repetitions of those so-
called spontaneous prayers that are babbled out without
thought or heart-intention! Imagine coming before a person
and saying Hallelujah over and over again as fast as you can,
without putting your heart and mind behind it! Yet some who
criticize us for praying a Psalm do just this and are themselves guilty of vain repetition. They do not direct their hearts
to God, but are emotionally "psyching themsleves up"
through fast repetition.

To cap the argument, Yeshua goes on to teach the apostles
a simple memorized prayer that can be said *with* meaning
and used with other prayers. This prayer is in mnemonic
form, as can be seen in modern translations that put it into
poetical form. Furthermore, the prayer is parallel in its con-

tent to the ancient Jewish prayer known as the *Kaddish* which Yeshua probably prayed in the synagogue:

Yeshua's prayer	*Kaddish*
Our Father in heaven, hallowed be your name.	Glorified and sanctified be God's great name in the world which he created according to his will.
Thy kingdom come. Thy will be done in earth as it is in heaven.	May he establish his kingdom during the days of your life and all the house of Israel.

The importance of heart-intention is crucial to infusing repeated prayers and Psalms with meaning. It is also crucial in keeping spontaneous prayer from degenerating into stereotypical phrases and cliches that have no meaning. The rabbis called such heart-intention *kavanah*, and taught that without it, all prayers are vain!

The best teachers of worship have always taught that both spontaneous prayer *and* repeated content are important to a balanced worship. Repeated content teaches us how to pray scripturally by making scriptural content the center of our prayer so our heart's desire is God's own desire. Spontaneous prayer then is enriched by biblical content and brings a freshness to the liturgy of worship. All worship should be offered to our God who is present, a real person before whom we bring offerings of praise and intercession.

The issue should not be primarily our boredom but God's (Malachi 2:1). We know from God's directives for worship in Torah that He enjoined acts of worship which were precisely repeated daily, weekly and annually. He also delighted Himself in spontaneous acts of praise and prayer. Problems in worship are not only matters of style, but issues of whether or not our spirit is open to the inspiration of the Spirit in all acts of worship so our love and imagination soar toward God! "God is a Spirit and those who worship Him must worship Him in spirit and in truth" (John 4:24).

COLOSSIANS 2:16-23

"Therefore do not let anyone judge you by what you eat
or drink, or with regard to a religious festival, a New Moon
celebration or a Sabbath day. These are a shadow of the things
that were to come; the reality, however, is found in Messiah.
Do not let anyone who delights in false humility and the
worship of angels disqualify you for the prize. Such a person
goes into great detail about what he has seen, and his unspir-
itual mind puffs him up with idle notions. He has lost connection with the Head, from whom the whole body, supported
and held together by its ligaments and sinews, grows as God
causes it to grow. Since you died with Messiah to the basic
principles of this world, why, as though you still belonged to
it, do you submit to its rules: 'Do not handle! Do not taste! Do
not touch!'? These are all destined to perish with use, because
they are based on *human commands and teachings*. Such
regulations indeed have an appearance of wisdom, with their
self-imposed worship, their false humility, and their harsh
treatment of the body, but they lack any value in restraining
sensual indulgence."

This passage is somewhat obscured by the fact that we do
not know the circumstances to which it was addressed. Some
quote the passage, however, as proof against celebrating Jewish festivals. Yet, the passage is far more complex, for the
situation evidently reflected not only those who were judg-
mental in regard to Jewish observances but who also worshipped angels (v. 18), "practiced asceticism" in a harsh
treatment of the body (v. 23), and were involved in superstitions of not touching or tasting. These superstitions involved
participation in the "elemental spirits" of the universe—
which are demons. All of this is called "philosophy and empty
deceit according to the elemental spirits of the universe." But
it is clearly *not* speaking about Biblical Judaism.

This has prompted *most scholars* who are students of the
passage to hold that Paul was not addressing a group of Jews
who were in the mainstream of Judaism, but one of those
heretical Jewish groups (or even superstitious Judaized non-
Jews) who were *influenced by pagan superstition* and seek-

ing to teach their doctrine at Colosse. Hence Paul could enjoin the Colossians not to be brought under judgment by those who would enforce Jewish observance on them. The very ones who are doing such mischief are engaged in superstition.

Jewish observances point to Yeshua, the substance of the faith which they already have. Therefore it is not incumbent on them to be forced into these practices. At the same time, Paul enjoins them to avoid clearly pagan practices connected to the disarmed "principalities and powers," a phrase which is usually taken to refer to the most powerful of demonic rulers. Paul would *never* call the content of Torah human commands and teachings.

Clearly, what is in mind *is not* the call of a Jew to maintain his celebration of God's gracious work in the history of Israel and the world. Rather, it is the imposition of such practices on non-Jews that is forbidden, as well as the whole *quasi-magical superstition present at Colosse.*

Paul does not contradict his own practice, as recorded in Acts. The passage says nothing negative to a Jew who, in light of the whole of biblical history, senses a call of God's Spirit to remain part of his people and to celebrate God's faithfulness to Israel through the festivals which are now used to extol salvation in Yeshua. God has faithfully preserved the Jewish people according to His Covenant, and the Messianic Jew is a unique witness to the Covenant-keeping God . . . which gives confidence to *all* people of God's faithfulness. As a witness to his own people as well, his involvement in the concerns of the Jewish community—as well as in the biblical heritage—is necessary if the love of the Messiah is to be demonstrated. Only then is the truth heralded that "God has not forsaken his people" (Romans 11). Israel is a unique people with a unique Biblical-cultural life. So far as it is consistent with Scripture, the Messianic Jew will be involved in identification with Israel—on every possible level. He should not shirk the work involved, for the Spirit can strengthen him to every good work. God did not spend 2000 years creating a context for understanding the gospel only to destroy the context of understanding.

TITUS 3:9

"But avoid foolish controversies and geneologies and arguments and quarrels about the law, because these are not profitable and are useless."

Paul here speaks of divisive people who will not submit themselves to spiritual authority. They are contentious, always looking for arguments, and therefore dangerous.

The phrase sometimes cited against Messianic Judaism is to avoid "quarrels about the Law." This is taken to mean that we are to avoid the Law or any discussion of its meaning or purpose since the Law no longer has relevance for us. How false is this view in the light of II Timothy 3:16 and 17, which call "all Scripture profitable" and II Timothy 2:15, which calls us to diligence in studying, to correctly handle "the Word of truth." To have a sincere concern to understand the meaning and purpose of the Law in the light of all Scripture is clearly a God-given mandate. This is indeed a major theme of Romans 2-8. Paul is not contradicting his own concern to understand "God's holy, just, good and spiritual law" (Romans 7) in the light of God's purpose for it. Quarrels and controversies we *are* to avoid; but those who are anti-Law also engender such quarrels and are similarly to be avoided as "lawless men."

SUMMARY

We have sought to explain many of the passages that are used by the critics of Messianic Judaism. Our summary of these passages—in light of all the evidence of Scripture—supports rather than detracts from Messianic Jewish conclusions.

Often the naive follower of Yeshua will find an erstwhile opponent stringing these passages together *out of context*. He is then shaken by the seeming weight these passages carry in contradiction of Messianic Judaism. However, we could just as easily string together pro-Messianic Jewish passages.

The problem is that prejudice and *pre-conceived* conceptions have caused the very picking and choosing of these passages. Bias illicitly uses Scripture for its own purposes. When *all* of the passages are seen in the light of the *whole* teaching of Scripture, in the *context* of the situation to which each passage was addressed, the problems dissolve. The Messianic Jewish understanding can then be seen to be that which is in accord with Scripture. May this chapter strengthen faith in the marvelous consistency and wisdom in the revelation of God.

It is principle that when Scripture seems to speak against the Law, it is generally speaking of the *misuse* of the Law as a means of gaining merit for salvation by works-righteousness or depending upon the Law for our relationship with God. Our obedience is rather the response of love produced by God's Spirit in us.

CHAPTER FIVE

Survey of the History of Judaism and Christianity

At the close of the New Testament period we find the following picture. Jewish followers of Yeshua maintained their identity through the practice of their Biblical heritage as part of their continued call from God. They were thus both witnesses to the world of God's historical revelation and witnesses of Yeshua to their *own people*.

Extra-Biblical records also prove the continued Jewish way of life among first and early second century Messianic Jews.[1] The very disciples of those who *knew* Yeshua maintained this lifestyle. The practice of New Covenant Jewish groups in the early second century, however, was not uniform. Several groups can be distinguished:

The Ebionites are discussed by Jerome and Eusebius. Apparently they carried on the anti-Paul stance of the New Testament Judaizers. They rejected most of the New Testament except for Matthew, which they produced in a unique version of their own. They also rejected the divinity of Yeshua. The name "Ebionite"—which means a "poor one"— could be a reference to a weak or poor view of Yeshua or to the fact that they lived with little material wealth.[2]

The second group was the Nazarenes. This group was probably closest in viewpoint to the disciples and those closest

personally to them. The work of recent scholars has capably
distinguished them from the Ebionites. They were Biblically-
oriented in a very full sense and accepted the central doctrines of the New Testament. They practiced their Jewish
heritage as part of their life in Yeshua. Messianic Jews today
identify most often with this group.[3]

The third group was the Assimilationists. These were
Jews in Greek-speaking lands which were spiritually distant
from their Jewish heritage. In accepting the Gospel while
acculturated in a predominantly non-Jewish setting, their
Jewish identity was eventually lost.

We are indeed thankful that God has provided us with
records by which we can understand the perspectives of these
communities.[4]

The writings of early church fathers preserved by Eusebius and the work of Josephus, the Jewish historian, provide
important information on these groups.

After the death of the disciples, leadership among the
Jewish believers in Yeshua passed to James' cousins. By the
middle of the second century, however, the situation had
vastly changed; change which occurred mostly between 68
and 100 C.E. Unfortunately, the exact nature of the process is
hidden by a lack of sources from this period. However, the
end of this period produced a church and synagogue at war
with each other—while Messianic Jews were rejected by
both groups.

The progress of this split can be mapped in basic terms.
First, the New Testament was written in Greek to convey the
message of God to a more universal audience. Although the
background of the New Testament was Hebraic in context,
Greeks often applied its content to a Greek context, leading
them to adopt teachings and perceptions that were essentially
Greek-oriented. Hence, the Church became more foreign to
Jewish people.

After the death of the apostles, the leadership of most of
the Church passed to non-Jewish leaders. Unfortunately,
many of these leaders did not appreciate Jewish people or
their Jewish Biblical heritage. The fall of Jerusalem was

evidence to them of God's *ultimate rejection* of Israel in spite of Paul's teaching in Romans 11. That "all Israel would be saved," was interpreted to mean that all Jews and Gentiles who accepted Jesus—and were thus spiritual Israel—would be saved. Judaism, to them, was dead. Passages in the New Testament which condemned the hypocrisy of the Jewish religious establishment were interpreted as condemning all things Jewish.

Hence we find in Justin Martyr's *Dialogue with Trypho the Jew* (130-150 C.E.), that a condescending attitude was often present. Although aware of the Jewish Nazarenes, he could not understand their continued practice of their heritage. He could accept that they were "saved" but found it inconsistent that they practiced what Yeshua fulfilled—which he took to mean eliminated.[5]

The Epistle of Barnabas (100 C.E.), according to H.L. Ellison, used such language about Jews, Judaism and the Law as to make any effective contact with the Synagogue impossible.[6]

Ignatius of Antioch (early 2nd century) spoke as well of the uselessness of all things Jewish.[7]

Yet in the midst of all this it is crucial to remember that the Nazarene Jews were the very relatives of Yeshua and disciples of the disciples who carried on their practices!

The continued development of official church doctrine concerning Jews in the centuries following brought a wider gap between the Church and Synagogue. The Church was not only "New Israel" but the only "true" Israel. Old Israel was reprehensible before God. Bishop Ambrose (4th Century) therefore allowed the burning of synagogues and stated that this was not a sin. Augustine argued that Old Israel served only one purpose: to exhibit the wretched plight of those who reject God.

These viewpoints led to the spiritualization (allegorization) of the prophecies and promises in Scripture which referred to the physical descendents of Abraham. All reference to Israel's promise of land forever was taken to mean the Church's inheritance of the Kingdom. That God would gain His ultimate triumph over the nations through Israel and then bless the world through Israel was taken to mean the triumph of and blessings for the Church. As one writer succinctly put it, the Church took all the blessings and left Israel with all the cursings.[8]

The Synagogue, on the other hand, rejected the Nazarene Jews and developed its viewpoint in opposition to parallels with church views.

Before the fall of Jerusalem to the Roman General Titus in the year 70, there were several divisions within Judaism. The Pharisees, the Saducees and the Essenes represented the three most prominent sects. The Nazarene Jews constituted an additional perspective within Israel. We do not know all of the reasons for the rejection of the Nazarenes by the Jewish community, but some prominent reasons stand out:

When the Roman armies approached Jerusalem to quell Israel's rebellion, the Nazarenes fled the city, taking up residence in Petra. They thereby avoided the terrible destruction and slaughter by the Roman army. The rest of the Jewish community branded the Nazarenes traitors, no longer to be accepted. Why did the Nazarenes flee? The major reason was the prophecy and command of Yeshua! In Luke 21 and Matthew 24, Yeshua predicted that Jerusalem would be surrounded by armies. His followers were told that when they saw this beginning to occur, they were to "flee to the mountains." They were not "traitors"; they were simply following Yeshua's teaching.

Another reason for their rejection, no doubt, was their theology. It was abhorrent to many Jews to think of their great king Messiah dying as a common criminal. The idea so went against the common idea of the Messianic role that any explanation of how the suffering role was a prelude to the kingly role was not allowed. So severe was the rejection of this view in some circles that there was no acceptance of the people who held it.

In addition, prominent synagogue leaders were angered because the preaching of the New Testament blunted their efforts to gain converts from Gentile ranks. A Gentile could accept Yeshua, worship the God of Israel and claim salvation without the stigma of circumcision or the necessity of adopting all the practices of the Jewish tradition. Many potential "converts" left the synagogue for the new movement.

After the Temple fell, only one party within Judaism—the Pharisees—had the strength to assert leadership. The Sadducees were too connected to the Temple system and the Essenes' losses were too severe in war. Pharisaical Judaism became the precursor to today's orthodox rabbinical Judaism. The rabbis moved to preserve and unify the Jewish community under their teachings and sought to exclude all other forms of Judaism. Orthodox rabbinical Judaism soon became normative Judaism. The Nazarenes received special condemnation by the rabbis. The Council of Jamnia (90 C.E.) not only defined Judaism; it also condemned heretics.

At this time the "Berkat ha Minim" was added to the 12th Benediction. It prayed a prayer of condemnation for heretics. Although this prayer was later altered by force under Christian rulers, it probably originally singled out the Nazarenes and prayed for their destruction.[9] A Nazarene Jew in the synagogue would not be able to pray this and would thus be excluded. Thus, the Nazarenes were cast out of rabbinical synagogues.

Further reflection of this rejection is found in the Talmudic story where a Rabbi Jacob was sick. Upon questioning, it was learned that his sickness was caused by once being pleased by a saying of Yeshua which a follower of His quoted.[10]

We recognize that the rabbis of this age preserved much of the great heritage of Jewish history. However, this was overlaid with material contrary to Scripture, including the interpretations which rejected the Messiahship and work of Yeshua.

The separation of the Nazarenes from the rest of the Jewish community was further intensified by the Bar-Kochba Revolt.

Bar Kochba, a ruthless military leader, spearheaded a second revolt against Rome around 135 C.E. He recruited the Jewish population still in the land for his revolt. At first, it seemed that the Messianic Jews followed Bar Kochba and

sought by this means to demonstrate their loyalty to Israel.
However, during the war, the venerable Rabbi Akiba proclaimed Bar Kochba the Messiah.[11] Other rabbis rejected this
proclamation, but the damage was done: Messianic Jews
could not follow a false Messiah. They threw down their
arms; only Yeshua was the Messiah. Bar Kochba massacred
those who would not give him total allegiance. The Romans
then quelled the revolt. A great loss of Jewish lives resulted;
Rabbi Akiba and Bar Kochba were slain. Despite the tragic
ruthlessness of Bar Kochba and the error of Akiba, the Nazarenes were again branded as traitors for not fighting in the
revolt. Over the next few centuries, the Nazarene communities dwindled and ultimately vanished.[12]

The result of this history was the loss of the testimony of
loyal Jews who believed in Yeshua. Without such a community within the Jewish community, the bridge of understanding between Jewry and the Church was lost as well. Messianic Jews could have kept alive the picture of a Jewish Jesus.
This would have done much to stem the tide of future anti-
Semitism. With the loss of this bridge of understanding
Church-Synagogue hostility increased. Both the Church and
Synagogue fought for proselytes among the Gentiles.[13] In
competition they formed their theologies in opposition to
each other. Christian theological positions were adopted
because they freed the Church from Jewish roots and were
contrary to Jewish teaching. To the theologians of the day,
there was no longer a Covenant with Israel as a nation; there
was no longer a purpose for Jewish identity. The Church was
seen as all in all in God's purposes. Some positions which
were adopted were *anti-Semitic* as the next section will
recount.

The Synagogue also honed *its* theology in opposition.
God's unity was thus a singular numerical unity that allowed
for no sense of plurality at all, this concept being contrary to
the Trinity.[14] All the passages of Scripture which pointed to
a suffering Messiah as well as any concept of substitutionary atonement for sin were played down.

Church ritual, statutary aids to worship and Greek theological concepts intensified the Jewish view that the Church was a semi-pagan institution. When the Roman Empire adopted Christianity as its official religion and institutional Christianity became a persecuting church, hope for understanding and reconciliation diminished.

A HISTORY OF ANTI-SEMITISM

"So, I ask, have they stumbled so as to fall? By no means! But through their trespass salvation has come to the Gentiles so as to make Israel jealous. Now if their trespass means riches for the world, and if their failure means riches for the Gentiles, how much more will their full inclusion mean. Now I am speaking to you Gentiles. Inasmuch then as I am an apostle to the Gentiles, I magnify my ministry in order to make my fellow Jews jealous and save some of them" (Romans 11:11-14).

Here we read the wonderful directive of God through Paul—that Jewish people see the riches of the Gospel in the lives of non-Jews and be moved to jealousy because of the reality which such a life and love so manifest. By this jealousy, they would turn to the Messiah and receive Him.

Sadly, the history of the Church hardly fulfilled this mission.

Soon after the Jewish apostles died, leadership of the Church was transferred to people who had no great respect for Jews or Judaism. Rather than seeing Jewish people as erring brethren to whom they were indebted for the gifts of Scripture, the Messiah and Old Testament saints, the Jewish people were looked upon as reprobates hated by God. Sentiment expressed against some Jewish leaders by Jewish followers of Yeshua was used by later non-Jewish leaders as an indictment of all Jewish people.[15]

The Epistle of Barnabas, from the end of the first century, reflects this negative attitude and applies it to Jewish practices as well. As H.L. Ellison put it, "Already the so-called Epistle of Barnabas, which may go back to the last decade of the first century, uses such language about Jews, Judaism and the Law, as to make any effective contact between the two sides virtually impossible. As soon as it had the power, the Church did its utmost to defeat God's purpose. It persecuted and bullied, thereby automatically putting itself in the wrong. It spread the vilest calumnies about the Jews."[16]

Many writers did not display an accurate understanding of the very things they criticized, including the nature of the Old Testament revelation. Ignatius of Antioch, in the same period, was clear in indicating the uselessness of all Jewish things.[17]

Justin Martyr, one of the famed leaders of the early second century, spoke of Jewish people and practice in condescending terms. In his dialogue with Trypho, he expressed dismay over the fact that Jewish followers of Yeshua still maintained their cultural identity and practice.[18] He accepted the possibility of their salvation, but could not understand Jewish practice as a way of expressing their faith. Justin believed that fulfillment by Yeshua eliminated Jewish things.

As the decades passed, the Christian polemic against Jews and Jewish practice continued. Bishop Ambrose, in the 4th century, even went so far as to suggest that burning a synagogue was no sin. Why? Because the Jews rejected Yeshua; therefore, what could be considered a crime against others would not be a crime against Jews. This interpretation overlooked the fact that it was the Jews who first followed Yeshua and who originally spread the Good News throughout the Roman Empire; it overlooked the great number of Jews who did follow Yeshua; and it overlooked Judaism as the original context of Christian faith.

John Chrysostom, however, is the author of the greatest virulence. Chrysostom was threatened because Christians in Antioch visited synagogues to gain a better understanding of the Jewish roots of their faith. Chrysostom held that the coming of Christianity eliminated the value of Jewish practice and identity. To destroy any Christian interest in Judaism, Chrysostom wrote eight sermons against the Jews. The poisonous hate of these sermons has not been surpassed. Nor was Chrysostom just an isolated individual. He was a renowned church leader. His viewpoint, therefore, became part of the attitude of institutional Christianity.

Augustine himself, the great theological giant revered by both Catholics and Protestants, added his own fuel to the fire. He explained the purpose of the continued existence of the Jewish community in strictly negative terms. The reprobate state of the Jews, who were under God's judgment, would provide a witness to the truth of Christianity, he said, as well as an example of what happens to people who turn against God.

Perhaps we could point to many parallels of religious and social prejudice. The venom released in intense religious dispute is great. Institutional Christianity became the state religion when Emperor Constantine converted to Christianity in the fourth century. Religious bigotry thus became part of state policy; severe economic and social sanctions were progressively applied to the Jews.[19] The church-state collaboration in discrimination was maintained for fifteen centuries.

When we come to our own age we find that Nazi leaders defended their actions by claiming to follow the history of church tradition. Luther's sermons against the Jews were widely recounted. The historical image of the "insidious Jew" prepared the way for Auschwitz. The Church found it difficult to recognize its own complicity; for although it had demeaned the value of Jewish people, it did not draw the implication that they had no right to exist. The Nazis drew this implication.

It is often asked, why did so many of the people of "Christian Europe" stand by during the Holocaust? Human weakness, ignorance, fear of taking risks for others, self protection and a crowd mentality are often mentioned. Some point to the very work of the Devil himself in blinding the minds of people. However, to all of these reasons, we must add another key reason: The historic tradition of the Church in its teaching on Jews and Judaism served to undercut concern for the Jewish people.

In all fairness, we must mention that there were individual Christians who stood with Jewish people against this tradition. In their close walk with Yeshua, they gained a deep

love for Jewish people, in many cases sacrificing their lives
for their Jewish friends.

We should note that some have traced the origins of anti-
Semitism to early Jewish persecutions of Christians. Although there was fierce persecution of Jewish followers of
Yeshua, this was an intra-Jewish battle. Jewish persecution
of non-Jewish Christians is now considered an unwarranted
assumption by the most competent scholars who deal with
this early period.[20]

The greatest irony can be seen in the fact that Yeshua's
disciples opened the door to anti-Jewishness by adopting a
liberal policy toward Gentiles and their admission into the
universal body of believers. They were permitted entrance
without the cultural restrictions of Jewish identity. This
freedom was a great spur to the spread of the Gospel among
the Gentiles. However, although the original identity and
way of life among Yeshua's followers were Jewish, when the
later non-Jewish majority was in control, they restricted
freedom and would not allow for Jewish identity within the
body of believers.

The most glaring example of this is the Inquisition in
sixteenth-century Spain. Those of Jewish origin who claimed
to follow Yeshua, but yet celebrated Passover, were burned
at the stake. We must also mention the Crusades to free the
Holy Land from Arab-Islamic control in the twelfth century.
The cross was used as a symbol on the implements of war. The
Crusaders were offered freedom from hell and purgatory by
participating in a Crusade. The cry went out that it was inconsistent to seek to rid the Holy Land of infidels when there
were infidel Jews within the midst of the lands of Europe.
Hence the Crusaders held their crosses high as they pillaged
and destroyed Jewish lives and property throughout Europe
on their way to the Holy Land. Many were burned alive and
tortured. In his book, *The Anguish of the Jews*, Fr. Flannery
made the perceptive statement that the cross—which was an
intended symbol of giving up one's life for another, a symbol
of pacifistic (in relation to violence) but active love—was
thoroughly adulterated. It was now a cross sharpened into a

sword to torture, kill and plunder.[21]

Who can evaluate the extent of suffering during the numerous explusions from many nations, from Spain in 1492 and throughout Jewish history? Who can evaluate the damage from forced conversions at the point of the sword from Charlemagne in the ninth century and throughout later centuries? Or how can we sum up the economic and social deprivation? Even the Reformation brought little relief to Jewry. The early Luther was sympathetic to the Jewish plight; but the later Luther attacked the Jews when they did not convert to Lutheranism. He called for making them into a caste of menial laborers for the rest of the nation.

The widespread nineteenth-century pogroms in Russia were devastating to Jewish life once more. Every government made Jews the scapegoat during difficult times.

The saddest chapter of all might be the Jewish turncoats. These supposed converts to Christianity led the pogroms and Torah burnings. Their purpose was self-serving. Joseph, Pfeferkorn in 16th-century Hungary was responsible for many Jewish deaths. When some Jews think of Hebrew-Christians, it's his image that comes to mind. How tragic! Yet could there be many who honestly converted to Christianity when the Church required the convert to renounce all things Jewish, to change one's Jewish name to a "Christian name," and to give up contact with Jewish people? Each "convert" had to sign a document swearing an oath to all of these requirements!

The major ground for this anti-Semitism was often said to be the New Testament. A closer examination of the New Testament shows that its passages are not at all anti-Jewish but can be classified instead as follows:

(1) *Statements which are negative to the established leadership* at Jerusalem consisting of Saducees (a party which did not accept the resurrection of the dead or the prophets) and Pharisees. These were criticized severely either for a narrow legalism that was oftentimes self-serving and contradicted the spiritual intent of Scripture or, (2) *comprised Scriptural statements which were critical of "the Jews" in the Gospel of John*, but which were actually refer-

ring to the *Judean* leadership establishment from the perspective of Galileans.[22] For example, Americans are known as
Yankees in other countries; but in the South "Yankee" is
used as a sectional term to refer to the North. In the same
way, Galilean Jews referred to the *Judean Jewish establishment* as "the Jews." The word in Greek for the Judeans is
the same as the word translated "Jews." (3) *Statements concerning the judgment that would fall on the nation due to the
blindness of the leadership at the time.* Nations as a whole
suffer under the blindness of their leaders. Thus, though
nations are judged corporately, there is no right to judge all
the individuals in the nation.

These statements were made by Jews but were never
intended to condemn all Jewish people. Most of the statements referred to only a particular group within the nation
and are not meant as universal statements. These are statements of criticism between family members and are totally
invalid when repeated by non-Jews as applying to all Jews.
Anti-Semites never quote John 4:24—"Salvation is of the
Jews"—and admit that Jesus, the Savior of the world, was, is
and forever will be a Jew descended from Jacob! Nor do they
quote Romans 11:28-29—"they are beloved for the Father's
sake the gifts and call of God are irrevocable." Neither do they
quote the Gospel statements which testify that "the common
people heard Him gladly," that many wept at Yeshua's death
and beat their breasts, and that the priestly establishment
feared all of Jerusalem following Him (Luke 20:19; 22; 23:7;
24:20). Nor is it mentioned that myriads of Jews followed
Yeshua (Acts 21) or that it was the Jewish blood of the Apostles and many other witnesses which was spilled by non-Jews.

The Jewish apostles spread the Good News of Yeshua
throughout the world. The debt of the Church is to Israel as
Paul states, and the proper Scriptural response is gratitude
and love. For as Paul says, "it is not you who supports the root,
but the root supports you" (Romans 11:18). The whole of the
Biblical testimony refutes the principles of anti-Semitism.[23]

Let us note that the reason the leadership of Jerusalem
handed Yeshua over to the Romans was that His popular

following caused Him to be a threat to this leadership. Let us also note that it was a Gentile *Roman instrument* of capital punishment, the cross, which was his place of execution.

Theologically, it was God's plan that Yeshua would die on the cross for the sins of the whole word (I Peter 2:24). It was our collective and universal sin which placed Him on the cross. He died not for our punishment, but that through Him we might be freed from condemnation.

Too few were those who gave their lives in love for Israel. How few were those like the ten Boom family who fearlessly gave themselves with courage.[24] This remarkable family lost a brother, father and sister in the Holocaust. Brother Wilem ten Boom was a writer against anti-Semitism and argued against the assimilation of Jews into Western Christian forms. He adopted Messianic Jewish conclusions back in the 1930's. Corrie Ten Boom has well recounted the marvelous story of God's grace in their service to Israel, stretching back to grandparents who supported Zionism.[25]

In the light of all this history, there is cause for much sadness. The bridge between the Church and the Synagogue, the Messianic Jews, to all intents and purposes, ceased to exist. The Church and the Synagogue were light years apart in understanding each other. Yeshua was seen as a false god of the Gentiles by Jews, and as a Gentile Savior by establishment Christianity. Gone was the great vision of Acts 15 of two great wings of one universal people of God: a Jewish wing and a non-Jewish wing, each part of one body, but each, in freedom, following their distinctive callings. Neither side would seek to dissolve the other, but there could be Hebraic congregations in Jewish areas, non-Hebraic in non-Jewish areas and mixed congregations where this was most feasible—all under the Lordship of Yeshua. Jews would be believers in Yeshua, but still loyal citizens of Israel. How Messianic Jews could have given the lie to anti-Semitism! How they could have reflected the Jewishness of Yeshua as a witness to the Jewish community and the Church! What a gain there would have been toward a deeper Biblical understanding of Israel and the Church in the purposes of God, thereby thwarting anti-Jewish theologies.

THE RESPONSE OF HEBRAIC CONGREGATIONS

Messianic Jewish congregations are forming in response to Scripture and the impact of history. Messianic Judaism is not a *completely* new movement, but rather the resurrection of a very old movement.

We have sought to show that the identity described under the term "Messianic Judaism" was the identity of the apostles and the community of Jewish "followers of the Way" in the first and second centuries. Since that time, many Jewish believers in Yeshua have enhanced the Church as pastors, theologians and laymen. It remains however, that a Messianic Jewish style of existence has been lacking subsequent to the early centuries. Indeed, the church sought to have its converts literally change their names and give up all identity as Jews.

The Synagogue, as well, sought to have followers of Yeshua ostracized from the mainstream community. A Jew who accepted Yeshua was considered no longer Jewish.

The early history of Jewish missions was often a sordid affair, with self-serving missionaries seeking to enrich themselves at the expense of gullible church members.[26] However, there were always some who understood the place and calling of Israel and whose lives were exemplary.[27]

In 1825, theologian J. Toland argued that a careful reading of Scripture would lead us to believe that Israel is still called by God as a nation and that Jewish followers of Yeshua should maintain their identity and heritage as Jews.[28]

In the mid-nineteenth century, the Hebrew-Christian Alliance of Great Britain was formed. It sought to bring Jewish Christians together in periodic fellowship so as to maintain their Jewish identity. In 1915, the Hebrew-Christian Alliance of America also began to foster a purpose of Jewish identity and witness within Israel. In 1925, the International Hebrew Christian Alliance was formed. In the original founders of the Alliances one finds a deeper appreciation of Jewish identity and practice than was sometimes to be found in later followers. Of note in those years was Mark John Levy, the General Secretary of the American Alliance. Levy argued indefatigably that Jewish Christians were called to maintain their heritage of feast, festival and Hebraic worship. He traveled worldwide and in 1914 convinced the Episcopal Church to adopt as its official position that congregations of Jewish believers should be formed for the preservation of Jewish identity and as the best means of witness to the Jewish community. Levy was himself a gentleman, scholar and saintly man. Even Rabbi Eichorn, who has researched the seediest aspects of Jewish missions, conceded his high character.[5]

Others of note during these early years of the Alliance included Rabbi J. Litchenstein of Hungary, who was a district head rabbi. He became a follower of Yeshua by reading the New Testament when the light of God's grace, love and power in Yeshua dawned on him.[6] This rabbi saw Yeshua as a Jew. He taught the New Testament from his pulpit and refused assimilation into any Christian denomination so as to remain with his people. So respected was he that for a time he could not be dismissed from his congregation—despite his unwillingness to recant his beliefs before higher authorities. He may be said to have had the first Messianic Jewish congregation in 1400 years. There was also Joseph Rabinowitz, who held similar views to Litchenstein and traveled in Eastern Europe and Russia.

Of special note is Theodore Luckey, who edited *The Messianic Jew* at the turn of the century. This Eastern European was a man of such kindness and piety that Dr. Henry Eimspruch called him a "lamed vavnik"; or one of the 36 righteous men of each generation who, by their saintliness, stave off God's judgment. Dr. Luckey lived a life of true Jewish practice and called Jesus "the bone of our bones and flesh of our flesh" in relation to Israel. Luckey argued our basic positions eighty years ago.

Strong currents were afoot in America, however, which would impede the new progress toward an authentic Messianic Judaism. Fundamentalist dispensationalism, a turn-of-the-century movement, discovered the truth of God's prom-

ises to Israel—to be regathered to their land, to recognize
their Messiah and to be the geographical center of His Kingdom. However, they held to a rigid distinction between Christians and Jews. To many, a "Christian" was a former Jew or
Gentile who became part of the Bride of Christ—the Church.
The converted Jew thus was to find his total spiritual identity
within the Church and not in the nation of Israel. The nation
had a separate identity and future salvation, but was not to be
confused with those "saved" during the present age. Hence, a
converted Jew, being part of the Church, could remember his
origins intellectually, but was to no longer practice Jewish
holidays and festivals, for these were said to be part of the
"Old" dispensation, while the believer was in the New dispensation of the Church. Although early Fundamentalists
were fine scholars,[8] many later dispensational Fundamentalists became narrow, legalistic and even obscurantist. This is
why many present day evangelical Christians will not accept
the Fundamentalist label.[9]

These narrow attitudes and rigid distinctions became
common in the American Alliance and progress toward a
more authentic Jewish movement for Yeshua was precluded. One of the casualties during these years was the
enigmatic figure of Hugh Schoenfield, who is notorious today
for his book, *The Passover Plot,* which discredits the resurrection of Yeshua. Schoenfield was also the author of *A History
of Jewish Christianity,* which is a fine historical account and
defense of the tenets of what we today call Messianic
Judaism. Schoenfield was a member of the Alliance and
sought to foster a more authentic Jewish expression.

When I learned of this I was mystified as to how he had
changed so radically. However, I had a sense in my spirit that
this sensitive young man was probably badly mistreated for
his viewpoint, left the Alliance and harbored bitterness
toward Jewish-Christians ever since. This bitterness would
explain his later skeptical writings. I corresponded with him
to see if my sense was correct. It was! Furthermore, he also
indicated another central problem which explained his writings. Schoenfield had occult abilities which he took to be

natural abilities, but which we as Bible believers know to usually have their source in Satan and from which a person needs deliverance. The later Schoenfield received visions of historical events and wrote the footnotes later to prove the truth of the visions. What a tragedy! What if Schoenfield had been treated discreetly and supportively? What if he had been delivered from occult bondage? Perhaps he could have been a great Messianic Jewish scholar. However, since that time for several years the Alliance made little progress toward Messianic Judaism.

This does not mean that progress was not made anywhere. Progress occurred mostly in the United States. The Holocaust eliminated many European thinkers and leaders who were tending toward an authentic Jewish identity among Jewish followers of Yeshua. In America, the United Presbyterian Church established several important works, some of which still continue. Hebrew Christian churches were established in Los Angeles, Philadelphia, Baltimore and Chicago. The latter three still exist.

By far the most influential work was the Peniel Center (est. 1921) and the first Hebrew Christian Church (est. 1934), which became Adat Hatikvah (1975). Rev. David Bronstein was the founder of both these works. Although they did not achieve an authentic Jewish expression of faith, progress toward this ideal was made. Accusations of re-erecting the "wall of partition" were made against Bronstein then, as today against Messianic Judaism. Although Christian hymnology and Sunday worship provided a church atmosphere, Bronstein's own teaching, the symbolism and design of the worship hall, and the remembrance of feasts by preaching and demonstration were closer to a Messianic Jewish style than anything else then in America.

The bridge to contemporary Messianic Judaism can be clearly seen as we look at the ministries of Edward Brotskey, Manny Brotman and Martin Chernoff. As a student at Moody, Brotman gained a vision for producing materials which would speak the Good News in a thoroughly Jewish way.

Space and time do not permit us to credit all who have had a significant role in Messianic Judaism. We would mention the spur given to Jews who are believers in the Messiah by the Jews for Jesus under the leadership of Moishe Rosen. We would also mention the theological help being given by Dr. Louis Goldberg of Moody Bible Institute, who has sought to provide balance to the Messianic movement theologically over the last ten years.

Beth Messiah of Washington, D.C., is typical of the progress of Messianic congregations. Beth Messiah was founded by a handful of Jewish believers including Paul Liberman, Sid Roth of Messianic Vision, and Sandra Sheshkin. It was spurred on by the outreach ministry of Manny Brotman, who was called as the first leader. Beth Messiah is presently growing in walking out a Biblical spiritual life style. Since 1973, this congregation has continued to see scores of Jewish people come to know the Lord. It was the first independent Messianic congregation to own its own facility.

Ed Brotsky headed the first Messianic Jewish congregation in Philadelphia. Rev. Brotsky came to the faith through the ministry of Rev. Kaminsky while he was still in Toronto. A significant work under Daniel Feinstone in Philadelphia also later developed into a congregation.

A prominent Messianic Jewish congregation was planted by the late Rev. Martin Chernoff in Cincinnati. He was also won to Yeshua by Rev. Kaminsky and had continued contact with Chicago. He next led a congregation in Philadelphia. His son Joel is known for pioneering Messianic Jewish music. Several Jewish missions also established small congregations of varying success and Jewishness.

In 1975, the Alliance changed its name to the Messianic Jewish Alliance, reflecting the growing Jewish identity of Jewish followers of Yeshua. It is at this point that a major question comes into focus: What is the distinction between Messianic Judaism and Hebrew Christianity, which was the traditional designation for Jewish believers in Yeshua?

Hebrew Christians, traditionally, have *not emphasized* the planting of Jewish congregations; but Messianic Jews have. Hebrew-Christianity, at times, saw Jewishness as merely an ethnic identity, whereas Messianic Judaism saw its Jewish life and identity as a continued call of God. Of course there are many exceptions for those who use either label. A total distinction cannot be drawn. In general, however, Messianic Judaism has emphasized the planting of Messianic Jewish congregations and fidelity to the Jewish biblical calling. The exact nature of this is still in process of outworking. Furthermore, Messianic Jews have tended not to use the "Christian" label because of its cultural sense—not being Jewish (which is a Jewish understanding of the word)—rather than its linguistic meaning, "One of the Messiah."

An interesting aside is the story of Willem ten Boom. He was the brother of the famous Corrie ten Boom. Willem ten Boom became a student of the history of the relationship between Jews and Christians. Through his studies, he came to the conclusion that it was God's desire to not have Jews assimilate, but that Jews under the Abrahamic Covenant were still chosen as a distinct nation. He came to believe that a Jew who comes to Yeshua should do so within a context of maintaining his own heritage.[10] This leads us to a practical question—how is this to be done?

The issue of Messianic congregations is a pragmatic answer to several such questions: How shall an ongoing Jewish lay witness to Israel be established? How shall a Jew be enabled to maintain his heritage of Shabbat and feast while holding to the capstone of revelation in Yeshua? How shall a Jew enable his children to grow up with a sense of heritage, to be Bar Mitzvah and maintain an ongoing involvement in the Jewish community? The Synagogue will not open its door to train his children and the majority of local churches will not provide for this. How then? The answer is clearly congregational, for achieving this individually or through a monthly fellowship may be inadequate or too difficult to sustain for the average person. Many who are brought up without a Jewish congregational context have little understanding of their heritage or felicity in its practice. Without such a strong context of a Jewish fellowship of believers, an effective outreach is also blunted. Furthermore, a congregation is the most effective center of discipleship for new Jewish followers of Yeshua.

Without a visible community of Jewish and non-Jewish followers of Yeshua in a clear Hebraic fellowship, how shall the truth of Israel's call be reflected for the Church? And how shall Israel see Yeshua *as her* own anointed King? Such a visible community, capable of fulfilling all these goals and drawing the full resources of God's power, is only to be found in the local body (Matthew 16).

A Messianic Jewish congregation provides the social and spiritual context to reflect the whole of Biblical truth. A congregation of Messianic Jews is as well a New Covenant congregation, whose membership is open to Jew and non-Jew who are called to it and who affirm its purpose and mission. Such a congregation is a local expression of the universal body of believers. It fully expresses Jewish heritage in the context of New Covenant fulfillment and truth. Yeshua only established one type of organization to be empowered to carry out his work: the Kehilah or Congregation. There need to be such congregations within Israel to carry out His commission of witness and discipleship, rather than only "professionals" doing the work of God. Lay people in a congregational base multiply witness.[11]

Furthermore, we have to ask what institution—outside of life in Israel—is able to help Jewish believers in Yeshua in their Jewish identity. In the light of God's supernatural preservation of Israel, in the light of untold Jewish suffering throughout the centuries, culminating in the Holocaust, and in the light of Romans 11:29—"the gifts and call of God are irrevocable"—we assert that the assimilation (loss of identity) of Jews is *not* God's will. It was the devil's desire to destroy the Jewish people as a distinct people. Can we in the light of all history diminish the Jewish nation by our own assimilation?

A Messianic Jewish congregation provides the social and spiritual context of discipleship in the Messiah without assimilation. Other examples of non-assimilation without congregational life usually manifest some marks of a congregation by having worship services, fellowship times, witness training and activities to foster Jewish observance. They have simply not yet been *named congregations*.

At the invitation of Adat Hatikvah and B'nai Macadeem, in the spring of 1978, a successful preliminary meeting of congregational leaders from nineteen congregations was held in Chicago. It was agreed that they would form a union of congregations. The official incorporation meeting was set for June. Finally, in June 1979, nineteen congregations joined together in Mechanicsburg, Pennsylvania and formed the Union of Messianic Jewish Congregations to help one another foster the goals of Messianic Judaism. This union has since grown to over fifty congregations.

The Messianic congregation is a practical answer to the two-thousand-year tug-of-war between the Church and the Synagogue. In the very teeth of controversy and anti-Semitism, it can adequately testify that Yeshua is the Messiah and Savior of Israel to the Jewish community and to the Church that Yeshua is a Jew, a son of Israel and that anti-Semitism is anti-Jesus. It can be a living bridge of understanding between the Church and the Synagogue. It can be, at once, part of the Jewish community and an expression of the single universal body of believers.

There is another model which also can bear much fruit. It is the model of a non-Jewish congregation which understands and encourages the Jewish identity of its Jewish members to the enhancement of the whole congregation. This option hardly seemed possible twenty years ago; but today, we have many examples of it. Messianic Jews must stand for—and with—the whole body of believers.

CHAPTER SIX

The Faith and Life of Messianic Jews

Messianic Jews live in the period between the "already" and the "not yet." *Already*, they know that the Kingdom of God has come spiritually in Messiah Yeshua. As communities, they seek to demonstrate this reality of the present Kingdom by lives of love, power, reconcilation and healing. The Kingdom has not yet come in its fullness to all the earth. Only when Messiah Yeshua returns, will the Kingdom be a reality in fullness over all the earth.[1] Hence Messianic Jews live in expectation of that Day of the Lord, when "His will shall be done on earth as it is in heaven" (Matthew 6:10). The life of Messianic Jews, however, is a life with definite concept of authority, the way of salvation, the work of God's Spirit, the Messiahship of Yeshua, what it means to be Jewish and how all this is manifest in one's lifestyle and practice.

THE AUTHORITY OF THE BIBLE

Messianic Jews accept the full authority and truth of the complete Bible. Whatever Scripture teaches is to be believed and obeyed. It is crucial, however, that there be an accurate understanding of the meaning of the authority of the Bible. The Bible is certainly true, *but how do we* ascertain its truth? What do we mean when we say the Bible is inspired?

Basically, the inspiration of the Bible means that God

superintended the Biblical writers in such a way that what
they wrote conveyed what God desired to convey. That which
was taught was all truth and not error. God did not usurp the
personalities of the writers by placing them in "trancelike"
states. Rather, He used their unique styles and personalities
to convey His truth. Paul can ask Timothy in a very human
way to bring his cloak and we gain a glimpse into the intimate
life of the Apostle. This was God's desire. However, Paul also
can write that his teaching is the commandment of God (I
Corinthians 14:37). Scripture therefore says, "All Scripture is
given by inspiration of God" (II Timothy 3:16). The Greek
sense of inspiration is "God breathed." And in II Peter 1:20-21
we read, "No prophecy of the scripture is of any private
interpretation. For the prophecy came not in old time by the
will of man: but holy men of God spoke as they were moved
by the Holy Ghost."

It is crucial to understand that the highest authority and
court of appeal for all teaching in Messianic Judaism is the
Bible. However, what a person understands the Bible to teach
varies from reader to reader. Each perceives within his own
limitations of knowledge and ability as illuminated by the
Spirit. What we seek to understand is the intended teaching of
the Biblical author.

The only *objective* means of sorting varying interpretations is to understand Scripture in *context*.[2] By context we
mean several things: The verse is to be understood in the
context of the whole Bible. As one writer aptly stated, "a text
without a context is a pretext." Secondly, part of the context
for better understanding is the original language of revelation (Hebrew or Greek). Thirdly, the original language,
words, sentences and literary styles must also be understood
according to the *usage* of the time of writing. To whom did the
author write? Why did he write? And *how would his audience*
have understood his writing in their circumstances and their
language usage? When we understand these things, we can
make more accurate applications of the Scriptures. It is crucial to respect Biblical scholarship and to avoid narrow *subjective* interpretations. These are the laws for understanding

any piece of literature.

Every Bible translator depends upon the above type of practice and seeks to ascertain all of the above information in making his translations. However, a translation is an abbreviation of the fullness of meaning. The translator uses cultural-historical studies, commentaries and linguistic-grammatical studies to produce an English translation. Messianic Jews must therefore eschew the rejection of scholarship. The Bible teaches only truth; but our understanding of the Bible depends upon a proper interpretation (see Acts 8, Philip and the Ethiopian eunuch).

Does not this place the Bible beyond the average layman and overlook the teaching ministry of the Spirit? Not at all. The Spirit does not teach us to parse Hebrew and Greek verbs; but He indeed illumines the Scripture to every sincere reader. Every sincere reader of a good translation receives much understanding of the basic teaching of the Bible on salvation, love and service. The Spirit reveals this to our hearts, empowers us and helps us to apply the Word. However, our perceptions of the Spirit are fallible: we see now through a glass darkly (1 Corinthians 13:12), and controversial Biblical issues require more information for solution.

Furthermore, it is crucial that we understand the Spirit's work, what He does and does not do. The Spirit illumines the Word; but He will not give us Hebrew lessons! He will give us insight; but his insight is a subjective perception unless it is tested by the objective tools of Biblical study. The Bible enjoins us to "test the spirits" and to not believe another gospel (I John 4:1-3; cf. Galatians 1:8-9). The only objective test for interpretation is the tools to accurately understand Scripture in context. The Word is the test of the Spirit; but without the Spirit, the Word is dead and unapplied to our lives. The Spirit and Word go together; but we must never elevate the Spirit and His illumination above the objective Word. We have seen groups give themselves to wholesale heresy and deception by having no objective test for their understanding in the Word. The Bible is for all to read and grow by. The Spirit is likewise given to all believers; but let us not be foolish in rejecting the tools for a more accurate understanding. All should read the Word in dependence on the Spirit.

Why do we believe the Bible? There are multitudinous reasons, of which we summarize only a few. There is first, the interior claim within the Bible, a unique claim in comparison with other religious literature: The Mosaic writings regularly testify having been written according to the *instruction of the Lord*. This is also the case with the prophetic books, in which the words, "Thus saith the Lord," are regularly found prefixing the message. The same is true in the New Testament, where we read in II Timothy 3:16, that "All Scripture is given by inspiration of God and is profitable for doctrine, for reproof, for correction . . ." Paul, the Apostle, writes in I Corinthians 14:37, "What I am writing to you is a command of the Lord." These claims are so unique that they give import to the unique inspiration of the Scripture.

We also find great evidence from the teaching of Yeshua. He who rose from the dead, on the best of historical evidence,[3] is our authority and teacher. He taught the inspiration and authority of all Scripture, stating that "until heaven and earth pass away, not a jot or tittle shall pass from the law until all be fulfilled" (Matthew 5:18). Further, He stated, "the Scripture cannot be broken" (John 10:35). His whole teaching demeanor demonstrated His attitude toward Scripture. He consistently used several words—"It says," "Scripture says," "It is written," and "God says"—as interchangeable. For Yeshua, a quotation from the Tenak (Old Testament) settled the matter. For Yeshua, then, the Old Testament was inspired and true in all its teaching. He also made provision for the New Testament by giving His apostles full teaching authority as witnesses and interpretors of His truth (John 16:12-14; 14:26). This is reflected in the apostolic writings as well, for Ephesians 2:20 says that Yeshua's congregation is "built upon the foundation of the apostles and prophets." Peter says, "we did not follow cleverly devised myths . . . but we were eye witnesses of his majesty" (II Peter 1:16).

Furthermore, the Bible through and through gives evidence of being the supernatural Book of God. For example, the Nation of Israel began with a miraculous deliverance from Egypt, the reception of the Law at Sinai and the conquering of the land of Canaan. Archaelogy bears out the conquest of the very cities described in Scripture.[5] Only the account of the Torah adequately explains the existence of this singular nation, Israel, which alone believed in one personal God, characterized by His justice and love. The archaeological record reveals the idolatry of Canaan and an amazing freedom from idolatry in the periods of Israel's righteousness, just as the Bible recounts.

The Bible amazingly predicts the future history of nations. For example, the Bible predicted the utter destruction of Tyre and even mentions the causeway which would be built to finally destroy the ancient city some 300 years later (Ezekiel 26). Yet the sister city, Sidon would have a sad, bloody history and still not be destroyed (Ezekiel 28). The Bible sketches history with amazing accuracy, predicting the progress of world empires—down to our own day! Daniel 2 and 7 predict and describe the successive empires of Babylon, Medo-Persia, Greece and Rome and a last-day confederation of nations which will oppose God.

The Bible also predicts the dispersion of Israel (Leviticus 26) and her last-day regathering from all over the earth (Isaiah 11). Bernard Ramm tabulates the amazing accuracy of the Biblical predictions of God's future judgments on nations and cities. All the references are given in his account.[6] The Bible predicts the following of nations:

Egypt will remain, but decline as a world power.
Israel (Northern tribes) will cease as a nation.
The Jews will remain.
Philistines will cease.
Moab and Ammon will continue after the Babylonian exile.
Edom will cease completely.
Of cities:
Tyre will be fully destroyed.
Sidon will remain.

Thebes will be destroyed.
Ninevah will be destroyed.
Babylon will be destroyed.
Jerusalem will remain.

Need we mention the incredible prophecies concerning today's regathering of Israel which we witness—the second regathering (Isaiah 11) during which the desert would bloom (Isaiah 35, Ezekiel 36)?

Even more supernatural are the Bible's predictions of the Messiah. He was predicted to be born in Bethlehem (Micah 5:2), to be born of a virgin (Isaiah 7:14), to be rejected, to die as a sacrifice and to rise from the dead (Isaiah 53, Psalms 22), to be cut off before the destruction of the Second Temple in 70 A.D. (Daniel 9:25-26) and many, many more.

Surely this is an incredible Book, inspired and unlike any in history! As to why we accept all the books of the Bible we mention the following: We know Yeshua accepted the Jewish Bible of His day. From Jewish tradition and Josephus, we know this Jewish Bible consisted of just those books today designated as the Old Testament. The Old Testament consists of the covenants of God with Israel and the records of prophets who called Israel back to Torah and instructed the nation on the basis of the Mosaic revelation (Deuteronomy 13, 18).

Provision for the writing prophets was made in Torah itself. The Old Testament is the covenantal record of the relationship between God and Israel.[8] As we said, the New Testament is the product of the apostles chosen by Yeshua. His resurrection, testified to by apostolic and other martyrs who died for the truth of their witness to His resurrection, authenticates His teaching. The early communities preserved and testified to those books which had true apostolic origins, and these became part of the New Testament, our foundation for doctrine and teaching.[9] The Bible thus stands alone among all ancient books, its historical accuracy tested by archaeology and its supernatural origin attested to by fulfilled prophecy and the resurrection of Yeshua.

Even more important, however, is the moral character of

the Bible and the spiritual nature of its message. No other book reads with the quality, majesty and depth of the Bible. It has the ring of truth. Only the Bible reveals a God who acts and speaks in history through Yeshua. Only the Bible has brought God's life-giving message to millions, turning them from despair to hope and purpose.

As Messianic Jews, we may gain wisdom and insight from our Jewish tradition. The tradition, however, is to be tested by the Bible, which alone is accepted as totally true. Tradition has not this authority. That which is consistent with the Scriptures can be accepted; that which is inconsistent must be rejected. The Bible is the final rule of faith and practice. It is our authority.

SALVATION BY GRACE

The popular use of the words "salvation" and "saved" is a distortion of the rich Biblical meaning of the terms. In Scripture, salvation includes the fullness of deliverance from a meaningless life of transgression, emptiness, alienation and darkness, concerning life after death to a life of fellowship with our Creator, as well as hope, healing, community with others and the assurance of everlasting life with God. Unfortunately, the word "grace" is a misperceived concept as well in much popular thinking. Many, for example, believe that grace means that God has suspended the moral standards of His Law to accept us. Because He has accepted us, we need only believe—it does not matter what. This is totally contrary to the Biblical view of grace.

In Scripture, grace is God's offer of unmerited forgiveness to us, despite the fact that we are sinners or lawbreakers. Yet God upholds His character and Law in His offer because Yeshua paid the penalty of the Law. In Him, we can be counted as fulfilling the Law. It is crucial to understand that God judges us as a people *in Him.*

We are "in Him" (Galatians 2:20) and are *in Him* accounted righteous. He is perfect according to God's Holy Law. Hence, David can say in Psalms 32:2, "Blessed is the man to whom the Lord imputes no iniquity." It is also clear in Psalm

51 that David cast himself totally on the mercy of God for
forgiveness and did not depend on his own merits. He said,
"Be merciful to me, O God, according to thine abundant
mercy, blot out my transgression . . . Purge me with hyssop
and I shall be clean, wash me, and I shall be whiter than snow'
(vv. 1, 7). Eternal life is God's gift (Romans 6:23) and no one
can earn it, for none are righteous (Psalm 53:3). Hence, God
can say of Israel that He did not choose them because of any
righteousness or might of their own (especially Deuteronomy
8-10).

However, the reception of God's gift in Yeshua requires a
response of faith. We can only be righteous before God
because *we are in Him, and He alone is perfectly righteous*
according to God's Law. Faith grasps the gift of God and by
faith we are born again and given a new Spirit (Ezekiel 36:26;
II Corinthians 5:17). The Hebrew word faith (emunah) cannot be divorced from the word faithfulness (emunah). A true
response to God issues in a heart or spirit whose desire is to
obey and please God. Salvation by faith never leads to moral
looseness when rightly understood. Paul can thus say in
Romans 3:31 as he recounts God's Law upheld in Yeshua and
our new heart to obey, "Do we then overthrow the Law by
this faith? By no means! On the contrary, we uphold the
Law." Ezekiel well reflected the relationship between faith
and faithfulness when he stated that the Spirit will write
God's Law upon our hearts (Jeremiah 31:33).

God's grace is effective. It is God's power within us, enabling us to do His will. God in Yeshua has delivered us from
the penalty of the Law; but we do not cast away the Law or its
value for teaching and guiding (II Timothy 3:16-17). I John 3:4
says that "Sin is the transgression of Law." Romans 6 says
that we are "not to yield ourselves to sin" or "continue in sin
that grace might abound." Obviously, if our hearts have
responded to God, we will not desire to break His Law. Sin is
the transgression of Law (I John 3:4). Because we are free
from the bondage of the penalties of the Law and our fleshly
efforts to keep the Law which end in failure (Romans 7), we
can now do the Law *by God's power* (Romans 8:1-4). We can

say with the Psalmist, "Oh how I love thy law, it is my meditation all the day long . . . sweeter also than honey and the
drippings of the honeycomb" (Psalms 119:97, 103). Scripture's
message never divides grace from obedience, but teaches that
the heart must be changed first.

"For by grace are you saved through faith, it is a gift of
God not of works lest any man should boast" (Ephesians
2:8-9); *"for God is at work in you to will and to do of his good
pleasure"* (Philippians 2:13).

James says, "Faith without works is dead" (James 2:20).

Titus teaches we are "justified by grace" (3:7), *and* then
exhorts us to be careful to "apply ourselves to good deeds"
(mitzvot) for "these are excellent and profitable to men"
(Titus 3:8).

The Tenach also records this relationship between faith
and works and the Law, for we read of Abraham, "Abraham
believed God and God accounted it to him for righteousness"
(Genesis 15:6), but Genesis 26:4-5 says, "by your descendants
all the nations of the earth shall bless themselves; because
Abraham obeyed my voice and kept my charge, my commandments, my statutes, and my Laws." We are justified
(accepted as righteous) by faith, but the justified one has a
heart for God's will and Law. (See James 2, which comments
on Genesis 26.) We desire to be obedient and to do His
commands.

SPIRIT AND LAW

Another subject of great contemporary misunderstanding is the relationship between the Spirit of God (within each
disciple of Yeshua) and the Law. Some put Spirit and law in
total opposition, which is a Biblical impossibility. The central
chapters of the Bible for understanding the correct teaching
are Romans 6-8. These chapters must be read with great care
or false conclusions may be drawn.

First, let us note that sin is the transgression of Law,
"whosoever committeth sin transgresseth also the Law; for
sin is the transgression of the Law" (I John 3:4). Paul clearly
shows that the relationship of the Spirit to the Law is not

antithetical. The Spirit revealed the Law; He will write God's Law on our hearts (Jeremiah 31:33; Ezekiel 36:26). So He can say, "Are we to sin (transgress the Law) because we are not under Law but under grace? By no means! Do you not know that if you yield yourselves to anyone as obedient slaves, you are the slaves of the one to whom you obey, either of sin (the transgressing of the Law) or of obedience, which leads to righteousness" (Romans 6:15-16).

What Paul has in mind is that the *Author* of the Law would dwell within, giving us an intuitive sense of right as well as a love which obeys the Law in its true spirit and intent. We would then serve not a set of external articles with do's and don't's (a written code) but in newness of the Spirit. In other words, the Spirit will make obedience a personal response of love, not legalism.

Romans 7 and 8 are the great chapters which summarize that the way of obedience is through the power of the Spirit. This is because, from our own power in our fallen nature (called the flesh), it is impossible for us to obey the Law. The problem is not the Law. That reflects God's eternal character and standard. Yeshua said that not a "jot" or "tittle" of the Law would pass away until *all* is fulfilled. Heaven and earth would pass away before God's Law (Matthew 5:17-18). Thus Paul can say "If it had not been for the Law, I should not have known sin . . . the Law is holy, and the commandment holy, just and good. Did that which is good, then, bring death to me? By no means . . . we know that *the Law is spiritual* . . . Now if I do not do what I want, I agree that the Law is good" (Romans 7:7, 12, 13, 14, 16). This should be enough to convince anyone of Paul's positive regard for the Law. The problem is not the Law, but our sinful nature which is bent toward transgressing the Law. So fallen is man that he even uses the commandment as an occasion to imagine the forbidden action and to be drawn, falling, into the act.

"I should not have know what it is to covet if the Law had not said, You shall not covet. But sin finding opportunity in the commandment, wrought in me all kinds of covetousness" (Romans 7:7-8).

So Paul describes the man who seeks to obey the Law by his own power as not able to do the very things he desires. This is the law "principle" of the sin nature and it perpetuates a state of spiritual and physical death (the law or principle of death).

The cry thus goes forth, "Oh wretched man that I am, who shall deliver me from this body of death?" (Romans 7:24). The solution is "Thanks be to God through *Yeshua ha Meshiach*" (Romans 7:24). For through Him, we are given a reborn spirit, and in recognizing that we died to our old self in Him and rise to new life, we are empowered by the Spirit to no longer be in bondage to sin. We may still fall; but we now have the power to obey. From our position in Yeshua, we can grow to progressive obedience in love. Hence, the Spirit enables us to fulfill the Law (Romans 3:31). Thus, "There is therefore now no condemnation for those who are in Messiah Yeshua. . . . for the law of the Spirit of life in Messiah Yeshua has set me free from the law of sin and death. For God has done what the law *weakened by the flesh*, could not do; sending his own son in the likeness of sinful flesh, he condemned sin in the flesh, in order that the just requirement of the law might be fulfilled *in us*, who walk not according to the flesh but according to the Spirit" (Romans 8:1, ff).

The issue is not a conflict between Law and Spirit but between flesh and spirit. Do we seek to please God by our own fleshly efforts to keep the Law, or do we depend on the resurrection power of His Spirit within? We are to set our mind on depending on the Spirit. By His power, we can please God.

With this understanding, the Messianic Jew has no ambivalence in approaching the *whole* Bible as "profitable for doctrine, for reproof, for correction and instruction in righteousness" (II Timothy 3:16-17). Truly he can say with the Psalmist "O, how I love thy Law." Yet, even more does he love the demonstration of the meaning of the Law in Spirit and in truth in Yeshua ha Mashiach.

SALVATION AND JEWS WHO DO NOT KNOW YESHUA

In recent times, it has become popular to believe that

Jewish people have a covenant with God and may have eternal life with Him by this covenant—even if they do not *explicitly* accept salvation by faith in Yeshua.

We must make a distinction between two groups who hold this viewpoint, the liberal theologian and the evangelical. To the liberal, this is often a reflection of tolerance which is maintained for all peoples and cultures. For the liberal of today, it is questionable whether religious truth can be discovered with any degree of objectivity. If pressed, he would give equal acclaim to Hindus and Buddhists, claiming that he only favors the Biblical tradition because it is his tradition. Because we believe the Bible to be the Word of the living God, we must judge all by its revelation. Our concern is with those who truly affirm the Scriptures. Do they have something to teach us on this issue?

Many hold that unless one consciously and explicitly makes a decision for Yeshua—Who is understood as the One Who lived, died and rose again in the first century—there is no salvation. Although Scripture is not teeming with verses to support this position, there are definitely Scriptures which seem to support this view:

Acts 4:12, "Neither is there salvation in any other, for there is none other name given under heaven among men whereby we must be saved." So also, "He that hath the son hath life and he that hath not the son hath not life" (I John 5:12), and "Whoever believes the Son has eternal life, but whoever rejects the son will not see life, for God's wrath remains upon him" (John 3:36, NIV).

However, our "two-covenant" theorist points to other passages to support his claims and gives a different slant to these verses. Elmer Josephson would be the most extreme of two-covenant theorists among evangelicals, believing that every circumcized Jew who does not repudiate the covenant with Abraham through explicit renunciation—or implicitly through gross immorality and assimilation—is saved under the Abrahamic Covenant.[10] We, of course, cannot elaborate all of the reasons given by two-covenant theorists. Basically, however, they would argue as follows:

Because of God's covenant with Abr ham, Jews are a covenant people under God's grace and salvation, just as Christians are saved under the New Covenant. Of course, the reason the Jew has salvation in the Abrahamic Covenant is because of the atonement provided by Yeshua. A Jew, however, may be connected to this atonement through the Abrahamic Covenant without explicitly accepting Yeshua. Josephson seems extreme in applying this to almost all Jews. Others would hold that unless there is a faith-response to God's offer of grace in the Abrahamic Covenant there is no salvation. A Jew may talk as though his good deeds save him, but in his heart of hearts he may really be depending on God's grace and mercy.

The two-covenant theorist would especially point to these Biblical facts to support his view. Jews were saved in the pre-Yeshuic period by faith, without *explicitly* accepting Yeshua. Implicitly, however, by accepting the Scriptures and God's mercy in the sacrificial system, they were joined to Him. Doesn't it seem, they would argue, that this is the case with Jews also today? Jewish prayer enshrines these principles. For example the *Al Het* Yom Kippur prayer asks for God's forgiveness and mercy. The petitioner admits that he has *no* merit of his own by which to claim salvation, but is a sinner who has broken God's Law in countless ways. Furthermore, he requests to be forgiven on the basis of past sacrificial offerings since there is presently no Temple. He even invokes the sacrifice of Isaac (which points to Yeshua's sacrifice) for forgiveness.

Further, the proponent would argue that God has hardened Israel's heart to the message of Yeshua for the purposes of his work among Gentiles (Romans 11:7). He can point to a multitude of verses that seem to support his position that God has not rejected His people (e.g., Romans 11:1). Israel is still God's people. So, also, Paul in Romans 11:16 seems to be saying that those of Israel who have accepted Yeshua are as first fruits, which make Israel, as a whole, still a chosen people and beloved. "If the dough offered as first fruits is holy so is the whole lump; and if the root is holy, so are the branches."

Yes, Paul recognizes that some branches were broken off through *explicit* unbelief and rejection; but Israel in general is still God's people. As the first fruits offered to God from the crop made the whole harvest holy and profitable in Israel, so also are the believers in Yeshua from Israel related to the whole nation.

Clearly, Israel will some day accept Yeshua; and this will herald the general resurrection from the dead (Romans 11:15), and so "All Israel will be saved . . . (for) they are beloved for the sake of their forefathers and *elect*; the gift and call of God being irrevocable" (Romans 11:26, 28-29). Thus, in conclusion, the proponents of this view would say that Jews can readily be saved under the Abrahamic Covenant as much as Christians are under the New Covenant.

How are we to respond to this mode of argument? It must first be acknowledged that preaching the Good News of Yeshua affords human beings everywhere the greatest opportunity to respond and be saved. It is God's clearest supreme revelation. The two-covenant theorist sometimes forgets this, for the Abrahamic Covenant is only possible because of the New Covenant in Yeshua. It is only through the truth that salvation is in Yeshua that grace was offered in the Old Testament period. We must not forget the words of Paul, that the "Gospel is the power unto salvation to everyone who believes, *to the Jew first* and also to the Greek" (Romans 1:16).

The two-covenant theorist is in danger of acting as though Jewish people do not need the Gospel, that what they have is adequate. Yet Jeremiah 31 and Ezekiel 36 make it clear that the New Covenant is offered to Israel and that Israel needs the New Covenant so that God's Spirit might be in them and the Law written upon their hearts. Indeed, aspects of New Covenant promises to Israel include their planting in the land and walk of faith with God, as well as these aspects of the New Covenant which followers of Yeshua have received (Jeremiah 31, Ezekiel 36). We still await the *totality* of the New Covenant's manifestation in the return of Yeshua. Clearly, however, the New Covenant is for Israel! Paul preached first in the synagogues! In the light of Western anti-Semitism and the desire to befriend the Jewish community, we can understand how our two-covenant theorist would desire to be unoffensive. However, we cannot blunt Scriptural emphases because of this desire. The Gospel provides the fullest opportunity for salvation to the Jew (Romans 1:16).

We must re-examine the evangelical certainty of being able to determine just who is and who is not hell-bound. Jews were saved under the period of the Old Testament through their response to the Covenant. Scripture makes it clear, however, that a personal faith response was necessary, as well as the outward sign of Jewishness: "For he is not a real Jew who is one outwardly nor is true circumcision something external and physical. He is a Jew who is one inwardly, and real circumcision is a matter of the heart, spiritual and not literal. His praise is not from men but from God" (Romans 2:28-29).

If Jewish people were granted fellowship with God and everlasting life in the Old Covenant period, why should it be precluded now? Let's say that a righteous Jew died an hour after the resurrection (or the gift of the Spirit at Shavuot or Pentecost, if you wish this to be the time of responsibility); would he be hell-bound then, but heaven-bound if only he had died an hour earlier? This is unthinkable, and indeed unscriptural. Scripture clearly teaches that lostness is a condition that results from rejecting the revelation of God that can be known. Romans 1 judges the heathen *not* for rejecting the Gospel, which they had not been given, but for rejecting the revelation of God in the created order which they have been given (Romans 1:19-21). Romans 2:1 points to the revelation of conscience as another means of rendering men without excuse.

To whom much is given, much is required. Jewry clearly was given a fuller revelation in the Old Testament (Tenach) than heathens (Romans 2). For this revelation, they were responsible. When the preaching of Yeshua was understood, they were responsible for this. However, at no time can we Biblically draw a line and say, "From this time forward, if a

Jew hasn't accepted Yeshua, he is lost." The time when people and individuals are responsible is when revelation is
given; and this time is different for everyone. It is only when
the Spirit-revealer is spurned that lostness ensues. The persecution of centuries has rendered the Old Testament the
main source of revelation and response for most Jews.

Does this not destroy the motive of giving the Gospel? Not
at all! For although we recognize a possibility of responding to
natural revelation and to the Abrahamic Covenant, *Scripture and experience show that most have not responded to
the revelation they have*. The pagan has eschewed true revelation for idolatry. Despite the clarity of the Tenach, the great
majority of Jews have not responded in faith to the Abrahamic Covenant. Modern forms of Judaism as well as the
religions of the world have taught salvation by a system of
works righteousness, "because they did not pursue it through
faith, but as if it were based on works" (Romans 9:32). Thus
the Old Testament message is not truly understood. The general condition of world Jewry today, in fact, is one of unbelief.
*Thus, the only way that they will respond to God at all is by
the preaching of the Gospel with power*. The preaching of the
Good News maximizes the opportunity of salvation. However, we cannot preclude the possibility of Jews responding
in faith to God's revelation in the Tenach. This view does not
blunt our zeal to spread the Good News, but blunts our judgmentalism as applied to individuals, which Scripture forbids
(I Corinthians 4:5). *Jewish people need the Gospel*; Jewish
people do have the Tenach, if they would pursue its message,
but most do not. To most, the Tenach is encrusted with false
interpretations; only the New Testament revelation can
break through.

Some might object to this presentation because Jews
under the Old Testament period had the means of atonement
in animal sacrifices; but today's Jews do not. However, the
animal sacrifices were only symbols of spiritual reality that
pointed to Yeshua's atonement. As Hebrews says, "it is
impossible that the blood of bulls and goats should take away
sins" (Hebrews 10:4). Rather it was faith in God's mercy that

connected the offerer to the Messiah! So, even though a Jewish person today does not have the sacrificial system, he can
still respond in faith to the *meaning of* the sacrificial system
as enshrined in the prayers of the synagogue.

What of the exclusionary verses which were quoted?
First, let us note that one can't reject something he or she has
not been clearly offered. John 3:36 says the wrath of God
abides on the one who *rejects* the Son. So also, I John 5:12, "He
that has the Son has life, he that hath not the Son of God hath
not life." Did the believing Jews of the Tenach in a spiritual
sense *have* the Son even though he had not yet come? Most
would say yes. Why not then Jews one hour after the resurrection, or one year, or one hundred years later? Let us also
remember that John teaches a spiritual reality to the Son that
is not limited to His sojourn on earth. He says of the Word,
Messiah, "That was the true light that lighteth every man
that cometh into the world" (John 1:9). The same meaning of
a universal light from the Messiah can be given for Acts 4:12.

In a day when our ancestors looked for many believers
from Roman oppression, Peter was able to say, "there is salvation in no one else." In other words, all saved people—from
Adam until the present—are saved only in Yeshua. "He is the
only name given under heaven among men by which we
must be saved."

Yeshua is the only *name* of the Reality by which all must
be saved. Indeed, when the Gospel is heard and understood,
there must be an explicit response to the Name. Otherwise, as
with the Old Testament saints, there must be an implicit
response to the Reality which the Name reveals. In the
semitic understanding, "The Name" stood for the inner
essence of the spoken-of Reality. God was simply called "the
Name." Peter was not only calling for an explicit response to
Yeshua in Acts 4:12, but was teaching *that all* salvation has
always been in Him. The same Peter could also say in Acts
10:34, "Truly I perceive that God shows no partiality, but in
every nation anyone who fears Him (faith) and does what is
right is acceptable to Him."

If a person still believes that a conscious, explicit response

must be made for Yeshua before death, we would point to the
possibility of further revelation even at the moment of death
for those who have responded in faith to the revelation they
have been given.

Considerations such as these as well as an examination of
the meaning of "remnant" in Romans 9-11 have prompted
H.L. Ellison, a venerable Messianic Jewish scholar, to come to
similar conclusions. He exposits the remnant to be that
minority within Jewry who have responded in faith and
therefore sanctify the existence of Israel (Romans 11:5). So
also, he argues that the "Christian" Church is full of unbe-
lievers; but it is the believers within the Church who sanctify
the existence of the visible Church.

It is crucial to see that Judaism is a religion with the
Tenach as a prime source. We grant that Judaism diverges
from the truth and quenches the light of the revelation.
However, some of the prayers and teachings are derived
from the Bible.

Some of the old time Hebrew-Christians through ignorance approached the Jewish tradition with total disdain. For
them, it was only a creation of hell-bound sinners, a tradition
with no value. Such an attitude bordered on anti-Semitism.
However, if the tradition (some of which is pre-first century)
was partially derived from the Bible, God's truth could be
seen therein.

How is it that some clearly saw that the Messiah suffered
for our sins in Isaiah 53?[12] How is it that prayer enshrines the
knowledge of salvation only by grace through no merit of our
own, even to the extent of appealing to the sacrificial system
and the sufferings of the Messiah?[13] So also the Talmud
teaches that Habbakuk reduced all the commands to one: "as
it is said, the righteous shall live by his faith" (Habbakuk 2:4).
Some of the traditions are so old that it would seem that Paul
drew from them to illustrate his teaching on faith.[14]

In conclusion, we have argued that the Gospel is for all

and "to the Jew first" (Romans 1:16). We have also argued that it is possible for a Jew to respond in faith to the Abrahamic Covenant and be connected to Yeshua. Yet in our view, most of Jewry is characterized by secularism and unbelief. Many religious Jews seem to be following a system of works-righteousness for salvation. (Therefore, the Gospel is a tremendous necessity and maximizes the opportunity for salvation).

THE MESSIAHSHIP OF YESHUA

Our purpose in defending a distinctive Messianic Jewish stance does not require a comprehensive summary of the reasons for our belief in the Messiahship of Yeshua. We only briefly recount here a summary of the Messianic hope and our reasons for affirming that "He is the One of Whom the prophets spoke."

The Messianic hope begins in Genesis 3:15, where God promises to the human race a seed of woman who will crush the head of the Serpent (Satan, the representative of evil), even though this seed will be bruised in the heel. The story fits the religious symbolic literature of the ancient Near East in recounting deep spiritual truths through natural phenomena. Although it is not of absolute proof value, there is evidential value in the fact that the verse teaches that a seed of a woman, not a man, bruises the head of the Serpent though Satan bruises *its heel*. Satan receives the fatal blow; the seed, a serious, but limited blow. How well this fits Messiah Yeshua, born of a virgin. Jewish writings also reflect this Messianic identification . . . as Targum Onkelos, which speaks of the seed as her son. The great expositor David Kimchi clearly identifies the seed as "the MESHIACH, the son of David, who shall wound his heel."[15]

We shall see that there are several promises in relation to

"seed" which, when traced, have great Messianic significance, although not limited to Messianic significance. The
next passage which talks about seed is Genesis 12. Abraham,
who is called to a new land, is told, "by your seed all the
families of the earth shall blessed." Blessing is to flow to the
world through the nation Israel. However, there are hints
that the seed-promise of Abraham looks forward to an individual. Sarah, Abraham's wife, is childless. The seed-promise
is to be applied to her offspring, not to any other. Sarah
herself gives birth to only one son, Isaac. Isaac is thus the
recipient of the seed-promise. The Messianic Jew cannot help
but see the parallels. Isaac, the only son of his father, is a child
of a miraculous birth (for Sarah was beyond child bearing
age—Genesis 18:12, 13). Most amazingly, Abraham is commanded to offer his son Isaac on Mt. Moriah as a sacrifice. This
is a test of his faith and obedience. Isaac is not killed, but the
symbolism of his being offered as a sacrifice is carried out in
Genesis 22. Moriah is the later site of the temple; traditionally, among Jews, it is the exact stone where the altar later
stood. That the image of Abraham's only seed is a sacrificial
image should make us note the parallel to Yeshua, who is also
a child of miraculous birth, the only son of his Father, who is
offered as a sacrifice.

The *seed-promise* is next passed on to Isaac's son, Jacob,
and then to the twelve children of Israel. However, there is a
promise to Judah which indicates that the Messianic ruler
will stem from Judah. "The scepter shall not depart from
Judah, nor the ruler's staff from between his feet, until he
comes to whom it belongs; and to him shall be the obedience
of the peoples" (Genesis 49:10). Either Shiloh in this passage is
a title of the Messiah or is "he to whom it (rulership) belongs"
comes. All of the Targums identify this promise with the
Messiah.

Many centuries pass before the seed-promise becomes
more explicit. The figure of Moses, a prophet, priest and ruler
of his people was considered to pre-figure the Messiah by
many Jewish people before Yeshua came.[16]

In II Samuel 7, we find the next great seed-promise: It

relates to the future ruler and representative of Israel. David is promised in this passage an *everlasting throne* through his descendants. Isaiah makes it clear that this will be fulfilled by one child. In Isaiah 7:14, a promise is given of a Messianic king who shall be named Immanuel, God with us. The contrast is drawn between this child and the wicked king Ahaz, who would not ask for a sign to prove God's will as requested by the prophet Isaiah. That Isaiah 7:14 has in mind the Messiah is clear since no other child of the time was given the name Immanuel. Hezekiah, the ancestor of the Messiah, might have also been born at this time as a sign of the greater birth to come. Lest there be doubt, however, in the Messianic character of Isaiah 7:14, we point out these two facts: The translations of the Septuagent recognized the passage to be predicting a virgin birth. "Almah," meaning young woman, is used of a young woman of marriageable age who is *presumed to be a virgin. They translated it "parthenos," virgin, before there was any debate.* Secondly, the title of the king, Immanuel, is a parallel title to those given King Messiah in Isaiah 9:6, 7 (v.5 Hebrew Bible). Other promises concerning King Messiah as the stem of Jesse are found in Isaiah 11:1-10.

In Isaiah 9:6, 7, we read, "For to us a child is born, to us a son is given; and the government shall be upon his shoulders and his name shall be called 'Wonderful Counselor, Mighty God, Everlasting Father, Prince of Peace.' Of the increase of his government and of peace there will be no end, upon the throne of David, and over his kingdom to establish it, and to uphold it with justice and righteousness, from this time forth and forever more" (R.S.V.).

Here we note that the Messiah is given uniquely divine titles in this passage, which will be explained in the next section. Our translation is very close to the literal Hebrew; other translations seek to blunt these titles by adding interpretive material. There is no disagreement on the Messianic character of these verses. We now see that blessing flows to the world through Israel and through the Messiah. Of the Messiah we read that the Gentiles, non-Jewish peoples, shall seek after Him. He shall be a sign to the peoples and "to it shall the Gentiles seek" (Isaiah 11:10 ff).

Of the "Servant of the Lord" in Isaiah 40-66, we read that He will bring forth justice and He will be *a light to the nations* (Isaiah 42:3, 4, 7). Though Israel is found in these passages as God's servant, so is the Messianic king. For the promise of the servant of the Lord here includes the same content as the promise of King Messiah in Isaiah 11.

There is a special connection of the Messiah to Bethlehem, not only because this was David's city, which was obviously known. Micah 5:2 connects the Messiah to Bethlehem to show that His birth there shall parallel David's. It is a sign. Hence the scribes of Matthew 2 could easily answer Herod's question as to where the Messiah would be born . . . "in Bethlehem." They then quoted Micah 5:2, which states that the ruler of Israel shall come forth from Bethlehem. Micah also says of Messiah that His "goings have been from of old, from Everlasting." Messiah in some way has a reality before His actual birth. Some traditional Jews see that pre-birth reality of the Messiah as in the being of God; He is in some special sense, part of God.

However, more astonishing than all these passages is the Scriptural indication that the Messianic figure must suffer and die before He rules and reigns. This gave rise to the Talmudic idea that a suffering Messiah, son of Joseph, would precede the triumphant Messiah.[17] We have already noted that the Servant of the Lord of Isaiah 40-66 has both reference to Israel and Israel's king. Of this "servant of the Lord" we read that He suffers as a sacrifice for sin (in Isaiah 53) and experiences many other sufferings.

Isaiah says—"He is despised and rejected of men, a man of sorrows and acquainted with grief, and we hid as it were our faces from Him. . . .

"All we like sheep have gone astray, we have turned every one to his own way, and the Lord has laid upon him the iniquity of us all . . ." (Isaiah 53:3, 6).

Of this One we also read that he is with both criminals and a rich man in His death. In the gospels we read that Yeshua was crucifed between criminals. Joseph of Aramathea, a rich man and member of the Sanhedrin, had Him buried in his own tomb.

Because of his sacrifice, we read "he shall see his off-spring, he shall prolong his days . . . . He shall see the fruit of the travail of his soul and be satisfied; by his knowledge shall the righteous one my servant, make many to be accounted righteous, and he shall bear their iniquities" (Isaiah 53:10 ff).

The One who dies as a sin offering lives again. How well this fits Yeshua. Jewish voices are not lacking who refer this passage to the Messiah, even though they do not accept Yeshua as the Messiah. The Talmud, in Sanhedrin 98b, gives a title to the Messiah, "the leprous one," because Isaiah said He bore our diseases in this chapter. The famous kabbalist R. Elijah de Vidas from Safed in Upper Galilee is most emphatic that this referred to the Messiah saying, "it follows that whosoever will not admit that Messiah thus suffers for our iniquities, must endure and suffer for them himself."[18] So also the Targum Jonathan, a most ancient source, sees the Servant as King Messiah.[19]

The One who is pierced is spoken of as well in Zechariah 12:10, where we read,

"And they shall look upon me whom they have pierced, and they shall mourn for him as one mourneth for His only Son, and shall be in bitterness for him as one who is in *bitterness* for His first born." That this refers to a suffering Messiah is clear in most ancient Jewish interpretation. The Talmud (Succah 52:1) refers this to the Messiah, the son of Joseph, as does R. Alschech and Kimchi.[20] However, what is the warrant for holding to two Messiahs instead of one Messiah who must first suffer before reigning?

Daniel 9:25, 26 gives an astonishing reference to the Messiah. For in this prophecy, the Messiah is predicted as cut off before the destruction of the second temple. Seventy weeks of years which were decreed from the time of Arta-xerxes would bring us to the time of the Messiah Yeshua (490 years). Even beyond this, however, "the Messiah the Prince" is cut off in the 69th week (483 years) and the temple and city are destroyed soon after. Many Rabbinic references show that this is the Messiah (cf. R. Moses Abraham Levi, Sanhed. Tal. 97.b, Nachmanidies, and Abarbanel).

When we observe all of these passages together, it is astonishing how precisely Yeshua fulfills the nature of the Messianic hope as it is developed in the Tenach. He is the seed of the woman who gives Satan his fatal blow (Genesis 3:15); He is the only child of Abraham, a child who, like Isaac, is the only son of His Father and is offered as a sacrifice by His Father (Genesis 12:1-3; 22); He is the prophet like Moses (Deuteronomy 18); He is a descendant of David (II Samuel 7), the one born of a virgin and given supernatural titles (Isaiah 7:14; 9:6, 7), born in Bethlehem but from Ancient Days (Micah 5:2); He is the source of light to the nations, for it is only by turning to Yeshua that non-Jews received God's Scriptural revelation (Isaiah 42:11); He is the One who is pierced and dies in the image of a sacrifice, but yet sees His offspring (Zechariah 12:10, Isaiah 53); and He is the One who comes before the destruction of the second temple, which occurred in 70 C.E.! (Daniel 9:25, 26).

Yeshua alone fits the Biblical hope. Furthermore, His life, miracles, death and resurrection multiply the strength of the evidence. Only the Spirit of God can open the eyes of those who are blinded, but the evidence is extraordinary. No man ever taught like Yeshua. Read His summary of the heart meaning of the Law, in Matthew 5-7, or His parables in Matthew 13. No one ever performed miracles of compassion like Yeshua. No other man ever was raised from the dead like Yeshua. The evidence for His resurrection is not just good evidence—it is the best evidence we have for any ancient event. We have only positive evidence for the resurrection, no negative evidence.[22] The sources are all early; the four gospels, the letters of Paul, Peter, James, Hebrews and Revelation were *independently* written and all testify to the resurrection. The early fathers of the Church maintain this testimony. Most of the disciples died for their faith in Yeshua's resurrection, never recanting under pressure. The Apostle Paul could testify that 500 brethren were witnesses to the resurrected Messiah at one time, most of whom were still alive (I Corinthians 15). The implication is that his readers could go and ask the witnesses about the truth.

There is no explanation of the resurrection by the early critics of Yeshua except the excuse that His disciples stole His body, the same disciples who died for the truth of their testimony! The dead body could not be produced because Yeshua was alive again.

Yeshua alone fits our hope and Scriptural expectations of the Messiah. He identified with Israel and personally paralleled Israel's life; His family fled to Egypt and was called out of Egypt (Matthew 3:15); He went through the waters of baptism, paralleling Israel going through the sea; He was tempted in the wilderness for 40 days, paralleling Israel's 40 years (Matthew 4); He exposited the Law on the mountain (Matthew 5). His life was integrated into all the Jewish feasts (John 5-10). He is certainly the One of whom the prophets spoke. He shall yet return to rule on the throne of David, fulfilling each of the prophecies which are part of Israel's Messianic hope.

IS THE MESSIAH DIVINE?

To raise the question of Yeshua's divinity is to open one of the greatest debates between Jews and Christians. This question leads to the whole debate about the Trinity, since the Messiah is said to be divine as one part of the Triune God.

Christians have locked themselves in Greek philosophical definitions of the Trinity. Jews ask, do Christian believe in one God or three? In reaction to what they perceived as tritheism (belief in three gods), Jews have also defined their God in opposing Greek categories of oneness. Maimonides, who is quoted and referred to for the Jewish doctrine of God, explained God's oneness or singularity, formlessness and simplicity after the thinking of Aristotle. The term "trinity" or "triunity" is not in the Bible. We therefore are not so concerned to argue for the term as for those aspects of the Biblical revelation which the term reflects. We have to begin with the salient fact that Jewish literature itself reflects something of the mystery of God. This is most evident in speech about the "Shekeenah," or Holy Spirit. He is spoken of

as God and yet as separate from God. When the Temple was
destroyed, the Shekeenah is said to have gone into exile with
Israel. The Shekeenah is also said to have moved from the
Temple mount to the Western Wall. It is this author's conten-
tion that the literature of Judaism and the Bible always
reflected this mystery of God, wherein God is spoken of as
one, but manifestations of God are spoken of as to some
degree separate from God. Jews spoke functionally and
never drew a theological conclusion concerning oneness or
threeness during all of the ages of history before Yeshua.
Christians, however, who were Greek-oriented, drew specific theological (ontological) conclusions from this functional
language. The Jewish reaction to the Christian doctrine was
to finally draw an opposite and contrary conclusion. God was
defined as "yachid," completely and totally singular.

In Genesis 1:26 God said, "let *us* create man in our own
image." "Eloheem" (God) itself is a unique uni-plural form
which takes a singular verb, but could be translated "gods." It
is possible that the "Let us" structure could be a regal plural
of majesty, such as found in Queen Victoria's speech. However, God says, "God created man in his own image . . . male
and female *created He them*" (1:27). The fact that male and
female *together* are in God's image must bear some significance. Further, God says of marriage, "For this reason a man
will leave his father and mother and be united to his wife, and
they will become *one* flesh" (Genesis 2:24). The word for one
here is *echad*, the same used in the Sh'ma, "Hear O Israel, the
Lord is our God, the Lord *alone* (echad)" (Deuteronomy 6:4).
One Jewish authority personally admitted in a class at a
prominent Jewish college that the Sh'ma was not a statement
at all about God's mathematical singularity, but that this
invisible God of revelation was to be worshipped apart from
all other idols. Furthermore, if the Sh'ma is an assertion of
God's oneness, it would be a statement counter to the obvious
indications of plurality in the Tenach. (See also Ezra 2:64 and
Exekiel 37:17). "Echad," however, does not connote singular
oneness in many usages.

The examples of plurality in the Tenach are arresting to

say the least. In Genesis 18, one of three angels is designated the LORD, the Holy name of God. Here is a manifestation of God, yet He is *not all of God Himself*. Is it God or an angel of God? It is both.

In Genesis 32, Jacob wrestles with the Angel of God, called a man in v. 24. Jewish literature explains this as only an angel. Yet how then do we explain Jacob's words in v. 30, "So Jacob called the place Peniel, saying, 'it is because I saw God face to face and yet my life was spared.' " Jacob was amazed because it was believed that no man could see God and live. Jacob did not see God *fully*; no one ever has. However, this was a manifestation of God in human form which cannot be put aside by calling it a powerful angel which, being from a divine level of reality, would cause the fear. This explanation completely ignores Jacob's own words.

In Exodus, the Angel of the Lord is distinguished from God Himself and yet is continually called by the holy name of God Himself, written The LORD (all caps) in English and (יהוה Hebrew):

Exodus 14:19—the Angel of God travels before the people in a pillar of cloud.

Exodus 13:17 ff.—God Himself leads the people.

Exodus 13:21—God is called The LORD who went ahead.

Exodus 33:14—God says *"My presence will go with you."*

Moses prays for God's presence to precede Israel, in verse 16. However, in verse 9, the presence is identified with the Lord, as Moses prays for the presence of the LORD to go with Israel. Clearly, the LORD goes with Israel in leaving the tabernacle, in Exodus 40:36-38.

There are several other examples where the Angel of God is distinguished from God and then called God or the LORD. In Genesis 22:11, we have the Angel of the Lord; but in 22:12, He is God (cf 16:7, 16:13).

In Exodus 23:20-23, God's name is said to be in the Angel in such a way that he can pardon sin. "Behold, I send an angel before you, to guard you on the way and to bring you to the place which I have prepared. Give heed to him and hearken to his voice, do not rebel against him, for he will not pardon your transgression; for my name is in him.

"But if you hearken attentively to his voice and do all that I say, then I will be an enemy to your enemies and an adversary to your adversaries.

"When my angel goes before you and brings you in to the Amorites and the Hittites, and the Perizzites, and the Canaanites, the Hivites and the Jebusites, and I blot them out, you shall not bow down to their gods, nor serve them, nor do according to their works, but you shall utterly overthrow them and break their pillars in pieces. You shall serve the Lord your God, and I will bless your bread and your water; and I will take sickness away from the midst of you. None shall cast her young or be barren in your land; I will fulfil the number of your days. I will send my terror before you, and will throw into confusion all the people against whom you shall come, and I will make all your enemies turn their backs to you. And I will send hornets before you, which shall drive out Hivite, Canaanite, and Hittite from before you. I will not drive them out from before you in one year, lest the land become desolate and the wild beasts multiply against you. Little by little I will drive them out from before you, until you are increased and possess the land. And I will set your bounds from the Red Sea to the sea of the Philistines, and from the wilderness to the Euphrates; for I will deliver the inhabitants of the land into your hand, and you shall drive them out before you. You shall make no covenant with them or with their gods. They shall not dwell in your land, lest they make you sin against me; for if you serve their gods, it will surely be a snare to you" (Exodus 23:20-33).

Judges 13 brings out the phenomenon clearly. Beginning with verse 9, we read, "the angel of God came to the woman while she was in the field . . . Menoah got up and followed his wife. When he came to the man he said . . . the Angel of the LORD replied" (v. 3). Menoah inquired of the name of the Angel of the LORD" (v. 17). Menoah said, "we are doomed to die. We have seen God" (v. 22). However, his wife assured him that IF they were to die, the LORD would not have accepted the offering. Just as in the story of Jacob wrestling with God, we have the Angel of God both distinguished from God *and* identified with God.

Most astonishing of all the examples is Exodus 3, where the "Angel of the LORD" appeared to Moses in flames of fire from within a bush. What did He say? "I am the God of your father, the God of Abraham, Isaac, and Jacob." As Menoah, Moses asked His name and God gave the inscrutable name which He did not give to Menoah in Judges 13 saying "I am who I am" (a variant of YHWH).

So the Angel is God and yet distinct from God.

Other references show forth similar mysteries. Is God's Spirit of Shekeenah somehow God and yet distinct from God? What of all those passages where it is spoken of in this way? We note especially Isaiah 48:12-16,

"Hearken to me, O Jacob, and Israel, whom I called! I am He, I am the first, and I am the last. My hand laid the foundation of the earth, and my right hand spread out the heavens; when I call to them, they stand forth together.

"Assemble, all of you, and hear! Who among them has declared these things? The Lord loves him; he shall perform his purpose on Babylon, and his arm shall be against the Chaldeans. I, even I, have spoken and called him, I have brought him, and he will prosper in his way. Draw near to me, hear this: 'from the beginning I have not spoken in secret, from the time it came to be I have been there.' *And now the Lord God has sent me and his Spirit.*"

In this passage, God is the speaker, but then at the end of the passage, says that He is distinguished from the LORD and the Spirit. And, as is commonly known, rabbinic literature regularly speaks of the Shekeena, the Spirit's presence, as a separate person with intelligence, will, purpose, emotions, etc.[25]

Furthermore, there are hints of the Messiah being more than just human. In Isaiah 9:6-7, the Messiah is given the names of God—literally in Hebrew, "Wonderful Counselor, Almighty God—Everlasting Father, Prince of Peace." This child who is born will rule and reign over all the earth. The Messianic king is addressed, "The Lord said to my Lord" (Psalms 110:1). Who is this that David calls Lord? How this question puzzled Yeshua's listeners!

" 'What do you think about the Messiah? Whose son is he?'

" 'The son of David,' they replied.

"He said to them, 'How is it then that David, speaking by the Spirit, calls him Lord? For he says, "The Lord said to my Lord, sit at my right hand until I put your enemies under your feet." '

" 'If David calls him Lord, how can he be his son?' No one could say a word in reply." (Matthew 22:42-46. See also Micah 5:22; The Messiah is from Ancient of Days.)

Some rabbinical responses to the literature of the Tenach are quite unconvincing. Jacob's wrestling with the Angel is overlooked or glossed over. The reason the Angel of God is called God is not because he is God, but because God's name is in Him. What is this supposed to prove? If we can call an Angel by the holy name of God (YHWH) because God's name is in Him, so also could we not call Yeshua divine because God's name is in Him? The evidence of Tenach leaves us with a belief in one God with a plural dimension seen in manifestations of God. This revelation provides for an understanding of the New Testament revelation and its teaching on God and Yeshua. In the Tenach we find the Angel of God, God the Father, and the Shekeenah distinguished.

In the New Covenant Scriptures, God's plurality is clearly manifest in a sense of threeness. The Spirit is spoken of as distinct from God and yet God. The Spirit will be given when Yeshua leaves (John 14:15-31). He will be given by the Father. (Note the personal pronoun "He" for the Spirit.)

Yeshua is not only a man, but uniquely carries the name, nature, or stamp of divinity which is not true of other men. He is born of a virgin as predicted in Isaiah 7:14 (which was translated *parthenos* [Greek for virgin] before Yeshua's time by the Jewish translators of the Septuagent version, 100 B.C.E.). As being born of a virgin, His origin is part human and part special creation by God to carry the nature of God. In the very Jewish virgin birth account in Luke, which continually talks of the hope of Israel and Israel's deliverance from oppression, the virgin birth is spoken of as the act whereby Yeshua will be called the Son of God. Let us note that Israel was called God's son (Hosea 11:1) and that David was promised that Solomon would be God's son (II Samuel 2). However, this is not in the same unique sense of Yeshua. Although the New Testament does not emphasize Yeshua's divinity in an out-of-balance way, it clearly brings out this truth. In John 8:58, Yeshua claims to be one with the "I Am" saying, ". . . before Abraham was I am" (cf., Exodus 3:15).

In John 5:17-18, Yeshua claims oneness with the Father, who, according to rabbinic teaching, did not rest on Shabbat because he had to maintain the world's order. He also called God His father in a special sense. We have already quoted Matthew 22:41-46, where Yeshua asked how David could call the Messiah, his son, his Lord. The writings of the rest of the New Testament also bring out this truth.

Matthew 28:19 commands the Mikvah (baptism) to be performed in the name of the Father, Son and Holy Spirit. So also the Messiah is called the One in whom "all the fullness of the Deity lives in bodily form" (Colossians 2:9). He was in the form of God (Philippians 2:6) but emptied Himself, becoming a servant. As a result of this every knee shall bow and every tongue shall confess that Yeshua the Messiah is Lord (Philippians 2:10).

Yeshua, however, is not all of God's totality. He is one person or one aspect of that plural manifestation of God (from the Tenach) who became a human being. He, therefore, is a man who depends on the Spirit, prays to the Father, gets weary and dies. His divine nature never dies, but He is human as well as divine. As such, prayer in the New Testament is not primarily addressed to Yeshua but to "Our Father" in the Name of Yeshua. For Yeshua is the human revelation of the Father.

This should not be thought so incredible. Man alone is created in the image of God. He alone, therefore, can be the

perfect revelation of God. A perfect man who carries God's
Name or nature but is not all of God fits into the whole
character of Biblical revelation. Yeshua, the man, did *not*
exist before the first century; but His divine nature did!
Yeshua is not all of God, but is a man embodying God's
nature. He gives preeminence to His Father (John 5:19; 17:1-5;
16:25-27. So Yeshua is described in Scripture as without sin
(Hebrews 4:15; I Peter 2:22; John 8:46). If God is a uniplural
being, this is perfectly sensible, although beyond our complete understanding. Jews shunned this doctrine; but it is
not at all impossible. They have rejected Christian prayer,
which seems to limit God to Yeshua—as if Jesus was in
Himself, the Christian God.

Sometimes Christians speak as if they have lost sight of
God the Father; what G.E. Wright called a "Christo
monism."[26] Yet the New Testament, although recognizing
Yeshua's divinity, recognizes that God is more than Yeshua.
It *only rarely* addresses prayer to Yeshua, while recognizing
that by His life, teaching, death and resurrection, He is the
fullest revelation of God to man.

Jewish ways of expression are needed, ways more consistent to the New Testament, if Jews are to penetrate Christian rhetoric to see the truth of Yeshua's divine nature.

Jewish literature is not totally silent on the mystery of
God's plurality. It should be mentioned that this literature
sometimes reflects the reality of God's plurality. The Zohar
mentions that the Ancient One is revealed in three heads
"which are united into one" . . . "described as being three"
. . . "But how can three names be one? . . . (This) can only be
known by revelation of the Holy Spirit"[27] (Zohar, Vol. # p. 288,
Vol. 2: p. 43).

Once we accept the divine nature of Yeshua—a teaching
both consistent with Tenach on the uni-plurality of God, as
well as the New Testament teaching on Yeshua—we might
ask other reasons why God would reveal Himself in this
way. There are several.

In terms of revelation, since man is created in the image
of God, only a man would be able to bring the fullest revela-

tion of God. A perfect man, however, would need to bear the
nature of God to maintain perfection when born of our race.
God reveals Himself in a man to benefit our understanding, a
level of revelation we indeed can comprehend.

As a demonstration of God's unity with and love for the
race of man, a revelation of God in a human being is the
greatest possible way God could personally and intimately
show His great love (John 3:16).

Such a revelation also has a unique redemptive significance. The sufferings of the Messiah are not the substitutionary sufferings of a separate agent being punished for sin
instead of the guilty party. Rather, the Messiah's suffering is
the suffering love of God revealed, which forgives in the
midst of devastating hurt—if man will only turn in repentance. "Father forgive," said Yeshua when He was crucified
(Luke 23:34). Such love awakens us to our sin and wins us back
in repentance. Yeshua as representative man—also in love—
carries the hurt and destruction of the race for them or in
their stead, as a parent would suffer in love to free his way-
ward children and turn them to the right. As the divine
Messiah, His sacrifice has infinite value. If we are spiritually
one with Him, *God accepts us in Him.* He thus is our mediator
and high priest, not in the sense that we pray to Him *instead
of* the Father, *but, because we are "in the Messiah" (Galatians 2:20), we can go directly to God.*

The divinity of the Messiah is not idolatry, but reflects the
fullest revelation of God. It is like the revelations of God in
human form in the Tenach, which also were not of an idolatrous nature. In the Messiah, the revelation is conveyed in a
human being that remains forever a human being.

The Scriptures thus communicate to us the impression of
one great divine reality of three inseparable manifestations
of God. The relationship of love and accord blends the three
into eternal oneness beyond human comprehension. Yeshua
prays to the Father, thanks Him for His love and asks that He
would be glorified with the love He had with the Father
before the foundation of the world (John 17:5). The love relationship then is the highest eternal reality. This love over-

flows in creation. God gives Himself in love to the creation and the creation gives itself back to God in love.

When we say that God is love, God was not before creation loving Himself narcissistically. Rather, a reciprocal *giving relationship* of love is eternally existent within the plural unity of God.

CHAPTER SEVEN

The Life of Messianic Jews

Much confusion comes because two questions are not distinguished: "Who is a Jew?" And, "What does it mean to live as a Jew?" According to Halakah (traditional Jewish legal interpretation), a person is Jewish if born of a Jewish mother, circumcised if male, and is not a convert to another religion. Some rabbinic authorities have been willing to consider the convert as still Jewish, but would definitely not consider his children Jewish. This definition is also expanded to include those who convert to Judaism through instruction, decision, the ritual mikvah (Jewish water immersion) and circumcision.

The major problem with this position is its contradiction of the Scriptural indications that Jewish descent was carried through the father. The Covenant was originally made with Abraham. The father clearly determined the religious identity of his family. The Covenant sign of circumcision was applied to the male sexual member, indicating that this was a Covenant applying to physical descendants through the father.

Many Israelites of prominence took non-Jewish wives as well, who then were part of the Jewish identity of the family—with no formal conversion. This is so with the wife of Moses, who was a Cushite. It is true of Ruth with Boaz, the

ancestors of King David. That Jewish identity can be passed
on through the father becomes notably clear in the case of
Athaliah, the wicked pagan queen descended from Jezebel.
Through her came Ahaziah, the king, an ancestor of the Messiah. Though Athaliah sought to destroy the royal Messianic
line, her grandson, Joash, survived and became king. Certainly, no one would claim that Jezebel and Athaliah were
legitimate converts to Judaism; yet Athaliah's son and grandson were Jews! Therefore, to the traditional definition of who
is a Jew, we must add the element of descent from the father.[1]

The definition of a Jew must be more inclusive than just
physical descent and circumcision, if we are to carry on the
identity of Jewishness. For even nations and tribes have converted to Judaism and were then part of the nation.[2] Over the
years by marriage, the children of these converts also became
partakers of the blood line from Abraham. What is important
to note, however, is that others could also become part of the
nation of Israel.

David Ben Gurion, when asked who is a Jew, was so loose
in his definition that he simply stated that it was anyone who
desired to identify himself as a Jew. This seems to overlook
the seriousness of taking on a Jewish identity with real
conviction.

We would conclude from this that a person is a Jew who,
(1) is descended from a Jewish father or mother; and (2) who
is circumcised as a Jew if a male, and (3) maintains that he or
she is a Jew. One is also a Jew by conversion and circumcision.

Why, then, did the Halakic definition define Jewish descent through the mother alone? The reason reaches back to
Ezra. At that time, the Jewish remnant which returned to the
land was disposed toward an adulteration of its religious purity through the influence of spouses. Ezra commanded the
men at the time to divorce and send away their non-Jewish
wives. The conclusion of rabbis was that their children would
then not be considered Jewish. It is also thought that the
mother's early upbringing of the child as well as the certainty
of the child's descent from the mother—but uncertainty in
the case of the father's identity—all lent weight toward adopt-

ing this viewpoint. Suffice it to say that the Scriptural role of the father and descent from the father is *also* crucial.

WHAT DOES IT MEAN TO BE JEWISH?

The question of who is a Jew is important when considering what it means to be Jewish or to live as a Jew. We are not saying that someone who does not live a "Jewish" life is not Jewish any more than an American who is not patriotic is not an American. We do maintain that one who does not live as a Jew weakens the link of Jewish identity within his family and undercuts the perpetuation of a unique and identifiable Jewish people.

Many responses are given to what it means to be a Jew. Some see support of Israel and Jewish community causes as central; other point to synagogue attendance or the celebration of the feasts. All of these aspects contain nuggets of truth, but the full truth can only be seen in the light of Scripture's own teaching. The fullest sense of what it means to be a Jew is Biblically defined.

As stated throughout this book, God has called Israel to be a unique nation among the nations, a witness to His truth and faithfulness. As a nation they were given unique practices such as the practice of the Sabbath and the feasts, so that the people would be unified by the memory of what God had done in graciously establishing the nation. The nation would also then be unified in recognizing its unique purpose in showing forth the truth of the Scriptures and the faithfulness of God. The Biblical heritage of feast and festival and identity with the nation is crucial.

If we ask what makes up a nation from a sociological perspective, we gain further insight. In light of the fact that God has committed Himself to preserve the nation of Israel, and that we desire to be in accord with this purpose, these insights are important. In its strongest sense, a nation usually requires three major elements: defined borders, a common language, and a common culture and heritage. Weakening of any of the strands that constitute a nation weakens the survival of the entity constituting a nation.

Presently, for example, we could note the weakness of Canada due to the cultural and linguistic differences between French and English-speaking Canadians. Historically, nations have disappeared when uprooted from their land. Israel is unique because she maintained her nationhood though uprooted in the Diaspora. Jews were not in Israel, but the land of Israel was within the Jews! Hence, the importance of national borders became lessened in Israel's case because the land of Israel became part of Israel's religious-cultural future hope.

Israel in the Diaspora was preserved by God through a common language and heritage. Although Hebrew was not Israel's spoken language, it was preserved as the language of the synagogue. A Jew could worship in Russia, Poland, France or England with no language barrier. In addition, the Biblical practices of feast and fast as well as the rabbinic tradition, provided for an amazing cultural continuity. This was the case even where the fullness of the Biblical meaning of Israel's call as a nation was lost. This common heritage gave rise to a universal sense of Jewish brotherhood which continues to this day in Jewish community concerns for those in need, support for Israel and maintaining of other Jewish cultural ties in music, dance and literature.

The full scope of being a loyal Jew thus includes involvement in the Jewish community and support for Israel. However, *even more*, it means the preservation of the very historic Biblical roots of her heritage which makes these involvements possible today. It includes Sabbath, the feasts, Hebrew language, unique tunes and sounds in worship, as well as Bible-based discerning appreciation of Jewish history, literature and wisdom. Not all will be able to as fully give themselves to the whole of the Jewish heritage, but as loyal Jews, we should do so to the extent that we can. God has preserved Israel; He has done so through the element of the Jewish heritage.

Being a Jew is not just a physical thing. Messianic Jews should be on guard against tailoring their identity to a meaning which is weak in heritage identification because of the influence of Jews who become believers and are themselves weak in their heritage identification. This weakness is to be countered if there is to be a dynamic Messianic Judaism. No amount of ignorant comment concerning the "dead nature of Jewish tradition," "coming under bondage to the Law," and all other such misapplications of Scripture should shake us from recognizing the essentially Biblical and spiritual calling which we have from God to love and be part of the heritage of our people. Israel's calendar is from God; her preservation through her heritage is also from God. She is therefore a unique witness to God's faithfulness and His lordship over all of history. The "gifts and call of God to Israel *are* irrevocable" (Romans 11:29, emphasis the author's).

We should also note that central to the Jewish heritage is the prophetic call to social righteousness, concern for justice, compassion and mercy. Biblical Law is a foundation of social law for many Western nations. Messianic Jews should be in the forefront of witnessing to these prophetic truths.

However, as Messianic Jews, there should be a creative appropriation of our heritage as we are led by the Spirit. It must come from within rather than being artificially and rotely imposed from without, because there is a feeling of bondage to do it exactly as some other group does it.

SHABBAT

The Sabbath is a central pivot of Jewish life. As taught by Yeshua, "the Sabbath was made for man and not man for the Sabbath" (Mark 2:27). It was never meant to be a day of legalistic conformity. However, Sabbath is a day of crucial significance to Jewish identity. The principle of weekly rest, worship and renewal is one with universal significance. In this sense, the Sabbath principle is a spiritual and humanitarian guide for all peoples. Christians are free to incorporate this principle on Sunday or other days. The seventh day Sabbath for Israel is a special *central sign of the Covenant* between Israel and God. Hence, to abrogate the sign of the Covenant as a Jew is to cast doubt on whether we uphold the continuing covenant of God with Israel. Sabbath itself antedates Israel's existence and is a reflection of the creation order. However, Israel is given Sabbath as a memorial of God's gracious rescue from slavery as well as a memorial of creation and God's resting in the seventh period.

Messianic Judaism looks to Yeshua, who proclaimed himself "Lord of the Sabbath" (Mark 2:28), to gain a sense of direction for observance. The day is meant to be a break from the routine of work, whereby we may be renewed by worship, fellowship and rest. By this rest and renewal, Messianic Jews testify that God is Lord of creation and that man need not be subject to work as though the economic sphere of life has a tyrannical control over our lives. The one who is a person of faith and knows the "rest of faith" in Yeshua, testifies to the world that God is gracious and kind and will provide for us by faith even if one-seventh of our lives is spent in freedom from providing for our own material needs.

In Exodus 20:8-11, the nature of Sabbath is described as a testimony to God's own Lordship over the creation. The Messianic Jew testifies against all theories of atheism, agnosticism, evolutionary naturalism and pantheism by upholding the truth that, "In the beginning God created the heavens and the earth" (Genesis 1:1).

In Deuteronomy the Sabbath as a memorial of the Exodus as well as the Sabbath as a humanitarian stipulation are stressed. On this day, rich and poor, free and slave achieved a measure of equality in freedom from the domination of work. The Sabbath is an essential faith principle. We believe God's Word sufficiently to let go of our anxiety for food, clothes and shelter, believing that He is our loving Father and provider; we need not fear!

When we turn to the Prophets, we find the basic importance of Sabbath reaffirmed. Isaiah says, "Blessed is . . . the man . . . who keeps the Sabbath without desecrating it, and keeps his hand from doing any evil" (Isaiah 56:2, NIV). The passage goes on to delineate the blessings which shall be received by those who love God's Covenant and express it in a heartfelt recognition of Sabbath.

We also read in Isaiah 58:13-14 these words: "If you keep your feet from breaking the Sabbath and from doing as you please on my holy day, if you call the Sabbath a delight, and the Lord's holy day honorable; and if you honor it by not going your own way, and not doing as you please or speaking idle words, then you will find your joy in the Lord, and I will cause you to ride on the heights of the land and to feast on the inheritance of your father Jacob. The mouth of the Lord has spoken."

The prophets knew that desecration of the Sabbath struck at the heart of Israel's faith as to whether He was Lord, as to whether Israel was God's Covenant people!

The pages of the New Testament do not at all contradict the sense of Sabbath given in the Tenach. Nor does Yeshua break the Sabbath in its true sense. He calls Himself "Lord of the Sabbath" in Mark 2:27, decrying the legalists who would make Sabbath a burden instead of a delight by multiplying legalistic restrictions! The Pharisees criticized His disciples for eating grain as they walked through the fields. Their action was a natural response, unconnected with work. However, in the legalism of the day, this constituted harvesting! Yeshua perceived that such legalism would cause people to be concerned with scores of restrictions, thereby missing the sense of the day—its joy, its refreshment, its renewal. As Lord of the Sabbath, He set the record straight.

Outside of a Jewish context, the Apostle Paul allowed for freedom in regards to worship days. But he nowhere speaks against Jews who follow the Sabbath. He would not, however, allow a legalistic imposition of Sabbath on non-Jews. Our historical documents show that the Jewish believers of the first several centuries continued to practice Shabbat as part of their heritage and witness.

In non-Jewish communities, the Jewishness influence was such that the seven-day week became universal. Even the Sabbath principle was adopted by the Christian Church, although its day of worship was Sunday. Yet we should note that Sunday in Christian practice is one day in seven for worship, renewal and rest.

How is it that Christendom adopted the "first" day as its day of worship? Some have held that the early believers gathered on Sunday morning to celebrate the resurrection and celebrated both the Sabbath and Sunday. However, it is said that the Church perceived that, under the New Covenant, the Sabbath had been abrogated and that Sunday was a proper replacement of the Sabbath.

The most recent scholarship suggests that this explanation for the switch from Saturday to Sunday is mistaken. Dr. Samuel Bacchiocchi has probably written the definitive work on all of the evidence involved. A summary of his work appears in the *Biblical Archaeology Review* (Sept/Oct 1978) and a fascinating debate ensued as recorded in future editions.[3] The basic evidence seems to be that Sunday worship was not introduced as an authoritative apostolic practice. Part of the evidence is that "Paul refused to take a stand on the question of observance of days, advising rather to follow one's convictions and to respect differences of viewpoint"[4] (Romans 14:3, 5, 6, 10-13, 19-21, 2:16-17). Sabbath was not imposed on Gentiles, but Sunday-keeping did originate in Gentile communities. However, if Paul *had* introduced such practices, this innovation would have caused great controversy, which, historically, is not the case.

Bacchiocchi traces the exclusive observance of Sunday to the time of Emperor Hadrian (117-135), when Roman anti-Jewish repression influenced a policy of deliberate differentiation from Jewish customs.

The only examples in the New Testament of a first-day meeting prove to be Saturday evening rather than Sunday morning! In Jewish reckoning, the next day begins at sundown! Hence, in Acts 20:7, Paul preached all night and left on Sunday morning! He was not taking a day of rest and worship on Sunday.

The early believers did gather in the evening to celebrate the Messiah's memorial supper as is indicated by Paul's description of the rite as "supper-deipnon" (I Corinthians 11:20). This could have occurred on Saturday night as a counterpart to the Jewish Saidah Shlishi (the third Sabbath meal) preceding the ceremony ending Sabbath (Havdalah). Non-Jews could have mistaken this celebration as a first-day Sunday morning institution, which it clearly was not. As part of the community of Israel, Jewish believers in Yeshua would have worked on Sunday, but not on Saturday. Jewish believers were part of other synagogues on the Sabbath and thus may have gathered for their meetings at various times.

Bacchiocchi finds Sunday observance coming about as part of an anti-Jewish reaction, in which Sabbath was even seen as a temporary institution imposed as a trademark of the divine reprobation of the Jewish race. At any rate, there is no Biblical evidence to suggest that Sabbath does not have its value as a sign of God's continued Covenant with Israel, originally made with Abraham. For a *Messianic Jew, it is a day which celebrates the Sabbath rest that is ours in Yeshua who is Lord of the Sabbath.*

Messianic Jews must avoid a legalistic approach to Sabbath, where rules are imposed ad infinitum. However, if Sabbath is to be taken seriously, there are some basic principles which may be applied by our people:

First, Sabbath should be a day of freedom from work, especially that work which is required for our economic and material security. Judaism has always recognized that professions providing help in emergency (doctors, firemen, etc.) must be exceptions. Even these people, however, need the principle of renewal and should seek a period of rest.

Secondly, it is of spiritual value to mark the day off from other days by a special Friday evening meal, the lighting of candles and prayer. This makes us conscious of entering into a special period of time. Some Messianic Jews bring special recognition to Yeshua, who is the light of the world, in their Friday evening Sabbath meal. Blessings over bread and wine for Sabbath are helpful additions.

Sabbath is also an appropriate day to gather for worship and share the word exposited. It is a time as well for friends, fellowship and family. It is a wonderful time for those restful quiet activities that we might otherwise overlook. Reading Biblical stories together, quiet games, even napping, and sharing with friends can all be interwoven to make Sabbath a joy. The Sabbath also may be ended with special prayer. The

Havdalah service is a meaningful way. Havdalah means a separation from Sabbath. A special candle is lit and extinguished in wine. Sweet spices are shaken in a spice box and sniffed by all as a reminder of the sweetness of Sabbath, a fragrance of beauty.

What is of primary importance is that our activity be a true renewal of life in God. We need not legalistically define what constitutes "work." However, activity which is wearing on us, which depresses, which is related to material security, is to be avoided. Sabbath should be a *real contrast* from other work days. Congregations with Sabbath schedules ought as well be careful to not tax their people with too much activity. To make Sabbath a delight, let our celebrations be creatively expressed and not rote.

Much material on Sabbath is available from Jewish publishers. Take note as well of the *Jewish Catalogue*,[5] which is a fine source for all the holidays.

THE FEASTS OF ISRAEL

Passover

Passover is the great feast which recalls the Exodus from Egyptian bondage. It recalls the birth of Israel as a nation into freedom. As a great feast of remembrance, Passover is a feast without equal. It is full of meanings which relate to all followers of the Messiah. The Exodus is a type or image pattern of all of God's redemptive acts and even of the final redemption and the establishment of God's Kingdom. Hence, we note these salient facts:

1. The slaughter of the Passover lamb sacrifice and the placing of its blood on the doorpost and on the lintel is used in the New Testament as the background for understanding the death of Yeshua. As the angel of death *passed over* the houses of the Israelites who were protected by the blood of the lamb, even so we are passed from death unto life by the atonement blood of Yeshua. Hence Yeshua dies on the eve of Passover in John 19, for He is "our Passover lamb" who is slain (I Corin-

thians 5:7 ff). In this same passage we are njoined to purge
out the leaven of malice and wickedness.

"Your boasting is not good. Don't you know that a little
yeast works through the whole batch of dough? Get rid of the
old yeast that you may be a new batch without yeast, as you
really are. For Messiah, our Passover lamb, has been sacrificed. Therefore let us keep the Festival, not with the old
yeast, the yeast of malice and wickedness, but with bread
without yeast, the bread of sincerity and truth (I Corinthians
5:6-8).[11]

Leaven was not eaten by Israel when they left Egypt
because the dough had no time to rise. Leaven also became a
symbol of that indwelling evil which pervades and affects life.
Passover symbolism is central to Paul's exposition of the
meaning of Messiah Jesus.

2. The 5,000 Israelites ate the loaves which were multi-
plied by the supernatural power of God in Yeshua. The feeding of the 5,000 is fraught with the Passover symbolism, recalling the manna in the Wilderness.

3. The early believers—*both* Jew and non-Jew—celebrated the resurrection of the Messiah on Passover, which
began the eight-day feast of unleavened bread. He replaced
the sacrificial lamb which was absent in their celebration.

4. The Messiah's memorial meal (the Last Supper) was a
Passover meal in which Yeshua made the wine of the cup of
redemption (3rd cup) and the bread of the afikomen (dessert)
symbolize His broken body and shed blood. Therefore, He
was telling His disciples to make the bread and wine of the
Passover meal a pointer to His redemption and a participation in its power and meaning.

In the light of this, we can see how Passover would be
celebrated by Messianic Jews. They, of course, would rejoice
in the eight-day festival in thanksgiving to God for their
redemption from Egyptian bondage, their birth as a nation
and their continued preservation. Eating only unleavened
bread for eight days, special services and the Passover meal
itself on the 14th of Nisan would all be a joyous part of their
celebration! However, their celebration would also incorpo-

rate all of the meanings of Yeshua's life in us. The bread and wine would stand for Him. He would be seen in all of the sacrificial images which were part of Passover.

This is a great annual teaching time for the family. The family and its guests gather for the meal on the 14th of Nisan. Each family would have a Seder (order) or Passover meal reading the stories of the Exodus and of our redemption in Yeshua. The festival would be an eight-day celebration of the resurrection with special days off from work to gather as a congregation on the first and seventh days as enjoined in Leviticus 23.

Passover is a great celebration of God's grace in both Old and New Testament times! We should note that, in our view, the proscription of guests who are not circumcised at the meal is not applicable to any believer who is clean (circumcised in heart) in Yeshua (Acts 10).

Passover celebrates the fulfillment of God's promise to Abraham to make him a great nation and to bring Messiah from his seed. There is no legalism involved in this joyous celebration.

Thousands of Messianic Jews around the world now celebrate Passover in this way.

First Fruits—Counting the Omer

In Leviticus 23:9-14, we read of the Feast of First Fruits, celebrated on the Sabbath day after Passover. The Feast includes an offering to God of the first produce of the year. As stated previously, Yeshua the Messiah now takes the place of all of the *sacrificial* dimensions of all the feasts. Although this feast is not as "major" in Scripture as other feasts, it does have important significance: For us, it is a celebration of the resurrection. We read in I Corinthians 15:20, 22b—"But now is the Messiah risen from the dead, the first fruits of them that sleep, even so in the Messiah shall all be made alive."

The meaning of First Fruits is the promise of more to come. Because he rose, there is more to come, namely the resurrection of all followers of Yeshua. Thus, we might recommend as part of Messianic Jewish practice, a gathering for worship either by congregation or families. Reading Leviticus 23:9-14 and I Corinthians 15 on the resurrection would be excellent. In addition, a special offering could be taken in our congregations or for other worthy spiritual ministries to show that all we have is God's.

In ancient Israel, First Fruits celebrated the beginning of the barley harvest. We, in remembering this, tie ourselves to our people and its land.

Shavuot (weeks)—Pentecost (50)

We are enjoined to count 49 days—or seven weeks—after First Fruits to commemorate the Feast of Shavuot. These days are actually counted in synagogues in Jewish liturgy. This is called the "counting of the Omer." The fiftieth day is the Celebration of Shavuot, one of the three major festivals during which men presented themselves before God at Jerusalem.

In Biblical times Shavuot originally signified thanksgiving for the first harvest of wheat. However, by the time of Jesus, this ancient feast was connected by rabbinic calculation as the time of the giving of God's revelation on Sinai. It is of value to connect ourselves to the land by this feast as well as to celebrate the giving of the Law in our worship.

However, there is a central meaning for Messianic Jews and Christians who have adopted this holiday as one of their own; for on this day, God sovereignly chose to give the Holy Spirit (Ruach ha Kodesh) to Yeshua's gathered followers. In Acts Chapter Two we read the marvelous story of how they preached the Gospel supernaturally to Jewish people from many lands who spoke many languages. The followers of Yeshua were able to communicate in these languages, even though they never learned them, the wonderful news of salvation. A great harvest of people were gathered into the new community of faith on this day.

How significant it is that God providentially gave His Spirit on this day, for only through the power of the Spirit can we actually harvest God's will. It is by the Spirit that God's law is written on our hearts (Ezekiel 36:25-27; Hebrews 10:16).

Shavuot is thus a great celebration of many Biblical meanings and events. It is a day of rest and worship. Homes and congregational buildings may be decorated with greens. The services of worship at home and in congregations will emphasize the truths of the relationship of the Law of God and the Spirit of God who inspired the writings of the Law. Special gifts to worthy ministries and needy people are also ways of showing gratitude to God. Furthermore, it is an ideal time to recommit ourselves to walk in the Spirit.

Rosh Hashana

The Feast of Trumpets—the Jewish new Year—takes place in the autumn, on the first of Tishri, on the Israeli calendar. Originally this day was not celebrated as a new year; but Rabbinic calculation fixed the anniversary of the creation of the world on this day.

Actually, Israel was originally to observe this as the day of the blowing of the Shofar (ram's horn) in preparation for Yom Kippur. Hence, Jewish tradition rightly incorporates prayers seeking forgiveness on this day as well as new-year memorials. Scripturally, our people were told to celebrate the month of the Feast of Passover as their new year. Tishri in the fall was actually the new-year festival of the surrounding nations of the near East, just as January first would be our parallel today. There is nothing wrong with remembering the creation of the world on this day, too, as long as we do not lose sight of the day as an *entrance into the days of self-examination and repentance before God.*

The Feast of Trumpets also reminds us of the return of Yeshua the Messiah to rule and reign. In I Thessalonians 4:16-18 we learn, "The Lord himself shall descend from heaven with a shout and with the voice of the archangel and the shofar of God and the dead in the Messiah shall rise first, then we which remain alive shall be caught up together with them in the clouds . . . and so shall we ever be with the Lord . . . therefore comfort one another with these words . . ."

We also read in I Corinthians 15 that we shall be changed in a moment at the resurrection, at the *last shofar,* in the twinkling of an eye.

Messianic Jews therefore celebrate Rosh Hashana as a day of rest, with services of worship emphasizing preparation for the return of the Messiah and the resurrection, as well as a preparation for Yom Kippur. Traditional and modern worship material may be creatively adapted to this end.

Yom Kippur—(The Day of Atonement)

Yom Kippur is the holiest day of the Jewish year. In ancient Israel, Yom Kippur was the day on which atonement was made for the whole nation (Leviticus 16). On this day, the high priest went into the Holy of Holies with the sacrificial blood to make atonement for the people's sins. He sprinkled this blood on the Ark of the Covenant. Prominent at Yom Kippur as well was the ceremony of the scapegoat. The priest laid his hands on the head of the animal, which then symbolically carried away the sins of the people. This is the only day in Torah specified as a day of fasting. In this day the nation was to "afflict itself" in repentance for sin. Traditional Judaism incorporates many great prayers of repentance for the seeking of forgiveness, some of which are fraught with Messianic significance. For example, the merit of the Messiah is appealed to for forgiveness.[6] Forgiveness is also asked on the basis of Abraham's offering of Isaac as a sacrifice (which Messianic Jews know to be a foreshadowing of the sacrifice of the Messiah Yeshua). (This is the case with daily services as well.)

Yom Kippur also has continuing central significance in Messianic Judaism. It is not that we seek atonement through our prayers or by the observance of a day: Yeshua the Messiah is our high priest, our atonement, and our scapegoat! The central chapters of the Book of Hebrews explicate the meaning of Yeshua in the light of Yom Kippur, and are central to us on this day.

Yom Kippur, for us, is a day incorporating several meanings:

1. It is a central celebration of the fulfillment of the Biblical meaning of *Priest* and *Sacrifice* in Yeshua.

2. It is a day of prayer, fasting and intercession for Israel, our people.

3. It is a day of self-examination and turning from sin in our own lives. Scripture enjoins us to "examine ourselves" (I Corinthians 11:28; I John 1:8-9, etc.).

It is a day to worship in community as well as to be apart, to take stock of the direction of our lives over the past year. Where have we missed God's direction? Where have we grown? Where have we slipped? As James 4:6-11 enjoins us, we repent and turn from these sins unto God. Confession and forgiveness form a daily part of our life in Yeshua. However, as individuals and as a community it is of value to have a special season for this purpose as well.

The services for Yom Kippur emphasize Messianic fulfillment as well as all of the above-mentioned elements. The break-fast is a special time of rejoicing and celebration for our forgiveness in Yeshua.

Two areas of special misunderstanding are worth noting in relation to Yom Kippur. One is "Kol Nidre" (All Vows) chant which begins the first evening service, called the Kol Nidre service. This particular chant asks forgiveness for all past and future vows which we might make and break. It is not that Jewish people intend to break vows; but under extreme duress and torture, Jews were often forced to take vows which they could not keep in loyalty to God. Messianic Jews have the promise of God's grace and the command of Yeshua to be totally truthful. Our Yom Kippur observance needs to emphasize this.

Secondly, both Rosh Hashana and Yom Kippur services have us pray to be inscribed in the Book of Life (for the coming year). Followers of Yeshua have sometimes had difficulty with both the prayer and the Rosh Hashana greeting, "may you be inscribed . . . ."

The Book of Life may refer to several books within Judaism. Some have thought that the reference must be to the symbolic book of eternal life found in the Book of Revelation. Other references, however, are only to the Book of Life in the sense of God's decrees concerning those who will be kept in life and health for the coming year. In the latter sense there is no problem with the greeting.

Succot—(Booths or Tabernacles)

Soon after Yom Kippur, the Feast of Succot begins. It is the third major feast in which the males of Israel traveled to Jerusalem. This is an eight-day festival during which the people of Israel dwelled in tents to recall their wilderness wanderings, when they had little in the way of possessions, permanent dwellings or natural provision for food. God supernaturally provided for their needs of food, clothing and shelter. When they had almost nothing, God provided! To dwell in tents is a vivid reminder of God's grace. When Israel dwelt in tents they remembered that, although they might have homes and land and other measures of wealth, their lives were just as dependent upon God. Security was not to be found in possessions. Nor was Israel to think that its might or wealth was a product of its self-righteousness or power (Deuteronomy 8-10). Israel was to love and trust God first and only. The eight day Celebration of Booths was to be a vivid reminder of all of these truths.

The Feast of Succot was also a celebration of the last major harvest period in Israel. It was a great festival of thanksgiving. Part of the tradition of this feast was the recitation of the Hallel Psalms 113-118 and the waving of fruit (etrog) and branches of palm and willow (lulav) before God (Leviticus 23).

Hospitality is an essential part of observing Succot. In gratitude for God's provision, we share with others. The first and eighth day of the festival are assemblies of worship.

The Feast of Tabernacles is also full of Messianic significance. In John 7-9, the teaching of Yeshua is better understood in the context of the feast of Succot. The last Day of Succot was the context of Jesus' statement, "If anyone thirst let him come to me and drink. He who believes in me as the Scripture has said, out of his heart shall flow rivers of living water. Now he said this about the Spirit . . . ." (John 7:37-39).

We know from the description of Succot in the Talmud that this was the day in which a great ceremony of pouring out waters of libation took place.

The joyful ceremonial of festival reached its climax in Temple times when the procedure known as 'the joy of water drawing' began on the second night of Succot and lasted for six days. Each morning a libation offering of water was made. It was taken in a golden ewer from the pool of Siloam, carried with great pomp and ceremony, and was poured into a perforated silver bowl placed on the west side of the altar, symbolizing the abundant rain for which the people prayed. Bonfires were lit and men of piety danced, holding lighted torches and singing songs and hymns to the accompaniment of harps, lyres, cymbals and trumpets played by Levites." (Tal. Succot)

During the last day of the Feast there was a magnificent lamp lighting ceremony in the Court of Women. The Temple thus shone with an incredible brightness of light. This, in all probability, was the context of Yeshua's statement, "I am the light of the world" (John 8:12).

Matthew 6 is also an excellent chapter as well to remember at Succot time, for it supremely recounts to us the nature of God's fatherly care.

How is Succot best celebrated by Messianic Jews? There are a variety of creative ways: First, as in all the feasts, the sacrificial dimensions are replaced by the centrality of Yeshua's sacrifice. In addition, services on the first and last days of Succot are a time for the gathered community to give thanks, to wave fruit and branches in thanksgiving, to read the Hallel Psalms 113-118, and to creatively worship using traditional and modern material. Evenings should be times of special fellowship through the sharing of meals and reading the Scriptures we have mentioned.

One of our dilemmas, of course, relates to the Biblical stipulation to dwell in tents: In Israel, with a warm climate, the practice is not only beautiful but practical. In some Diaspora climates, this becomes less possible. The rabbis, in realizing this, have sought to instill the practice of building a Succah and at least taking meals in the Succah.

As we look at Messianic Jewish practice we note as well the importance of conveying the meaning of this feast in an enjoyable way, recognizing that the command to dwell in booths was given for the nation dwelling in its land, possessing houses and security. In the Diaspora, there is a great measure of freedom. Climate permitting, we would indeed recommend the building of a Succah by families and the eating of meals in it. Decorating the Succah is a great joy to children; a festive spirit prevails. Some Messianic Jews have sought to take a camping trip during part of Succot so as to really get a greater sense of the bare necessities and of God's provision for us through the produce of the land; for He gives the rain and sunshine. The first and last days of the eight-day festival are special days of rest and community gathering for worship celebration. Traditionally, this was a period of especially looking forward to the Messianic Kingdom. God will some day be seen as the provider for all the earth; hence, according to Zechariah 14, this feast is to be universally observed. All nations will send representatives to Jerusalem to observe this feast with Israel.

Minor Feasts and Fasts
Simchat Torah—(Rejoicing of the Torah). Since we have just described *Succot*, it is fitting to describe Simchat Torah as well. Simchat Torah is not a Biblically prescribed feast. It occurs immediately after Succot and celebrates the transition from the last to the next reading of the annual Torah cycle. The Jewish community created a great festival of joy on a day that could have been only a day of the tedious re-rolling of the community's scrolls from the end to the beginning. We might also ask, is it not a great cause for rejoicing to complete a reading of the Scriptures by the community and to have the opportunity to begin reading again!

The festival includes music and dancing with the Torah scrolls. Among some of the Orthodox Hasidic communities, the celebration soars into great heights of joy and energy. For Messianic Jews, there is further cause of rejoicing—for in the Messiah we are accounted righteous and have the joy of God's own Torah written on our hearts by His Spirit.

Purim—celebrates the deliverance of Israel from a wicked plot of annihilation during the days of the Persian Empire. The Book of Esther records the account of the wicked plans of Haman and the efforts of the Jewish Queen Esther (Hadassah) to influence the king to save her people. Purim falls near the end of winter in the month of Adar. It is characterized by plays, songs, costumes, and the reading of the Scroll of Esther (the Megillah) during which children make noise with "gregors" to drown out the name of Haman. Other great periods of danger and deliverance in Israel's history are also recalled. The creative possibilities of the Messianic Jewish celebration of this day are unlimited. Special plays, dialogues, concerts, spiritual parties and more have been successfully undertaken.

Yom Ha Shoah—Day of Calamity. This day, occurring in the spring on the 25th of Nisan, recalls the destruction of European Jewry under the unspeakable horrors of the reign of the Nazis. The day is marked in both synagogues and larger communities by services which include memorial prayers, readings from concentration camp poetry and literature and recommitment to the survival of Israel. Messianic Jews join in mourning and memory with the whole Jewish community on this day as well as affirming the ultimate hope of justice and peace in the reign of the Messiah.

Lutheran Franklin Litiell also suggests a service for Christian churches in his book, *The Crucifixion of the Jews.* The Church would thereby repent of its past silence in the face of this atrocity while yet showing a solidarity of mourning and memory with the Jewish community.

Israel Independence Day—(Yom Ha Atzmaoot). Later in the spring, the 5th of Iyar marks the rebirth of the State of Israel in 1948. It is a day of prophetic fulfillment and celebration. Congregations and communities all over the world celebrate this miracle!

Tisha B'Av—(The Ninth of Av). This date, which occurs in mid-summer, is a day of fasting and sadness. On this day, supernaturally—by any standard of unbiased reasoning—the first Temple of Israel was destroyed in 586 B.C.E. by the

Babylonians and the second Temple was destroyed in 70 C.E. by Titus. Incredible as it seems, both Temples were destroyed on the same date 656 years apart! Also on this day, the decree of the Expulsion of the Jewish community from Spain in 1492 went into effect.

Messianic Jews on this day should seek identity with their people, mourning in prayerful intercession as we reflect on such judgments. We should also note the passages of comfort and hope in the Scripture. Let us pray for the peace of Jerusalem as well as for the salvation of friends and of all of Israel.

Chanukah (Hanukkah)—The Feast of Dedication. This feast celebrates the amazing victories in Israel's overthrow of its tyrannical Syrio-Greek rulers during the days of the Maccabees. The Syrio-Greek Empire sought not only to rule Israel, but to destroy Israel's unique religious fidelity to Scripture. They imposed pagan customs and rites on Israel, even in the Temple itself. Many were martyred for their faith. Hence, in the 160's (B.C.E.) the Maccabee family led a great revolt, eventually culminating in the rededication of the Temple and the independence of Israel for the first time in over 400 years. Chanukah itself, which usually falls in early winter—on the 25th of Chislev—marks the rededication of the Temple. Prominent during the eight-day festival is the lighting of the candles of an eight-branched menorah. Every day one more candle is lit. This recalls the reported miracle of oil in the Temple lamps. When the Temple lamps were relit, there was only enough to last for a day, yet the light burned for eight days until new oil could be obtained. Messianic Jews celebrate the victories of those days with the rest of the Jewish community. They retell the stories of Chanukah from the books of the Maccabees as well as reliving these events through Chanukah plays.

Messianic Jews would do well to also recall that this feast was the occasion of Yeshua's profound teaching on the relationship between Himself as the Good Shepherd and the rest of His sheep who "hear His voice," know Him, and follow Him (John 10).

We cannot overlook the fact that it is in a similar time
frame that most Christians celebrate Christmas. Although
there is no ambivalence among Messianic Jews toward the
Biblical meaning of Christmas as a time to celebrate the
entrance into this world of the Messiah Jesus, Christmas
itself brings ambivalent feelings to Messianic Jews. First,
scholars usually hold that this date is *not* the time of the birth
of the Messiah. Usually, the date is explained as one which
correlated to the old pagan winter solstice festival in which
pagans symbolically sought to magically assure the resurrection of spring. Perhaps the reason for the Church's date was to
counter such paganism with a Christian holiday. Yet the
ambivalence persists. The Puritan Christians forbade the
celebration of Christmas in the 16th and 17th centuries
because of supposed pagan connections.

The Jewish community has actually tended to emphasize
Hanukah, which was a minor feast, to counter the influence
of Christmas by having a parallel gift-giving holiday. The
story does not end here, for recently Cardinal Jean Danielou
proposed the opinion that the reason December 25th (a solar
calendar date) could be proposed as a date for the birth of the
Messiah in the light of its pagan connections must be sought in
the fact that the *25th of Chislev* (a lunar calendar date)
already possessed great significance to Messianic Jews. In
latter times this connection was lost and the 25th of Chislev
became identified with the 25th of December and the birth of
Yeshua. Danielou holds that the 25th of Chislev was the birth
of James.

Is there a solution to the problem of these dates and the
ambivalence they cause, a solution that also meets the special
need to recognize the birth of Yeshua as well as reading with
special festivity the passages so profoundly recording the
details of his birth (Matthew 1-2; Luke 1-2)?

If we note the practice of Messianic Jews of today and
yesteryear in celebrating the resurrection of Yeshua, we
might gain a hint at a solution. Messianic Jews celebrate the

resurrection in connection to the 14th of Nisan which is Passover. Thus they follow the Jewish lunar calendar for religious observance. If we note that there is no agreement on the date of the birth of the Messiah, we can perhaps make some creative new suggestions.

Without Chanukah and the preservation of the Jewish community by God, Yeshua would never have come. Chanukah is a festival of lights and Yeshua is the light of the world. Perhaps then for Messianic Jews, the climax of Chanukah could be the celebration of the birth of Yeshua. However, this celebration would be set by the Jewish lunar date of the 25th of Chislev. It would also be well to then read the birth narratives. Also, during Chanukah, the life of James, the great leader of the Messianic Jewish community in Jerusalem can be recalled. Messianic Jews need to produce story books and celebration ideas incorporating all of these significant events in the light of Yeshua. These books would then be of help to families and congregations. This is only a suggestion, but it is put forth with the hope that it has merit.

OTHER COMMON WORSHIP PRACTICES

The Tzizit (Fringes). "The Lord said to Moses, speak to the Israelites and say to them: throughout the generations to come you are to make tassels on the corners of your garments, with a blue cord on each tassel. You will have these tassels to look at and so you will remember all the commands of the Lord, that you may obey them and not prostitute yourselves by going after the lusts of your own hearts and eyes. Then you will remember to obey all my commands and will be conse-

crated to your God. I am the Lord your God" (Numbers
15:37-41).

The meaning of this command is quite simple. The
ancient Israelites wore four-cornered garments, almost like a
sheet with cutouts for head and arms. Upon each corner of the
garment was to be sewn a fringe or tassel with a cord of blue.
This cord of blue was to be a memory tool to remember to do
all in commitment to God, not for selfish desire, to be consecrated to God and to obey all His commands. Whenever it was
looked upon it was to recall the Israelite to his commitment.

Our desire as Messianic Jews is to recapture the *Spirit*
(the reason and application for today) of the Law and not just
the letter. This command does not mean that we as Western
20th century people have to return to the dress of 3500 years
ago and sew tassels on the corners of our garments. It does
mean that we should seek means of constantly reminding
ourselves of our commitment to God and to His commandments, that the love of God be constantly remembered.

Messianic Jews may find value in the prayer shawl
(Tallit), a garment developed for the purpose of keeping this
command, even though we do not wear four-cornered garments today. As they place the prayer shawl upon themselves, they return to their first love. Some Messianic Jews
find value in the Tallit Katan worn under the shirt so that
fringes are worn in all waking hours. We would also recall the
words of Yeshua, "If you love me, keep my commandments."
Thus the fringes still have value. However it is the principle
of memory that counts, not enforcing the particular means of
memory. Messianic Jews who wear fringes might well
consider departing from the Rabbinic laws of mystical knots
and to make fringes blue!

The fringes were worn by Yeshua, and those who sought
healing from Him would seek to touch the fringes of His
garment (Mark 5:28; 6:56). Some also use the Tallit as a symbol
of being clothed upon with the righteousness of Yeshua in
whom we are accounted righteous. By His power in us we
fulfill God's commands.

H.L. Ellison argues that Paul certainly wore fringes all of

the time or would not have been heard at all in the synagogues.[9]

Tefillin—Phylactries. In Deuteronomy 6:4ff—"the Sh'ma
Passage"—we read the words "You shall love the Lord with
all your heart, with all your soul and with all your might,"
and that these words "should be bound as a sign upon their
hands" and as a "sign on their foreheads." They are to be
"written on the door frames of the houses and . . . gates" as
well.

The traditional means of fulfilling this command is a
small box with leather straps which is placed on the arm, the
straps being woven around the arm and hand. Another box
with leather straps is placed upon the head. The command in
relation to gates and doorposts is fulfilled through use of the
mezuzzah, a small container affixed in the proper place on
the door. All three contain the Biblical verses enjoined by
Scripture. The *tefillin* is worn daily during daytime prayer
services.

Again we have a significant memory device in Scripture.
Jewish tradition rejects the use of tefillin on Sabbath because
Sabbath is also called a "sign" between God and Israel of
God's Covenant relation with Israel. Jewish reasoning
eschews the use of signs in any way that one sign could detract
from the significance of the other; the tefillin are also taken to
be a Covenant sign.

The Spirit of the law allow freedom in the usage of these
memory practices and emphasizes the memory purpose of
the command. Perhaps a modern rendition would be to write
the Sh'ma on our dashboards so as to remember it while
driving to work, or to place it in other visible spots (e.g., the
bathroom mirror while shaving). We are strictly warned to
not make any sign an ostentatious disply to call attention to
ourselves (Matthew 23:5-6).

The Yarmulke—the Kippah—Head Cap. The head cap is
an essentially non-biblical tradition that is also a sign of
contemporary Jewish identification among orthodox Jews.
Freedom prevails in such usage. However, there is some
question as to whether the Kippah is allowable in prayer since

I Corinthians 11:4-7 says that a man who prays "ought not to
cover his head since he is the image and glory of God" (NIV).
However, we need to remember that various cultures give
opposite meanings to various objects of use; we cannot
universally say that a head covering shows self-submission
and abnegation as in Paul's day. In one tribe in Africa sticking
out one's tongue is a friendly greeting, but Paul might have
forbidden it among believers in America. The cultural meaning of head coverings is no longer understood as conveying
anything in many cultures, but in Paul's day the meaning was
a part of their symbolic language structure. The Spirit of the
Law principle applies here as well as to the Tenach. We are to
show the proper reflection of God's image and His forgiveness
in the Messiah as men and not to act as though we are
unforgiven and rejected before God. This is the essence of
Paul's meaning and if the kippah does not convey a contradiction of this meaning to our culture it can be worn.

The following passage from *The American Messianic
Jew*, Spring, 1979, is republished here to bring out the probability that there is little relationship between the head covering of Paul's day and the kippah:

THE "YARMULKE"

"One of the symbols of Jewish piety has been the *yarmulke*. This head cap, required in Orthodox Jewish circles, is
a sign of reverence before God. In Jewish Reform circles, it is
now becoming common as a symbol of identity with Israel
and the Jewish people. This practice has become popular also
with some Messianic Jews.

"Recently, some have raised objections to its use on the
basis of the Scriptures. Some Christians have rebuked Messianic Jews for this practice, and some 'babes' in the Messiah
become confused by the interpretation of the biblical evidence, for they were told that they could keep their Jewish
identity in the New Covenant faith. Since Scripture is our
ultimate authority, only a deeper look into the passages at

issue can solve the problem.

"The passage in question is I Corinthians 11:4-15. Paul is here arguing for the distinction between the sexes, based upon the creation order. He speaks of hair length as a reflection of the creation order, and then goes on to speak of head coverings as another reflection of this order. Although the yarmulke was not in vogue at the time, we still need to see whether the passage has relevance to this issue and summarize it for this purpose:

" '. . . but any man who prays or prophesies with his head covered dishonors his head . . . (v. 4 ff). If a woman will not veil herself, then she should cut off her hair; but if it is disgraceful for a woman to be shorn or shaven, let her wear a veil. For a man ought not to cover his head, since the image and glory of God is he; but the woman is the glory of man. Neither was man created for woman, but woman for man. That is why a woman ought to have a veil on her head, because of the angels . . . Judge for yourself, is it proper for a woman to pray to God with her head uncovered? Does not nature itself teach you that for a man to wear long hair is degrading to him, but if a woman has long hair, it is her pride.'

"As we look into this passage, the first thing we notice is the inconsistency of those who criticize the practice of wearing the yarmulke. These people do not require women to cover their heads as required by this interpretation."

Text and Context
One of the first rules for Biblical understanding is that we must understand the passage in its original historical and cultural context. This text involves the whole gamut of issues relating to male and female distinctions, including styles of dress and grooming. The question is what Paul meant by the veil or headcovering and its relationship to hair length. The evidence is very strong that Paul was not speaking to any-

thing relating to the yarmulke. Rather, he was speaking of a
particular kind of veil, a large size veil that would cover all of
the woman's hair. The hair of a woman was considered her
glory as a covering. It was her glory because it was itself
beautiful and attractive while gracing and covering her head.
A woman's hair was not to be let loose for this was indicative
of a loose woman. Jewish literature is clear on this point
(Isaiah 3:17; Numbers 5:18; III Macabees 4:6; Talmud Ned. 30b;
Numb. R. 9:101). If a woman walked bare-headed, the husband could divorce her without question (Ketubot 7:6).
Women were not to have their heads uncovered after marriage (Ketubot 2:1). Indeed, Talmud Berachot 24a compares
the exposure of hair to be like an exposure of one's private
parts. There is even the concept that beautiful uncovered
hair tempted the angels. Thus Paul probably had in mind a
total head covering that would cover the face also, to be used
while praying, and speaking in the public meeting.

How are we to apply our evidence? The rule is that we
must follow that which the Biblical writer *intended to teach*.
A majority of Biblical exegetes believe that there are two
levels of intent in this passage: There is a universal principle
that male and female distinctions are part of the creation
order. These distinctions are to be reflected in dress and
action. Such is a valid principle for all times. However, there
is also a particular application. In Paul's day, the way to
maintain this order was by the headcoverings and other symbols which reflected sexual distinctions and purity. If a man
was to wear a woman's full headcover, this (at the time)
would have been a blatant "transvestite" act. Paul did not
intend his particular instructions to be binding for all times.
Therefore, the yarmulke is permitted under the concept of
Biblical liberty. We trust that liberty in the Messiah shall
prevail. It seems that the headcovering of Paul's day has little
relation to the yarmulke.

Of greater concern is the danger that wearing a yarmulke might profess submission to Rabbinic tradition and
orthodoxy. Messianic Jews need to weigh this in their
practice.

Biblical Food and Cleanliness Laws
Leviticus 11-16; Deuteronomy 14

It is a difficult task to understand the food and cleanliness laws of these chapters. There are many possibilities of interpretation. There is the "health" explanation repeated by Elmer Josephson in *God's Key to Health and Happiness* as well as in many other publications. This view holds that the avoidance of the foods on these lists prevented disease since the various animals forbidden as unclean were dangerous for human consumption. The ban against touching dead bodies, animals and the rule of uncleanness in regards to issues of blood, leprosy, and emissions of all kinds are interpreted as safeguards against contamination and possible disease. Some animals on the list certainly are known today to have adverse health effects. Some critics argue that even the best preparation of pork does not prevent trichinosis. However, although God's stipulations here do have a connection with health, one has to stretch an argument a bit far to find hygienic reasons for every rule. Why for example, is a mother unclean only 33 days after giving birth to a male, but 66 days after giving birth to a female? Other laws in the list are also problematic. Why is one unclean after sexual intercourse?

A second explanation, which is still held widely, was given great scholarly support in the *Old Testament Commentary* of Keil and Deiletch. They argued that the clean and unclean distinctions were symbolic reminders of sin or fallenness. Since death entered the world through sin, and all those born since Adam would be transgressors, all things connected with birth and death render one unclean. Unclean animals are scavengers; they feed off death. Touching that which is dead is an intimate contact with "the wages of sin." Sexual intercourse is itself not sinful, but will be the means of perpetuating a race that is fallen, although in the light of redemption such perpetuation is desirable. In addition, birth falls under the same symbol of making unclean. Leprosy is symbolic of that indwelling sinful nature. Other disease conditions also reflect fallenness and render one unclean. The woman sinned first, so a 66-day period of uncleanness is a reminder of this fact, while a 33-day period reminds us of Adam's sin.

A third explanation is that of Mary Douglas, who holds that the lists reflect something of a distinction between the ancient ideas of wholeness and fit and that which did not fit and was therefore abhorrent. Hence, fish have scales, but that which is like a fish but lacks scales is lacking in wholeness.

Perhaps these three explanations for the clean-unclean distinctions and the forbidden food lists all have some value. The evidence is certainly not so clear as to justify dogmatism. We should note, however, that the unclean person was in some cases isolated, a clear disease preventative, and was *forbidden during the specified period from participation in the Temple and its sacrificial system.* This system was to reflect purity, holiness and the wholeness of redemption. One could be unclean until evening, and then take a bath and become clean, or unclean seven days, or for the duration of the disease. In some aspects, therefore, the clean-unclean distinctions are for the age of the Temple which has been superseded for us in Yeshua during this age.

THE IMPORTANCE OF
MESSIANIC JEWISH CONGREGATIONS

Some having read thus far might conclude with us that it is valid and expedient for Messianic Jews to maintain their Jewish identity and practice. They would, however, question why it is important for Messianic Jews to form congregations. Wouldn't it be possible for Messianic Jews to be part of non-Jewish New Testament fellowships while maintaining their individual and family Jewish identity as well as their involvement in the Jewish community? Yes it is possible. There are some strong individuals who have done this, even maintaining regular synagogue attendance. We do not desire to dissuade these people from their patterns, but invite them to simply weigh their stance in terms of effectiveness for God's kingdom.

For most people, however, such a strong individualistic

stance is simply not practical. Messianic congregations can
provide many necessary functions for God's Kingdom. They
provide a unique corporate witness of the Messiahship of
Yeshua to the Jewish community. They are the most forceful
visible testimony that Jewish believers have not forsaken
their love of Israel, for their lifestyle and worship is Judaic.
They also testify—by the presence of non-Jewish members—
that Jew and Gentile are one in the Messiah.

In addition, Messianic congregations can uniquely provide for the special ongoing discipleship needs of Jewish
believers who wrestle with the questions of their Jewish
identity and practice vis-a-vis New Testament faith.

The Messianic congregation has the potential to provide
the worship, social, and educational context for raising children of Jewish New Testament believers as Jews with a
strong and secure identity in Yeshua. Additionally, Messianic
Jewish congregations provide the practical means of an ongoing and growing lay witness for Yeshua in the Jewish community. For most people, it would be simply too difficult to
give adequate time to their Jewish heritage and Jewish
community involvements as well as to be adequately involved
in a non-Jewish congregation. But in a Messianic congregation, one is in the universal body and his involvement dove-
tails with his call as a Jew. The eventual end for many not in
Messianic congregations would be slippage from a Jewish life
resulting in a large chance of assimilation for the children of
these Jewish believers in Yeshua. Many Jewish practices are
congregational in nature. The only model other than the
Messianic Jewish congregation which is practical is a congregation that is not Jewish but has a Jewish wing of believers in
Yeshua who maintain their Jewish life together. Some Jews
would not respond to this as well since one of the great testi-
monies of Messianic congregations is that they are self-
supporting and not a missionary arm or "front" for a non-
Jewish group. Yet this certainly is a valid Biblical model.

The studies in missionology in recent times have shown
that the greatest potential for the spread of the Gospel is the
planting of indigenous congregations adapted to the culture

of the people whom they seek to reach. If such indigenous congregations have a strong emphasis on witnessing and discipleship, they are far and away the most effective means of spreading the Kingdom. The Biblical method of spreading the Gospel was just this, to plant congregations that were able to adapt to the needs of the various cultural communities in which they were planted.[10]

LIFE IN A MESSIANIC CONGREGATION

A Messianic congregation is involved in all the tasks of any truly Biblical congregation. It seeks to provide a home of fellowship for its members. This congregational home should be a central focus of the commitment of each member. Indeed, the questions of where we live, work and how we spend our time and money should relate to our primary involvement in the congregation. We are to seek to become one in love, fellowship and mutual ministry. Secondly, we need to seek to use our gifts to build up the Body. We applaud the nationwide movement of believers to live in proximity to one another and to share their lives more deeply on a day-to-day basis.

Additionally, we as congregations need to seek to be witnesses of our faith through a high quality of life in the community of faith. We seek to disciple others in the Scriptures as well as to find the best means to spread the Good News.

The congregational tasks of education, worship services, preaching and counseling are ours as well. Indeed, the Messianic congregation needs to provide the full orbed means of healing and growth which is part of Biblical congregational life. The means of physical healing, inner healing, freedom from oppression, the Messiah's memorial, and the Mikvah of Yeshua (Baptism) are all intrinsic parts of congregational life.

We believe very deeply that life in the Body—with the operation of the ministry gifts of the Spirit in the Body through love (I Corinthians 12-14)—are means of growth which a believer in Yeshua must not forego. Congregational life is the means used by God to encourage, correct, and enable us to grow into maturity, to be like the Messiah! Elder-leadership in congregational life is necessary, as well, to give the congregation direction. Within the bounds of Scriptural truth, we are called to be accountable to one another and to our leaders (Hebrews 13:7,17; I Peter 5). Hence, elder insight and counsel should be a crucial part of our growth and decision-making. Our desire is to teach the walk of faith, to confess the Scriptures that God's gifts and promises would be ours. The victory is ours in Yeshua.

RABBIS, SCHOOLING, AUTHENTICITY

Many have questioned the nature of training for spiritual leaders or congregational leaders who would need to be thoroughly trained in Biblical studies, practical leadership and Jewish studies. There are both institutional and non-institutional means of such training. Presently, many congregations have leadership training and independent supervised study as part of their program. However, we should not eschew the value of an intensive period of study in the best of Jewish and Christian institutions. While we reject intellectual pride, we also recoil from the pride of ignorance, the sin of those who presume to know and cannot see the value of a "formal" education. It is true that a congregational leader is not made by academic training. He must have a call from God that is recognized in the Body. However, superior training for the one so called can produce greater quality, a person with a deeper understanding of the complexity of life and Biblical issues. Such a person is one of deep convictions without dogmatic narrow-mindedness. Liberal Arts training from a Biblical point of view as well as graduate level theological training can be very helpful in producing a person who can relate to others from all walks of life.

The interpretation of difficult Biblical passages, for example, is aided by an understanding of the meaning of the language of the passage(s) in their cultural-semantic context of meaning usage. Archaeological and linguistic studies are helpful here. Further help is available in seeing how others have spiritually perceived the passage throughout history. This will lead to a prayerful conclusion that has a measurable degree of objectivity. If we are to test the Spirit by the Word, objective means of interpretation are crucial. Such information is required by our very Biblical translators in their work; so we eschew such study to our detriment (as the proverbial man who saws off the limb on which he sits).

A knowledge of Jewish and Christian history provides us with a knowledge of the gains and mistakes of the past, even vividly illustrating the terrible results of destructive paths of interpretation and action. God has worked in the history of His people and he who will not learn from history is bound to repeat its errors.

At present, several schools of training have come into existence. A list of schooling opportunities is available through the Union of Messianic Jewish Congregations. The Union also sponsors its own summer yeshiva program. Those who do not choose such options must prayerfully seek the best education they can receive in the various needed areas of theology, Bible, Judaica, and practical leadership. Reading, courses at nearby schools, and guidance from a spiritual leader all can be part of a general program of training. We would suggest that the trainee and his mentor keep a record of all practical and theoretical training.

Should Messianic leaders be called rabbis if they have adequate training and fulfill the leadership position? The title originally implied "Master," "my great one" and is applied today to ordained Jewish spiritual leaders. In seeking a close identification with Jewish community practice, some believers might desire to call their leaders Rabbi. Yeshua, however, said,

"But you are not to be called Rabbi, for you have one Teacher, and you are all brethren. And call no man Father on earth; for you have one Father, who is in heaven. Neither be called masters, for you have one Master, the Messiah. He who is greatest among you shall be your servant, whoever exalts himself will be humbled and whoever humbles himself will be exalted" (Matthew 23:8-12).

Some Messianic Jews have held that such a structure was given in the light of those who sought the title for pride; but most Messianic Jews use the term only out of love for the Jewish community. Furthermore, they argue the term today connotes teacher and elder, not "great one."

Men desire titles of acclaim. Yeshua teaches us to forego them. Perhaps Messianic Judaism is meant to contrast with other forms of Judaism in regard to titles. We, at least, should feel a sense of uneasiness in the use of titles in the light of Yeshua's teaching. Elder brothers seem to be the highest titles of use among the first Jewish believers because of Matthew 23:8, perhaps we would do well to follow their example. If the term Rabbi is used with this in mind, in a humble context, we would not, however, object.

CHAPTER EIGHT

Extra-Biblical Practices

From the lighting of candles to inaugurate Shabbat to an order of prescribed liturgical services, Judaism has developed many extra-Biblical traditional practices. In addition, Jewish rabbinical leadership has developed a host of applications of Torah, as recorded in the Talmud and the Responsa (body of Rabbinic literature in response to community questions). This application material is known as Halakah (way).

Messianic Jews may value some of the traditions of Judaism. We note that any expression or practice must be judged on the basis of Scripture. Therefore, seek to understand and evaluate Jewish practices and teachings. However, we are not bound by tradition as a legalistic straitjacket, but follow the leading of the Spirit in practical reflection.

For example, Orthodox Judaism prescribes the number of daily services so as to keep accord with the periods of sacrifice in the ancient Temple. Must Messianic Jews be concerned to keep Shacharit (morning), Mincah (afternoon), and Maariv (evening) services according to the Rabbinic directives? We could perhaps conceive of a situation in an Orthodox community where Messianic Jews would desire to do so, especially remembering how all the sacrificial periods find their locus of meaning in Yeshua. However, for most Messianic Jews it is not practical or desireable to be so rigidly tied.

All practices and traditions are to be evaluated according to Scriptural teaching, taking great pains to study it with depth and care. Each community of faith must seek God's leading in ministering to the unique situation it serves.

Messianic Jews should respect the Jewish application of the Torah, Halakah, while at the same time reserving the right to criticize it in love. Yeshua Himself warned, "You make vain the Word of God by your traditions." Traditions must never blind us to the heart intent of the Word. They would then become more prominent than the Word.

There are some guidelines for approaching Halakah: The reapplication of Scriptural teaching for new situations *is an absolutely necessary task in every generation.* A little maturity of thought shows this to be the case. Scripture commands us to build a fence on our roofs (Deuteronomy 22:8). It also advises a full veil over the head and face for women who give prophecy (I Corinthians 11:5). Most believers today follow neither of these commands literally. Why? Because Scripture advises us to *follow the Spirit of the Law,* which gives life, not the letter, which kills. We recognize that the command of fence-building was given for those who lived in flat-roofed homes and used the roofs as porches. This law was an application of the command to "love thy neighbor" (Leviticus 19:18). We would apply the Law today by advising the repair of sidewalks and keeping them free from ice in winter.

The head veil was commended in an age when, for many, it was an important symbol of marital faithfulness. The foregoing of the veil caused new believers in Yeshua to be spoken of negatively by the unbelieving community, since it supposedly brought shame to the body. With no such common connection of the veil to fidelity or to submission, some communites today forego the practice as of no modern relevance. Others have advised, instead, a small symbolic headcovering to recall what they see as a truth concerning fidelity and submission. In all of these examples the believing communities have sought the Spirit—or heart intent—of the Scripture in their application of the Law. In other words, they have engaged in Halakic reasoning.

Halakic reasoning is as necessary today as ever. Halakic reasoning is pre-Yeshuic: Since Moses, Jewish leaders have applied the principles introduced in the Law to new situations. The body of Oral Law found in the Talmud is sometimes most ancient and at other times reflective of very late applications (1st-4th century). Although the principles of Halakic reasoning date back to Moses by his designation of judges who would produce a tradition of legal applications (just as the record of judicial canon in the United States), we cannot hold the belief that is held by some Orthodox Jews that the basic content of the whole Talmud was orally delivered by Moses and passed on generation to generation. We respect Halakah as ancient, but never as Scripture's equal.

We must also note that the Halakic tradition is a "mixed-bag." Sometimes there are brilliant applications of the Scriptural heart intent of the Law. At other times, however, the tradition seeks to maintain the letter and multiples structures and directions that tend to contradict the very intent of Scripture. Yeshua, for example, saw the multiplication of non Biblical Sabbath restrictions as destroying the intended joy and peace of the seventh day. On the other hand, there are Rabbinic applications of justice in business dealings which are brilliant in maintaining a true sense of Scripture's call for just weights and measures.

How does a Messianic Jew approach Halakah? He seeks to return to the original Biblical teaching and understand it in context. Is the Law (or command) a direct universal moral principle (e.g., "Thou shalt not commit adultery"), or is it an application of moral principle, building a fence on the roof (Deuteronomy 22:8). Universal moral principles are to guide all believers in the Spirit. This holds for both Old and New Testament commandments.

Is the particular Law part of Israel's heritage in celebrating God's grace in her history? Is it part of Israel's God-given national-cultural identity rooted in the Abrahamic Covenant (Feasts, Shabbat, circumcision) which has application to Jews today? Can it be followed practically both in the land

and in the Diaspora? Is it so intended?

Or, is the Law part of Israel's priestly Temple sacrificial system which has been fulfilled during this age in Yeshua and is observed by recalling how His work is the essence of the practice?

Having ascertained the basic sense of the Biblical teaching in the light of its original historical context and New Testament teaching, we can next look at Rabbinic tradition. We may here find an illustration of the *wrong* road to take. This would be helpful in clarifying our direction. Or we may find a brilliant application that helps us to appropriate the teaching in our day. The issues of our society—medical-ethical issues, divorce, environmental concerns, food adulteration, war and vast armies, community destruction—all require our best logical and prayerful efforts as mature believers.

The Christian Church has its own halakic tradition in a sense; and we need to recognize its particular historic involvement in seeking to apply Old and New Testament Scriptural truth. Our approach should also take into account the Christian tradition, recognizing its strengths as well as its departures from a Biblically-specific approach to the issues involved. A comparison of Jewish and Christian interpretations can therefore be most instructive.

Our goal, however, should always be to discern the Spirit. Our minds should be submissive to the Word of God, humbly seeking God's direction—without pride or narrow dogmatism. If we love Israel, our involvement will show respect as well as disagreement.

Kashrut —"Do you keep kosher?" This is a common question addressed to Messianic Jews. The usual answer is yes; but not rabbinical kosher—Biblical kosher! Keeping Biblical Kashrut was explained in the last chapter and mainly involved avoiding the forbidden foods listed in Leviticus and Deuteronomy. However, the Rabbinical meaning of the word "Kashrut" or Kosher is much more extensive. Rabbinical Kashrut is built on the command, "You shall not boil a kid in its mother's milk" (Exodus 23:19).

The ancient rabbis adopted the principle of building a fence around the Torah. This meant creating additional laws—which were actually more rigid than the Torah—to prevent the breaking of Torah itself. This, however, produced a great burdensome legalism. The reasoning went as follows: How can we know for sure that the animal we cook in milk is not the offspring of the mother from whom we get the milk? Couldn't this accidentally happen? Well, it is remote but possible! Therefore we will never cook meat in milk. However, to make sure we don't cook meat in milk we should perhaps avoid eating meat and milk together. But what constitutes eating meat and milk together? There may be a particle of a dairy product left on the plate which mixes with a later meat product. To avoid this, why not separate dishes for meat and for milk? Furthermore, a prescribed number of hours between meat and milk meals should be followed to avoid mixing milk and meat by mouth. A Kosher product therefore has no blood and no mixture of milk and meat in it. This is the progression of reasoning.

As for Kashrut in this Rabbinical sense, we believe that everyone should be led by the Spirit. Is God leading the person to a special level of identification whereby he or she will practice the full rules of Rabbinic Kashrut? Or would this be too restrictive even for our general social relationships in the Jewish community to which we minister? Everyone must seek God in this. Certainly there is no requirement in these matters for Messianic Jews. If one wishes to entertain Orthodox Jews in one's home, Rabbinic Kashrut becomes a necessity.

The Life Cycle—(Birth, Puberty, Marriage, Death). As in many cultures, Judaism has developed its "rites of passage." These are traditions and ceremonies which mark the passage from one stage of life to another. Such ceremonies and traditions enhance the meaning of these events.

The first of these rites are connected to birth. They include circumcision for the male on the eighth day, and synagogue dedication for the female. In both cases, the child is offered to the service of God. Messianic Jewish parents

commit themselves to raise the child as part of Israel as well
as in the *fullness* (this is a time for the whole community to
rejoice) of New Covenant faith and life.

The *Pidyon ha ben* (redemption of first-born son) is a
ceremony recalling the redemption of the first-born son. In
ancient Egypt, the first born of Israel were spared in the
judgment of God over the land of Egypt. The destroying angel
passed-over (Passover) the homes that had the Passover
lambs' blood upon the door. Later, the Levites as a tribe were
chosen to serve God in the work of ministry in place of all the
first-born sons of Israel. God, instead, commanded a special
gift and sacrifice for the redemption of the first born. The
Jewish tradition symbolically enacts the payment of five
coins to a cohen (priest) as the redemption of the first-born
son. This reminds us that the ancient sacrifices and offerings
were used for sustaining the priesthood.

Messianic Jews may symbolically engage in the *pidyon
ha ben* as well, recalling that the ancient Israelites were given
a system of sacrifice whose central meaning was to point to
Yeshua. We recall also the Passover, for the first-born sons
spared in Egypt were our ancestors. However, our rite should
extoll the fact Yeshua is now our redemptive sacrifice and
our Passover. He is our high priest, and in Him, not only our
first born, but all who come to Him in faith may have
redemption.

The second rite of passage is from childhood to adulthood.
Most cultures mark this time at the age of 13, when children
reach puberty. It is the age of early sexual ability wherein the
children, if married, would be capable of producing offspring.
Maturity should be not just a physical attribute, but an
entrance into more mature adult responsibility. Hence, after
a period of training in Scripture and Judaism, the child is
invited to participate in the Sabbath service as an adult to
read the Torah, and to affirm that he has made Israel's faith
and responsibility his own: he is "bar mitzvah" or "son of the
Commandment." Bat Mitzvah, daughter of the Commandment, is also applied to young women in Reform and Conser-
vative traditions. In a Messianic Jewish context, we seek to

avoid the greed and materialism that hav~ ᴊecome so prominent in the Bar Mitzvah rites of today.

Rather, it should be a time where the child is seriously, in
conscience, confirming his faith in God and Yeshua. He
would then be committing himself to live in accordance with
the Scriptures. The Bar or Bat Mitzvah child should have a
basic Scriptural and Jewish knowledge. The involvement in
major parts of the service is a recognition of the child's commitment and our renewed desire to respect him or her as a
young adult. Specific materials for training in Hebrew and
other areas are readily available at Jewish bookstores.

One significant question is the need for rites of passage
for the non-Jewish members of the Messianic congregation.
Non-Jewish babies should also be dedicated to God. In addition, because we are one in the Messiah, the non-Jewish child
should be confirmed, not as a Jew, but as one who is a spiritual
child of Abraham, an ingrafted branch. Commitment to God
can thereby be expressed. The child also can participate in
those parts of the service which are not specifically connected
to affirming a Jewish identity. Such a child is affirming his
support of God's work in the world through Israel, his special
call of love and solidarity with Messianic Jews, and his faith in
God's work in the true Christian church.

Marriage is the next major rite of passage. It is in marriage that a man and a woman leave their parents to cleave
unto one another and become "echad," one flesh. In the Jewish tradition, marriage is a gala joyous event. Ancient customs have become a significant part of Jewish weddings.
Some of these are:

The Vows of Betrothal, which are today incorporated
into the marriage vows themselves. However, in ancient
times, the betrothal (engagement) took place a year before
the marriage. It was as absolutely binding as marriage, even
though the couple did not marry and consummate their relationship until a year later. Unfaithfulness during betrothal
was considered adultery. Thus we find that when Joseph
discovered his wife Miriam (Mary) was pregnant before they
had come together, he was desirous of divorcing her pri-

vately. Later of course, he found that the child was a super-natural product of the Spirit of God.

The Hupah is a very special canopy under which the marrying couple exchange vows. It is either free standing or held up by the groom's attendants. His prayer tallit would be on top of the canopy. This symbolizes the groom taking the bride under his roof, she becoming part of his house. It also symbolizes their desire to be a faithful family of Israel.

The Seven Benedictions are often chanted. They prayer-fully give thanks for the marriage as well as voicing special hopes for the family and the community.

The Blessing Over the Wine, a great symbol of joy, enhances the wedding as one of the most joyous events in Israel.

The Breaking of the Glass at the end of the wedding by the groom is an ancient symbol of sorrow. Even in the midst of our joy, we are not to forget the destruction of the Temple and of Jerusalem. Others have seen in the shattering of glass a symbol of finality in which the marriage vows are expressed.

In a Messianic Jewish context, such symbols are present along with Scriptural material pertaining to marriage. The couple also tends to tailor their ceremony to individually express themselves as well as their faith in Yeshua. The congregational spiritual leader guides them in this process.

The Ketubah is a marriage covenant agreement which now comes in several forms. In ancient times, the Ketubah emphasized the promissory price to be paid the bride in the event of divorce. Such was meant to be a preventative in the light of a looser Jewish interpretation of the meaning of divorce than found in the New Testament. Yeshua only allowed divorce between believers on the ground of adultery (Matthew 5:31-32).

The largest question in Messianic Judaism as regards marriage is the question of intermarriage: Jews were forbid-den to marry "pagans" and assimilate. However, any fol-lower of Yeshua is no longer unclean and is certainly not to be considered a pagan. Many have been hurt by what have been taken as insensitive statements against Gentile singles seeking to marry Jews.

In the Messiah, the primary question is one of calling, not physical origin. Since Jews are called to maintain their identity with Israel the main question is: Is God truly leading the non-Jewish person to take up a Jewish life-style and adopt a Jewish family as a lifetime commitment? We cannot preclude such a match because of physical origins any more than the match of Ruth and Boaz. Each couple and individual should prayerfully seek God's leading for their life in this serious step. For the non-Jewish partner this entails a public commitment to identify as Ruth ("your people shall be my people"). For the man, this could entail circumcision. Care must be taken to assure that the calling is from God and not a rationalization of some romantic or marital desire.

It is very possible that God's Spirit may lead many to marry only those with physical Jewish roots for a special witness to Jewish people, who might not accept the Jewish calling of a non-Jewish believer. However, this should be by the leading of the Spirit, not by legalistic principles. We, both Jews and Gentiles, are one in the Messiah. In Him we are called to different lifestyles and to perhaps witness to and through different communities. However, we must be "up front" in our witness and honestly convey that we are New Covenant congregations where Jew and Gentile have become one in the Messiah.

Special recognition of commitment to Jewish identity for a non-Jewish partner (conversion) is presently a matter for each Messianic community to decide since there is no central authority to which Messianic Judaism looks.

Death—The last great rite of passage in Judaism is, of course, death. Many of the practices surrounding death are for the benefit of those who are left behind to carry on in this realm of space and time.

In no area do we find the Jewish traditions to be more consistent with Biblical values than in the case of the treatment of the bereaved in death. Jewish practices in regards to death are not Biblically consistent in every area; but in most areas, a great deal of wisdom is found. We reject, for example, the Jewish practice of praying for the dead since the Scripture indicates that our destiny is fixed in this life.

Judaism prescribes simplicity in funeral practices. When a relative dies, the family is not to seek an ostentatious funeral. Expenses are to be kept to a minimum to reflect that in death all are equal. We brought nothing into the world and we can take nothing out of the world. It is thus traditional to bury the deceased body in a white shroud; and, although this is not necessary, to do so is in accord with the Biblical perspectives. It is also culturally traditional to only have the closest friends and relatives involved with the mourner during this period. Many Jewish communities have burial societies that will voluntarily prepare the body for burial. This would be preparation for a traditional burial without embalming. Helping in this way is considered a great privilege.

During the mourning period, it is customary for the closest friends to bring meals to the immediate family.

The Jewish funeral is a closed casket memorial service. Since the person is no longer in the body, it is taught that we should not seek to glorify and attach ourselves to the body. Instead of flowers, it is recommended that gifts in memorial of the deceased be given to charity or worthy ministries.

After the funeral, a friend would often provide food and hospitality to those who come from out of town. Another friend would provide a meal for only the closest friends and relatives of the immediate family. This shelters the mourners from dealing with crowds of people. The first mourner's meal is usually simple, an egg traditionally being the first food (the egg is a symbol of mourning and sacrifice). The funeral service itself is a simple reading of Scripture and a time to recall the life of the deceased.

The seven days after burial are the Shivah period. During this time, the mourner receives callers at home for comfort. The institution of a mourning period is Judaism's recognition that, although the deceased lives with God, the separation is a difficult trial to be faced. The separation of death is not natural but is part of the Fall. Rather than suppressing mourning by spiritual platitudes, we need to be able to honestly cry, to face the hurt of loss and to share this burden with others. The New Covenant Scriptures, for example, never teach that we are not to mourn, but that because of the hope of the resurrection, "we mourn not as those who have no hope" (cf. I Corinthians 15:19; I Thessalonians 4:3-18).

The practice of Saying Kaddish is a common tradition. The Kaddish *is not* a prayer for the dead and was not instituted to be a prayer for the dead. It is a prayer of praise to God and of longing for His Kingdom. It was instituted to teach that we are to praise God at all times, whether in joy or in sorrow. Thus the Kaddish gives glory to God and reflects well upon those who have died if prayed with this understanding. Rather than saying Kaddish *for* the deceased by a son, etc., Messianic Jews need to recover these original intents of the Kaddish. Any mourner may say the Kaddish in praise to God: husband, wife, child, parent, or friend. The Kaddish is here translated:

"Glorified and sanctified be the Great name of God in the world which He has created according to His will. May He establish His Kingdom during your days and during the days of the whole house of Israel at a near time speedily and soon, and say Amen.

"May His Great name be praised forever, glorified and exalted, extolled and honored, and praised and magnified be the Name of the Holy One, blessed be He, whose glory transcends, yea is beyond all blessing and praise and consolation which is uttered in the world, and say Amen.

"May there be great peace from heavens upon us and upon all Israel, and say Amen.

"May He who makes peace from the heavens, grant peace upon us and upon all Israel, and say Amen."

The basic structure of the Kaddish is most ancient. Yeshua himself repeated the content of the first two lines of the Kaddish when he taught His disciples to pray saying,

"Our Father who art in heaven, hallowed be thy name. Thy Kingdom come, thy will be done on earth as it is in heaven . . ."

It is traditional for the Kaddish to be said by the closest

appropriate kin for eleven months; but there need be no limit
to its use in a Messianic context. Messianic Jews may see the
Lord's Prayer as more appropriate than the Kaddish. I have
composed a New Covenant Kaddish on this basis.

After the seven-day mourning period, the mourner
enters back into the usual pattern of life, albeit a quieter life.
In this period, other friends may visit. For eleven months the
mourner is especially reminded to praise God and recall his
loss. After eleven months the mourning period ends.

The spiritual and psychological value and sense of these
practices is incalculable. It recognizes our need to express our
loss, to be emotionally and mentally honest. We know that
suppressing mourning produces later emotional and psychological damage. The New Covenant directs us to look to God
for comfort, to trust Him and praise Him despite our loss. In
Yeshua this is possible because of the clearer knowledge of
the resurrection to eternal life in Him. Judaism counsels us
to have a real period of mourning, intense for seven days,
moderate for 30 days, and 11 months for progressively coming
out of our mourning. However, after 11 months the mourning period is over. The New Covenant shows us not to wallow
in sadness forever, but to get on with the business of living
and loving God!

Judaism also includes Yiskor or memorial services during various holiday seasons as well as memorial practices for
the anniversary of death. The New Covenant reminds us of
departed saints to inspire us with the memory of those whose
lives are spiritual examples to us.

KABBALISM AND HASIDISM

The Kabbalah is an ancient Jewish mystical tradition.
This tradition is primarily based in the Zohar, a late Middle-
Age compilation of mystical ideas of God and creation, nume-
rology, concepts of redemption and magic. From the Messianic Jewish perspective, the Kabbalistic tradition is truly a
mixed-bag. At times, one can find within Kabbalism the most
profound and Biblically-valid thoughts on everything from

the Messiah's suffering for sin to even a Triune concept of the unity of God. However, Kabbalism also contains concepts from magic and paganism.

Gershom Shalom, in his monumental book, *Major Trends in Jewish Mysticism*, shows that Kabbalism has roots in second and third century gnosticism. Gnosticism was a religious approach from paganism that influenced *heterodox* Christianity and Judaism. Gnosticism was a system that taught salvation by the way of a secret knowledge of spiritual and magical realities which was only to be conveyed to initiates. This secret knowledge assured passage after death unto salvation as well as a means to tap into spiritual powers whereby current events and situations could be manipulated. When the Kabbalah partakes of these magical and gnostic viewpoints, the Messianic Jew judges it to be dangerously occult and to be avoided. Yet not everything in Kabbalism is of this nature. No one but the most spiritually mature should seek to discern the difference between the strands of tradition.

The Chasidic Movement flourished in the eighteenth century and continues to this day. It traces its origins to the Baal Shem Tov, the Lord of the Good Name. Today's Chasidim are strictly Orthodox Jews; but in the beginning, the Chasidic Movement was considered to be heterodox. Martin Buber has sought to give us an appreciation for this movement.

Chasidism was a renewal movement within Judaism which brought exuberance, passion and dance back into a religion that many considered arid. However, the Chasidic leaders, although greatly interested in Torah and Talmud (traditional Jewish areas of study and practice), also were greatly influenced by and involved in Kabbalism. The Mitnagdeem, the Orthodox establishment of the day, condemned Chasidism. Usually a picture is painted of the Mitnagdeem as dry scholars with no spiritual life who rejected the Chasidim, who were themselves full of love, fervor and energy. It was not so simple. The Mitnagdeem not only recoiled at the untraditional actions in Chasidic life and worship, but at what they considered involvement in magic and heretical concepts!

In the Chasidic literature, we find many stories of rabbis who lost their minds in Kabbalism. There were many who dabbled in magic. However, there were other leaders who eschewed the magical aspects of Chasidism. Stories in the literature note the extreme dangers for even the most spiritual who became involved in magical means to produce certain ends or to bring the Kingdom of God. Some almost lost their lives. The dangers of Kabbalism are certainly at least reflected in the stories; yet, via the Zohar, the dangers exist even to the present day.

The Chasidic stories also recount teaching and examples that are closer to New Testament teachings and attitudes. The incredible example of Zusia, who allows himself to be abused for the sake of others, but thoroughly loves his enemies, is a primary example. The love of God and of neighbor, mercy and justice, are reflected in profound yet simple stories of great beauty. These aspects of Chasidism make it a great attraction to the rootless young today.

CHAPTER NINE

Jewish and Biblical Worship

Jewish worship historically has been based on a traditional prayer book called the *Siddur*. However, the earliest Talmudic statements also call for recognizing the importance of spontaneous prayer as well. The Talmud also eschews the use of written prayers in a rote way, requiring that in our meditations, the prayer truly becomes the prayer of our hearts. Today's society is anti-institutional. Organized religion is rejected and so are its trappings. A prayer book to many is just one of those expendable items from "dead" institutional religion. This is especially the case for those who grew up in Judaism and recited the prayers in Hebrew without understanding a word of what they were saying. The viewpoint which arises from such experiences is biased as we shall see. Action taken on this basis is absolutely unbalanced.

Our age is media-crazed and entertainment-oriented. Entertainment is fast-paced and active. We have no patience for more delicate pleasures and subtle joys. We require the ubiquitous television—not a good biography; a pummeling drumbeat, not classical Mozart. This, in part, influences our disenfranchisement with traditional worship forms which use prescribed materials.

Biblical worship has a place for dance and exuberance; but it *also* has a place for the softer joys of quiet reflection and written prayer.

God has revealed Himself in a written Word, in classical communication. Closeness to God requires recapturing a reading and meditative ability that our culture has lost. Our mass media culture produces shallow people who cannot think for themselves, who are easily manipulated. This culture is opposed to the values of the Word of God.

God, too, gave the first prayer book, which is known as the Book of Psalms. Why are there written prayers to be recited, memorized, chanted and sung? So that we might learn to pray more deeply, with a greater content of praise and intercession! The Psalms teach us from one of the greatest praying giants in history, King David. They also teach us from the best of Israel's prayer warriors. Evidently, God certainly considers written prayer of value. Nothing is so boring as the same "spontaneous prayer" without depth, rotely repeated week after week! Written and spontaneous prayers can both be rote!

We note, first, that the Psalms make up a good bulk of the Siddur. The second greatest concentration is made up of prayers composed of *Scriptural* verses and phrases interwoven. The rest of the Siddur is comprised of prayers composed by various leaders throughout Jewish history. Some of these prayers are truly in the spirit of the Scriptures; others are not. In responding to these non-biblical prayers we must use discernment.

A few sentiments expressed arise from a Kabbalistic background: Dangers are present in the Kabbalah. When a person uses the *content* of the Siddur in Messianic Jewish worship, he should only pray with Scriptural content.

"Teach us to pray," the disciples asked Yeshua. Yeshua then taught them the prayer recorded in Matthew 6:9-13, "Our Father who art in heaven, hallowed by thy name . . . ." The value of the Siddur's prayers and the Psalms as well as other prayers that Messianic Jews may compose is that they teach us to pray with a depth of Scriptural *content* and beauty which improved the level of our own spontaneous prayer. Scripture teaches, ". . . if we ask anything according to his will he hears us, and we know that if he hears us, we know that we have obtained the things requested of Him" (I John 5:14-15). As our heart in prayer is akin to God's heart, we pray in His will. We are aided in praying in His will if we learn to pray according to the Word.

Messianic Jewish worship should therefore incorporate the best Biblical content of ancient prayer and Biblically-based hymns from the ancient Psalms to new Messianic Jewish compositions. This material may be used with newly-written modern Jewish music. The material can be used in Hebrew or English. What is of importance, however, is that the material conveys *meaningful content,* not just that a ritual form is maintained.

Traditionalism, as contrasted with drawing upon rich traditions, feels constrained, however, to maintain the same prayer forms with exactitude—week after week. Those under the power of traditionalism are offended if the ancient material is used in new ways. For most Jewish people today— especially in America—there must be a freshness in worship. Hence, there should be a place for celebration, spontaneous worship and praise, as well as using traditional content in new ways. We can vary which traditional content is included in services and how it is used as the Spirit leads worship. Will it be a choral piece, or a meditation, or chant? Stewart Dauerman, musical director of Jews for Jesus, is working on putting the Amidah, the great ancient Jewish prayer of Nineteen Benedictions, to modern-sounding Jewish music. His rendition of the second Benediction on the promise of the resurrection, called "Melek Ozair," is a beautiful worship song. Hebrew and English are both sung in this song. Recently, *David and Lisa Lodan* (in Israel) have also put the Amidah and other Jewish prayers to music for congregations there. We can indeed mediate valuable ancient content in new ways.

It is important for Messianic Jews to seek a balance between the value of tradition and that of spontaneity. We must neither fall into rote traditionalism nor contentless emotionalism in worship. We must flow with the Spirit while allowing the richness of the Biblical and Jewish heritage to

take root among us. Those with differing gifts can blend har-
moniously. The modern guitarist can be used as well as the
cantor to bring an offering in righteousness to the Lord.

A few words should be said about the specific nature of
prayer in the Jewish tradition. The pre-second century
Jewish tradition is well in accord with Philippians 4:6-9,
which teaches to give thanks in all things. Hence, the basic
form of Jewish prayer is the benediction which begins with
this opening: "Blessed are you, O Lord our God, King of the
universe, who . . ." then adds the content of the praise or the
request. The prayer closes with a *seal,* which repeats the
"Blessed are you, O Lord, king of the universe . . ." a phrase
in accord with the basic prayer. If the blessings are part of one
prayer—as in the great prayer known as the Amidah—an
opening will suffice for a whole group of blessings and only
the seal will be included to end the blessing before new
content begins the next blessing. Ancient Judaism's prayers
were faith confessions. God is not just requested to heal the
sick; He is blessed as the healer of the sick: it shall be done,
since it is according to God's character and promise. God is
not just requested to restore Jerusalem, but is thanked for
that restoration since it is assured in His promises.

Most basic to Jewish prayer are the Psalms. Central to all
Jewish services are Scripture portions known as the "Sh'ma,"
which incorporate Deuteronomy 6:4 ff, Deuteronomy 11:13-21
and Numbers 15:37-41. Israel is herein reminded to remember
that the Lord alone is God, and we are to love the Lord with all
our heart, soul, and might. These passages also call the nation
to obedience to God in every area of life. Two blessings lead to
the Sh'ma and praise God for his love and wisdom. They are
"Creator of luminaries" and "with abounding love."

The prayer known as the "Amidah" or "Shemoneh
Esreh," also known as *the prayer*, is similarly central to Jewish worship. This prayer of Eighteen Blessings (actually 19
since the fifteenth was later added), praises God for His faithfulness as the God of our fathers, for the resurrection, for His
healing, for His restoration of Israel and much else.

Other great prayers or chants which are part of the

service are: the "Kaddish," the prayer of praise said by mourners as well as by the congregation in various parts of the service; the "Yigdal," the confession of faith, based on Maimonides' Thirteen Articles of Faith, which has been revised for Messianic Jews in "The God of Abraham Praise," the "Alenu," a prayer of praise and call to responsibility for Israel as a witness people; the "Adon Olam" hymn on the majesty of God and His faithfulness; and many others.

In summary, the major traditional service elements would, in order, be: the Psalms, the Sh'ma, the Amidah, the Kaddish, Yigdal, Alenu and Adon Olam. Also central to Jewish worship on Shabbat, Monday and Thursday is the Torah service. This includes blessings which praise God for giving the Torah as well as ancient songs which celebrate the giving of the Law. The prophets (Haftorah) are also read and, in Messianic Jewish congregations, New Testament readings are added. Messianic congregations which have a Torah service tailor various elements of ancient and modern worship into a meaningful period of praise. The Scriptures are read in Hebrew or English, sometimes concurrently. A commentary ties together the readings in the light of New Testament fulfillment.

Many prayers of confession and praise are also especially used on Holy days, and a special prayer book, known as the *Matzor*, has been issued for these holidays. It incorporates the daily and Shabbat content with all the Holy Day additions.

Some of the High Holyday prayers are noteworthy for their content. After the "Al Het" (for the sin) prayer of confession, congregants ask to be forgiven in the light of Abraham's merit and the sacrifice of Isaac. The sacrifice of Isaac is a great pointer to the sacrifice of Yeshua; and the truth of the Messiah's suffering for sin. Prayers of confession are the the purpose of self-examination as required by Scripture (I Corinthians 11:28-"Let a man examine himself . . . "). We pray for forgiveness, not only for ourselves, but for the whole community of Israel which has sinned. We do not pray as those whose forgivenss is in question, for the Scriptures say "If we confess our sin, he is faithful and just to forgive our sins and to cleanse us from all unrighteousness (I John 1:9). "Scripture calls us, as believers, to confess our sin. Such times of prayer can be used as meaningful occasions for the Holy Spirit to search our hearts by the Word and these Biblically-based prayers. The time can also be used to redirect our steps, priorities and commitments on a more solidly Biblical basis for the following year in the light of a self-examination of the previous year.

Messianic Judaism is developing a worship "in Spirit and in truth" that truly reflects Messianic Jewish calling and identity. It is a worship that primarily glorifies God and His Messiah. It has the verve and exuberance of the Spirit along with the depth of Biblical content. It avoids a simplistic chorus worship without recounting great Scriptural truths, while having a place for simple and beautiful songs.

The times of Orthodox Jewish worship services parallel the times of various ancient sacrifices in the Temple. "Musaf," the additional service, for example, parallels the additional sacrifice on Shabbat. Most Messianic Jews have not tied themselves to these times. However if they do gather at any of the traditional times—such as the Shachreet (morning sacrifice time) service—they would do well to recall the times of sacrifice as an occasion to remember Yeshua's sacrifice and His fulfillment of the meaning of sacrifice.

The daily service also includes the reading of Genesis 22, the sacrifice of Isaac, which is considered to be a sacrifice that merits our forgiveness. This is a harbinger of Yeshua's sacrifice, in detail, and easily causes us to rejoice in Him. Prayers for grace after meals also appeal to the memory of Messiah for forgiveness.

CHAPTER TEN

Dangers To Be Faced

Messianic Judaism faces trials and tribulations in many areas. As a relatively new—yet ancient—movement, the presence of mature, discerning leaders and congregants is proportionately lower than in other groups. There is a need for theological maturity so that the Scriptures will be a solid foundation for all our endeavors.

These dangers are instrinsic in the fledgling Messianic Jewish movement:

Legalism. In some quarters, a legalistic sense of "ought" in relation to tradition has taken root. Indeed, we should draw upon the richness of the Jewish traditions. However, we must, under the Spirit, choose our use of the traditions as He leads. Tradition must not rule us. When the latter occurs, there is a sense of "must" which destroys a sense of freedom and joy. "Must" is a word for Biblical commands; "expedient" is a word for non-Biblical but recommended procedures. Even for Biblical command, however, the sense of obedience must flow from the power of the Spirit in us and our identification with the Messiah.

This sense of "must" produces a feeling of great restraint. Members of the Body who have a legalistic, critical bent (which is all too common among human beings) use conformity to a tradition as the basis for judging others. If a phrase is

changed in a service, or a substitution made, or if a particular
order is changed, there is a response of anger and intolerance.
Others buckle under and conform. However, it will be with a
diminished joy and a sense of feeling manipulated. Most Jewish people today are undesirous of a demand for regular conformity in all of the details of their life and worship. In addition, judgmentalism and rigid conformity requirements in
life and worship destroy creativity. Where will there then be
room for new prayers, songs, drama, and dance that God
would desire in our midst?

Worship material of value can be produced today as well
as it was a thousand years ago. New material and style reflects
our identity and expression *today* as Messianic Jews. It is also
necessary. Ancient material roots us in our history.

Love should be predominant in our midst. We should
allow the Spirit of God to inspire one another toward the
practices He lays on our hearts. It should be at God's pace, not
by peer pressure. I personally may not eat shrimp, but if
another Messianic Jew does, not thinking that the food lists
have continuing validity today, I should not look at him with
an eye of disapproval. We can share our leading in the Lord,
but we must seek obedience or conformity only in clear Biblical directions. Legalism says "my way is the only right way,"
whether that way be modern or ancient. Legalism seeks to
control others and cannot trust the Spirit to bring about God's
desired ends. We must be on guard.

Shallowness. Another danger in Messianic Judaism can
be shallowness. There is, in some Messianic Jewish quarters,
a desire to be free of all tradition. However, this goes to such
an extreme that the richness of our Jewish heritage as well as
the value of historical Jewish and Christian theology and
tradition is ignored. Messianic Judaism would therefore not
have the capacity to recognize the theological and methodo-
logical pitfalls of the past. The greatest minds and pious saints
of history are ignored, leaving Messianic Judaism shallow
and bereft. Shallowness is reflected in all areas of life: Worship becomes a mix of fast-paced choruses which are great
fun but that do not convey either the depth of Scripture or the

wisdom of Judaism in its Biblical dimensions.

Our theology becomes overly simplistic. We are unable to grapple with the complexity of the issues we face. Having eschewed scholarship, we misinterpret the Bible by not gaining an accurate sense of the cultural-linguistic background of the text. Without this background, we cannot understand the meaning as it would have been grasped by the original readers of Scripture.

The rejection of education causes a corresponding inability to be broad-minded, to be able to understand with love a wide variety of peoples and to respond to the social, political and aesthetic issues of our day with a Biblical perspective. Instead of being salt and light in the world, we isolate ourselves by our attitudes and bring little of value to the daily marketplace of living.

In some quarters, this shallowness manifests itself in anti-institutionalization. The spiritual way is thought to be apart from having anything to gain from Jewish and Christian agencies, colleges and seminaries. Yes, God can prepare a congregational leader outside of the means of traditional institutions. To this we should be open. A person's position in the Body should be by calling, not by an academic degree. Yet, a period of intensive study under the best Biblical and theological scholars is invaluable!

Separatism. Although Messianic Jews have a distinct calling from God, they *are* part of the Body of the Messiah universal! We cannot fall into the danger of compromising Biblical truth for the sake of cultural identity. This is manifest by words and deeds. Words can be used so as to put distance between Messianic Jews and other believers so that the Jewish community will not perceive us to be one with the Body. *But we are one with the Body.* Jews and Gentiles are one in Him, and a Messianic congregation has non-Jewish members too. Although we seek to be part of Israel, we are also one with the Body of Messiah Jesus. Our words should reflect this. Our deeds should reflect this as well. There should be joint services, cooperative fellowship with leaders, etc. We can learn from the whole Body as we hopefully enrich it as well.

Heresy. The danger of heresy comes from two sources:
First, that the desire to identify with the Jewish community
will be so strong that it would influence us to compromise our
Biblical values and views because such views are more com-
patible with Jewish thinking. The Scriptures must remain
our absolute authority. Under this danger we would place
Ebiontism which denies the deity of Yeshua. The denial of the
substitutionary atonement of Yeshua for a doctrine which
sees the value of Yeshua's life and death in terms of moral
influence alone is another example of heresy. Yeshua is not
just our perfect pattern; "He died for our sins according to the
Scriptures." There is also danger from those who would not
seek to test prophetic gifts rigorously by the Scripture. How
common it is today that doctrine is formed in groups by a
prophetic sense which spiritualizes the Scripture and finds
allegorical meanings not intended in the text! This is the root
of strange heretical doctrine. If the Scripture, in context, is
not the basis for testing, then we enter into a subjective mode
of doctrinal formation that leads to chaos. We should hold as
suspect all teachings which pull phrases out of Scripture to
show some great new revelation not intrinsically present.

Control. Messianic Judaism is a movement of the Spirit.
The Spirit has independently brought many of us to see the
same truths. He will also unify. One of the dangers in the
national and international scene is a feeling that *we* have *the
right* sense. When a group has the *attitude* of superiority,
even if they *are* superior (in age, by numbers, etc.), they
alienate others. We all have much to learn from one another.
God can unify and blend us without any group or individual
controlling and manipulating others. Prayer and sharing will
bind us together. If we talk and act as if our group alone is of
value, if we do not seek concrete means to edify other groups,
or if we seek to make other groups like our own, or seek in
every way to benefit our group to the hurt of others, we
produce alienation.

If there are heresies inherent to Christianity, there will
be heresies from Messianic Judaism as well. May God guard
us from these dangers and many others that are not yet clear

to us. May He guard us from gullibility as we seek to apply the
Word with maturity.

CHAPTER ELEVEN

A Messianic Jewish Vision

When one speaks of a vision, he has in mind the basic picture to be developed on the canvas of living. Messianic Judaism is, as yet, in its embryonic stage. Without a vision, it will not have direction for growth. What is our vision of Messianic Judaism?

It is nothing less than to recover the dynamic power of the Gospel in the midst of the Jewish community. From the spread of the Good News will come an authentically Jewish expression of the New Testament faith. This expression will take various forms from independent congregations to Jewish wings of other New Testament groups. Yet it is our hope that all of these groups will grow over time in an affirmation and practice that has continuity with the beginnings of the faith in the first century. In the beginning, we read in Acts 2:44-47 that the Jewish believers gave themselves to the apostles' teaching, to prayer, and to the breaking of bread in the homes of one another. Let us expand upon these themes.

First, may there be a dedication to apostolic teaching. We should seek to understand the Word in its original context of language and culture and to apply it to our lives. To love in the power of the Word and the Spirit as a demonstration of the present reality of God's Kingdom is truly our call.

Secondly, the first believers gave themselves to "the

prayers." This includes praises, written prayer as teaching
models, intercession and fellowship with God in prayer. We
must truly be a praying community.

Thirdly, they were found in one another's homes, breaking bread. These early Jewish believers in Yeshua shared
their lives. They sold property and moved to be near one
another and under apostolic teaching. In a day of anonymity,
a day in which the economic motive determines where we
live and how, we need to recapture the sense of community
held by the early believers in Yeshua. We ought to consider of
prime importance choosing where we live, where we work
and how we spend our time in relationship to how we can best
serve God in the community. If we are to truly share and be
available and involved, distance from one another is to be
avoided. Moving for selfish reasons, without being led to
another congregation, should also be questionable. Why do
we consider our relationships so expendable and our part in
the body of such little consequence to our decisions? This is
certainly not in accord with Scripture. We ought rather be
giving ourselves to build that spiritual, healing community in
which the life of God can be recognized in the Body; we are to
do the work of the Messiah while there is still time. In the
Body, we are accountable to one another without binding
each other's conscience. We seek to build up one another.
From the Body, we reach out to others. This is the clear
model of John 17 and Acts 2:44-47. When we love deeply, then
the world will know the truth according to Yeshua's teaching. If we love, we no longer act as isolated individualists. We
are our brothers' keepers and we no longer direct our lives
without sharing our directions any more than we would
ignore our immediate families in such matters.

What of the Jewish heritage? I will fight those who would
make of this heritage a legalistic burden. We should be free to
experiment, to use new tunes, to use English as well as
Hebrew in English-speaking lands, to use music, drama and
dance in new ways. However, my vision is that if we truly
love Israel—*past, present, and future*—we will have a heart
desire to identify in a biblical way with our people's heritage.

Messianic Jews ought to be zealous to learn Hebrew; this is our national language. If Ben Yehuda could revive a language speaking nation, surely we can develop Hebrew as a second language. Surely we can learn to appreciate singing and praying in Hebrew as well as in English. Anyone who loves France studies French and learns French literature and culture. Isn't this obvious? We should have a Messiah-given love for our people far beyond our compatriots in their zeal for Hebrew. Hebrew is the language of the Tenach itself!

Secondly, we should see a *creative* appropriation of Jewish heritage to the extent that it is consistent with Scripture and can be used to extol the grace of God in history and the fulfillment of the Messiah Jews. We could be the leaders in times of joy. We could have a love of traditional melody, in *identification* with *the historic expression and experience of our people.* Our involvement would be with understanding! However, we could develop new expressions of music, dance and drama drawing from the Scripture and Jewish tradition. Because of the Holy Spirit, we could be the expression of our heritage that has life, verve, meaning and joy to such an extent that our people would say, "It is Jewish, but it is so much more full of life!"

Our desire is not to destroy the Jewish community, but to recover the means by which Jewish people could be part of the universal Body of believers, while yet remaining part of their people and the nation of Israel. It is not true that the Jewish nation must be apart from the universal Body of the Messiah to assure their distinctive continuance. Rather, all that is required is an expression of the Body which is Jewish and maintains the national identity and call of Israel.

As we have said, Messianic Judaism is in an embryonic state. How shall we judge it? Hopefully, with broadness and tolerance. We need the help of all New Covenant believers; we need their input and wisdom, not just to be cut off as odd. The Scripture says, "by their fruits ye shall know them" (Matthew 7:20). What are the fruits of Messianic Judaism fairly judged?

First, in comparison with congregations and movements which have been in existence for centuries and have mature, seasoned believers, we could seem as though we are lacking in fruit. Congregations of predominantly new believers in Yeshua, without trained leadership, are not going to match up to that which is seasoned. Indeed, things are said and done in ignorance and controversy is engendered. But let us not forget that this is the case with *all* new religious movements. The Corinthian congregation was so full of division and carnality that it makes us look quite good! Yet Paul did not dismiss the Corinthian Church as not of God. He called them to maturity.

The Reformation was a great back-to-the-Bible movement. The great reformers would not speak to one another. Religious wars followed the Reformation in which thousands were killed. Messianic Judaism has not fostered war or immorality. Do we really judge this new movement fairly from the outside? Yes, I know of tendencies to error; but allow me to make a personal statement from my own observations of the real inner fruit of Messianic Judaism:

When I began my work in the ministry, I had occasion to observe the practice of the old Christian missions to the Jews. Praise God, many have changed their style dramatically since those days. How vividly I remember. Many of the people who attended were spiritually and socially crippled. Some even hated themselves for being Jews, but felt they could not gain acceptance in the Jewish community. Being in the Hebrew-Christian mission was the closest to compromise between their self-hatred and their fear of Jewish rejection. How few were those coming to know Yeshua! Pathetically, we would see the same group make the rounds of all four missions in town. Each mission would print the stories of the same person as if it was responsible for the "conversion."

At that time, I did some figuring in regard to the budget of a large mission. From their own statement of finance and "conversion" we found their cost to be approximately $30-$40,000 per convert. Yes, a small fee to pay for a person's eternal life! However, how many reported decisions stick?

When I fairly judge the fruits of Messianic Judaism, I must keep all this in mind.

These have been my experiences in Messianic Judaism: First, Messianic Judaism is not a heresy, but affirms the clear doctrine of the New Testament as do all believing faiths. Secondly, people are being won to Yeshua, both Jew and non-Jew because of Messianic Judaism. Over the last year, our own congregation has seen over 50 people commit their lives in the waters of the Covenant. Over two-thirds were Jewish and most have stuck as members and attendees of the congregation. Proportionately, in my previous congregation, our results were also good, though not quite up to our present level. Those ambivalent to their Jewish identity cannot find a comfortable niche here unless they work through their self-rejection. People by this become healthier. What is the cost of this response? $1,500.00 per person (on the basis of total congregational budget).

What are some other fruits besides that of salvation? Let's look at the inner evidence: We have seen dozens of mixed-up kids forsake the occult, drugs, and Eastern religions. We have seen such kids reunited with their families and their families accepting them because of their renewed involvement with their heritage. What a joy to see whole families in Yeshua. I remember well the tears one day as we saw the father of one believer in Yeshua accept Him also. The whole family cried. He was an older man who taught Hebrew for the United States State Department.

Time does not permit us to recount the stories of some who were healed of paranoia, schizophrenia, depression, anger, and all sorts of confusion. Then there are the healed families. In fourteen years of Jewish congregational ministry we have seen broken homes united and unstable marriages stabilized. I don't know of many who could say this, but in fourteen years of ministry not one marriage of any congregationally-involved couple has ended in divorce, *not one*! Most marriages that have taken place seem solid. We see people moving to be closer to one another, to help and to serve.

Have there been problems? Of course. Immature Jewish

believers not recognizing the equality of non-Jews in the Messiah have made statements which have hurt. Some have misunderstood. Yet, I have no doubt that the fruits outweigh the dross. People are growing to be more like Yeshua!

As I look at the people of our congregations, we see people from all walks of life; what a miracle! We have homemakers, secretaries, government bureaucrats, doctors, corporate executives, repairmen, a tow truck driver, lawyers, biologists, social workers, an editor, teachers, a professor of traffic engineering, a real estate entrepreneur, etc. Here is an incredibly diverse group being made one in the Messiah! I, for one, am convinced that the fruits are good and shall remain so, and improve, if we keep our eyes on Yeshua, and discipline ourselves by the Word, keeping an open mind to learn from all sources.

Messianic Judaism must be an ensign of the final redemption and of the uniting of the Jewish community to the Body of believers, while preserving Israel and its unique contributions to the Body. Praise God for all His work, for His consistent revelation in the Word.

"For the gifts and call of God are without repentance" (Romans 11:29).

When God speaks, there is no double tongue in His promises, calling or purpose. It is His desire to have mercy on all. To that end, He has and will use Israel; to that end He has and will use the Church. May we all be in accord with His purpose. May we be light and salt in the Jewish community, a visible representation of Yeshua's Kingdom. May we be salt and light to the world.

APPENDIX I

The 613 Laws

There are over 1,000 New Testament commands. Some are of difficult application, but most are clear. Paul, however, taught that *all* Scripture is profitable for doctrine, reproof, for instruction in righteousness. This includes Torah commands. Therefore we seek to know how to apply the 613 Torah commands to our lives. Following is a brief delineation categorizing these laws by purpose to facilitate their application.

Key:

T (Temple)—Part of the Temple sacrificial system replaced by Yeshua's priesthood and sacrifice. Of teaching value in pointing to Him; but can only be kept during this age through receiving Him, no longer by practice. (For example, Thanksgiving sacrifices are paralleled by prayer and offerings during this age).

U.M. (Moral Universal)—Direct commands of personal and social morality which either apply directly to us or have underlying principles which do apply to us.

U.R. (Universal, but *revised*)—Intensified and deepened in New Testament. (For example, *Swear by His name* Deuteronomy 10:20. *Swear not but say yes, yes, and mean it.* Matthew 5:37.)

J (Jewish)—Part of the Jewish heritage which celebrates

God's fulfillment of His promise to make Israel a nation. Valid as part of Israel's national and cultural identity when done so as to show Yeshua's fulfillment, Yeshua replacing the sacrificial dimensions of the practice.

J (Ancient)—Applies to ancient nation.

?—Unclear as to the purpose or application—at least in part.

C (Combination)—A combination of above categories: (e.g., 1) food lists may have a moral dimension if they are valid for health reasons; may be part of a cultural distinction in Israel; and may be part of the Temple sacrificial system by making a person unclean. (e.g., 2) Sabbath is both J as well as having a moral significance for all people who need to rest one day in seven on some day of the week.

N.A.—No longer can any application be found.

There are also over 1,050 New Testament commands. Neither the continuingly valid commands from the Torah or the New Testament commands can be approached for merit or as if we seek to fulfill them in our own power. Only dependence on God's grace and atonement—resurrection power—enables us to obey from the heart. Commands deepen our humility and sense of dependence on God's mercy and power.

MANDATORY COMMANDMENTS

God

[1]Ex. 20:2	UM
[2]Dt. 6:4	UM
[3]Dt. 6:5	UM
[4]Dt. 6:13	UM
[5]Ex. 23:25;	UM
Dt. 11:13	
(Dt. 6:13;	
also 13:15)	
[6]Dt. 10:20	UM
[7]Dt. 10:20	UR
[8]Dt. 28:9	UM
[9]Lev. 22:32	UM

The Jew is required to [1]believe that God exists and to [2]acknowledge His unity; to [3]love, [4]fear, and [5]serve Him. He is also commanded to [6]cleave to Him (by associating with and imitating the wise) and to [7]swear only by His name. One must [8]imitate God and [9]sanctify His name.

Torah

[10]Dt. 6:7	UM
[11]Dt. 6:7	UM
[12]Dt. 6:8	CUMJ
[13]Dt. 6:8	CUMJ
[14]Num. 15:38	J
[15]Dt. 6:9	J
[16]Dt. 31:12	J
[17]Dt. 17:18	J
[18]Dt. 31:19	UM
[19]Dt. 8:10	UM

The Jew must [10]remember the Shema each morning and evening and [11]study the Torah and teach it to others. He should bind tefillin on his [12]head and [13]his arm. He should make [14]zizit for his garments and [15]fix a mezuzah on the door. The people are to be [16]assembled every seventh year to hear the Torah read and [17]the king must write a special copy of the Torah for himself. [18]Every Jew should have a Torah scroll. One should [19]praise God after eating.

Temple and the Priests

[20]Ex. 25:8	T
[21]Lev. 19:30	T
[22]Num. 18:4	T
[23]Num. 18:3	T
[24]Ex. 30:19	T
[25]Ex. 27:21	T

The Jews should [20]build a Temple and [21]respect it. It must be [22]guarded at all times and the [23]Levites should perform their special duties in it. Before entering the Temple or participating in its

²⁶Num. 6:23 T
²⁷Ex. 25:30 T
²⁸Ex. 30:7   T
²⁹Lev. 6:6   T
³⁰Lev. 6:3   T
³¹Num. 5:2   T
³²Lev. 21:8 T
³³Ex. 28:2   T
³⁴Num. 7:9   T
³⁵Ex. 30:31 T
³⁶Dt. 18:6-8 T
³⁷Lev. 21:2-3 T
³⁸Lev. 21:13 T

service the priests [24]must wash their hands and feet; they must also [25]light the candelabrum daily. The priests are required to [26]bless Israel and to [27]set the shewbread and frankincense before the Ark. Twice daily they must [28]burn the incense on the golden altar. Fire shall be kept burning on the altar [29]continually and the ashes should be [30]removed daily. Ritually unclean persons must be [31]kept out of the Temple. Israel [32]should honor its priests, who must be [33]dressed in special priestly raiment. The priests should [34]carry the Ark on their shoulders, and the holy anointing oil [35]must be prepared according to its special formula. The priestly families should officiate in [36]rotation. In honor of certain dead close relatives the priests should [37]make themselves ritually unclean. The high priest may marry [38]only a virgin.

Sacrifices

³⁹Num. 28:3   T
⁴⁰Lev. 6:13   T
⁴¹Num. 28:9   T
⁴²Num. 28:11 T
⁴³Lev. 23:36 T
⁴⁴Lev. 23:10 T
⁴⁵Num. 28:26
   -27   T
⁴⁶Lev. 23:17 T

The [39]tamid sacrifice must be offered twice daily and the [40]high priest must also offer a meal-offering twice daily. An additional sacrifice (musaf) should be offered [41]every Sabbath, [42]on the first of every month, and [43]on each of the seven days of Passover. On the second day of Passover [44]a meal offering of the first barley must also be brought. On Shavuot a [45]musaf must be offered and [46]two loaves of bread as a wave offering. The additional sacrifice must also

[47]Num. 29:1	
-2	T
[48]Num. 29:7	
-8	T
[49]Lev. 16	T
[50]Num. 29:13	T
[51]Num. 29:36	T
[52]Ex. 23:14	T
[53]Ex. 34:23;	
Dt. 16:6	J
[54]Dt. 16:14	C-JT
[55]Ex. 12:6	C-JT
[56]Ex. 12:8	T
[57]Num. 9:11	T
[58]Num. 9:11;	J
Ex. 12:8	J
[59]Num. 10:10	
Num. 10:9	T
[60]Lev. 22:27	T
[61]Lev. 22:21	T
[62]Lev. 2:13	T
[63]Lev. 1:2	T
[64]Lev. 6:18	T
[65]Lev. 7:1	T
[66]Lev. 3:1	T
[67]Lev. 2:1;	
[68]Lev. 4:13	T
[69]Lev. 4:27	T

be made on [47]Rosh Ha-Shanah and [48]on the Day of Atonement when the [49]Avodah must also be performed. On every day of the festival of [50]Sukkot a musaf must be brought as well as on the [51]eighth day thereof.

Every male Jew should make [52]pilgrimage to the Temple three times a year and [53]appear there during the three pilgrim Festivals. One should [54]rejoice on the Festivals. On the 14th of Nisan one should [55]slaughter the paschal lamb and [56]eat of its roasted flesh on the night of the 15th. Those who were ritually impure in Nisan should slaughter the paschal lamb on [57]the 14th of Iyyar and eat it with [58]mazzah and bitter herbs. Trumpets should be [59]sounded when the festive sacrifices are brought and also in times of tribulation.

Cattle to be sacrificed must be [60]at least eight days old and [61]without blemish. All offerings must be [62]salted. It is a mitzvah to perform the ritual of [63]the burnt offering, [64]the sin offering, [65]the guilt offering, [66]the peace offering and [67]the meal offering.

Should the Sanhedrin err in a decision its members [68]must bring a sin offering which offering must also be brought [69]by a person who has unwittingly transgressed a karet prohibition (i.e., one which, if done deliberately, would incur karet). When in doubt as to whether one has transgressed such a prohibi-

70Lev. 5:17
-18   T

71Lev. 5:15,
21-25;
19:20-21   T

72Lev. 5:1-11 T

73Num. 5:6-7 UM

74Lev. 15:13
-15   T

75Lev. 15:28
-29   T

76Lev. 12:6   T

77Lev. 14:10   T

78Lev. 27:32   T

79Ex. 13:2   T

80Ex. 22:28;
Num. 18:15 T

81Ex. 34:20   T

82Ex. 13:13   T

83Dt. 12:5-5   T

84Dt. 12:14   T

85Dt. 12:26   T

86Dt. 12:15   T

87Lev. 27:33   T

88Lev. 6:9   T

89Ex. 29:33   T

90Lev. 7:19   T

91Lev. 7:17   T

tion a 70"suspensive" guilt offering must be brought.

For 71stealing or swearing falsely and for other sins of a like nature, a guilt offering must be brought. In special circumstances the sin offering 72can be according to one's means.

One must 73confess one's sins before God and repent for them. A 74man or 75a woman who has a seminal issue must bring a sacrifice; a woman must also bring a sacrifice 76after childbirth. A leper must 77bring a sacrifice after he has been cleansed. One must 78tithe one's cattle. The 79first born of clean (i.e., permitted) cattle are holy and must be sacrificed. The firstborn of man must be 80redeemed. The firstling of the ass must be 81redeemed; if not 82its neck has to be broken.

Animals set aside as offerings 83must be brought to Jerusalem without delay and 84may be sacrificed only in the Temple. Offerings from outside the land of Israel 85may also be brought to the Temple. Sanctified animals 86which have become blemished must be redeemed. A beast exchanged for an offering 87is also holy. The priests should eat 88the remainder of the meal offering and 89the flesh of sin and guilt offerings; but consecrated flesh which has become 90ritually unclean or 91which was not eaten within its appointed time must be burned.

[92]Num. 6:5	JT	

Vows

A Nazirite must [92]let his hair grow during the period of his separation. When that period is over he must [93]shave his head and bring his sacrifice.

A man must [94]honor his vows and his oaths which a judge can [95]annul only in accordance with the Law.

(Acts 18)	
[93]Num. 6:18	T
[94]Dt. 23:24	UR
[95]Num. 30:3	URJ

Ritual Purity

(Health reasons for following, thus Temple and C.)

Anyone who touches [96]a carcass or [97]one of the eight species of reptiles becomes ritually unclean; food becomes unclean by [98]coming into contact with a ritually unclean object.

Menstruous women [99]and those [100]lying-in after childbirth are ritually impure. A [101]leper, [102]a leprous garment, and [103]a leprous house are all ritually unclean. A man having a running issue is unclean, as is [105]semen. A woman suffering from [106]running issue is also impure. A [107]human corpse is ritually unclean. The purification water (mei nidah) purifies [108]the unclean, but it makes the clean ritually impure. It is a mitzvah to become ritually clean [109]by ritual immersion. To become cleansed of leprosy one [110]must follow the specified procedure and also [111]shave of all of one's hair. Until cleansed the leper [112]must be bareheaded with clothing in disarray so as to be easily distinguish-

[96]Lev. 11:8, and 24	T-C
[97]Lev. 11:29 -31	T-C
[98]Lev. 11:34	T-C
[99]Lev. 15-19	T-C
[100]Lev. 12:12	T-C
[101]Lev. 13:3	T-C
[102]Lev. 13:51	T-C
[103]Lev. 14:44	T-C
[104]Lev. 15:2	T-C
[105]Lev. 15:16	T-C
[106]Lev. 15:19	T-C
[107]Num. 19:14	T-C
[108]Num. 19:13 & 21	T-C
[109]Lev. 15:16	T-C
[110]Lev. 14:2	T-C
[111]Lev. 14:9	T-C
[112]Lev. 13:45	T-C

[113]Num. 19:2-
    9   T

able. The ashes of [113]the red heifer are to be used in the process of ritual purification.

[114]Lev. 27:2-8 T

Donations to the Temple

[115]Lev. 27:11
    -12   T
[116]Lev. 27:14 T
[117]Lev. 27:16,
    22-23   T
[118]Lev. 5:16   T
[119]Lev. 19:24 T-J
[120]Lev. 19:9   UM
[121]Lev. 19:9   UM
[122]Dt. 24:19   UM
[123]Lev. 19:10 UM
[124]Lev. 19:10 UM
[125]Ex. 23:19   T
[126]Dt. 18:4   T
[127]Lev. 27:30;
    Num. 18:24 T
[128]Dt. 14:22   T
[129]Num. 18:26 T
[130]Dt. 14:28   CUMJ
[131]Dt. 26:13   T

If a person [114]undertakes to give his own value to the Temple he must do so. Should a man declare [115]an unclean beast, [116]a house, or [117]a field as a donation to the Temple, he must give their value in money as fixed by the priest. If one unwittingly derives benefit from Temple property [118]full restitution plus a fifth must be made.

The fruit of [119]the fourth year's growth of trees is holy and may be eaten only in Jerusalem. When you reap your fields you must leave [120]the corners, [121]the gleanings, [122]the forgotten sheaves, [123]the misformed bunches of grapes and [124]the gleanings of the grapes for the poor.

The first fruits must be [125]separated and brought to the Temple and you must also [126]separate the great heave offering (terumah) and give it to the priests. You must give [127]one tithe of your produce to the Levites and separate [128]a second tithe which is to be eaten only in Jerusalem. The Levites [129]must give a tenth of their tithe to the priests. In the third and sixth years of the seven year cycle you should [130]separate a tithe for the poor instead of the second tithe. A declaration [131]must be recited when separating the various tithes and

[132]Dt. 26:5	T
[133]Num. 15:20	T

[132]when bringing the first fruits to the Temple.

The first portion of the [133]dough must be given to the priest.

[134]Ex. 23:11	CJUM
[135]Ex. 34:21	CJUM
[136]Lev. 25:10	CJUM
[137]Lev. 25:9	CJUM
[138]Lev. 25:24	CJUM
[139]Lev. 25:29	
-30	CJUM
[140]Lev. 25:8	CJUM
[141]Dt. 15:3	CJUM
[142]Dt. 15:3	CJUM

The Sabbatical Year

(Universal principle of care for poor and business mercy is part of 136-141)

In the seventh year (shemittah) everything that grows is [134]ownerless and available to all; the fields [135]must lie fallow and you may not till the ground. You must [136]sanctify the Jubilee year (50th) an on the Day of Atonement in that year [137]you must sound the shofar and set all Hebrew slaves free. In the Jubilee year all land is to be [138]returned to its ancestral owners and, generally, in a walled city [139]the seller has the right to buy back a house within a year of the sale.

Starting from entry into the land of Israel, the years of the Jubilee must be [140]counted and announced yearly and septennially. In the seventh year [141]all debts are annulled but [142]one may exact a debt owed by a foreigner.

[143]Dt. 18:3	T
[144]Dt. 18:4	T
[145]Lev. 27:21,	
28	T

Concerning Animals for Consumption

When you slaughter an animal you must [143]give the priest his share as you must also give him [144]the first of the fleece.

When a man makes a heren (a special vow) you must [145]distinguish between that which belongs to the Temple (i.e., when God's name was mentioned in the vow)

[146]Dt. 12:21	CT UM	and that which goes to the priests. To be fit for consumption, beast and fowl
[147]Lev. 17:13 *(Reverence for life)*—UM	TUM	must be [146]slaughtered according to the law and if they are not of a domesticated species [147]their blood must be covered with earth after slaughter.
[148]Dt. 22:7	UM	
[149]Lev. 11:2	TC JUM	Set the parent bird [148]free when taking the nest. Examine [149]beast, [150]fowl, [151]locusts
[150]Dt. 14:11	CTJ UM	and [152]fish to determine whether they are permitted for consumption.
[151]Lev. 11:21	CTJ UM	The Sanhedrin should [153]sanctify the first day of every month and reckon the
[152]Lev. 11:21	CTJ UM	years and the seasons.
[153]Ex. 12:2; Dt. 16:1		*(147-149—unclean relates to Temple (T)— food laws of health value (J) and also distinguish Jews.)*

Festivals

[154]Ex. 23:12	JUM	You must [154]rest on the Sabbath day and
(Sabbath has a univ. prin. of rest pds.)		[155]declare it holy at its onset and termination. On the 14th of Nisan [156]remove
[155]Ex. 20:8	JUM	all leaven from your ownership and on
[156]Ex. 12:15	J	the night of the 15th [157]relate the story
[157]Ex. 13:8	J	of the Exodus from Egypt; on that
[158]Ex. 12:18	J	night [158]you must also eat mazzah. On
[159]Ex. 12:16	J	the [159]first and [160]seventh days of Passover you must rest. Starting from the
[160]Ex. 12:16	J	
[161]Lev. 23:35	J	day of the first sheaf (16th of Nisan)
[162]Lev. 23	J	you shall [161]count 49 days. You must
[163]Lev. 23:24	J	rest on [162]Shavuot, and on [163]Rosh Ha-
[164]Lev. 16:29	J	Shanah; on the Day of Atonement you
[165]Lev. 16:29, 1	J	must [164]fast and [165]rest. You must also
[166]Lev. 23:25	J	rest on [166]the first and [167]the eighth day
[167]Lev. 23:36	J	of Sukkot during which festival you shall [168]dwell in booths and [169]take the

[168]Lev. 23:42	J	
[169]Lev. 23:40	J	
[170]Num. 29:1	J	

four species. On Rosh Ha-Shanah [170]you are to hear the sound of the shofar.

[171]Ex. 30:12		**Community**
-13	T	
[172]Dt. 18:15	JUM	
[173]Dt. 17:15	NA	
[174]Dt. 17:11	T	
[175]Ex. 23:2	CJUM	
[176]Dt. 16:18	UM	
[177]Lev. 19:15	UM	
[178]Lev. 5:1	UM	
[179]Dt. 13:15	UM	
[180]Dt. 19:19	UM	
[181]Dt. 21:4	T	
[182]Dt. 19:3	CJUM	
[183]Num. 35:2	T	
[184]Dt. 22:8	UM	

Every male should [171]give half a shekel to the Temple annually. You must [172]obey a prophet and [173]appoint a king. You must also [174]obey the Sanhedrin; in the case of division, [175]yield to the majority. Judges and officials shall be [176]appointed in every town and they shall judge the people [177]impartially. Whoever is aware of evidence [178]must come to court to testify. Witnesses shall be [179]examined thoroughly and, if found to be false, [18]shall have done to them what they intended to do to the accused.

When a person is found murdered and the murderer is unknown the ritual of [181]decapitating the heifer must be performed.

Six cities of refuge should be [182]established. The Levites, who have no ancestral share in the land, shall [183]be given cities to live in. You must [184]build a fence around your roof and remove potential hazards from your home.

[185]Dt. 12:2;		**Idolatry**
7:5	JUM	
[186]Dt. 13:17	JUM	

Idolatry and its appurtenances [185]must be destroyed, and a city which has become perverted must be [186]treated according to the law. You are commanded to

[187]Dt. 20:17	NA
[188]Dt. 25:19	NA
[189]Dt. 25:17	NA

[187]destroy the seven Canaanite nations, and [188]to blot out the memory of Amalek, and [189]to remember what they did to Israel.

[190]Dt. 20:11	
-12	T
[191]Dt. 20:2	NA?
[192]Dt. 23:14	
-15	UM
[193]Dt. 23:14	UM

War

The regulations for wars other than those commanded in the Torah [190]are to be observed and a priest should be [191]appointed for special duties in times of war. The military camp must be [192]kept in a sanitary condition. To this end, every soldier must be [193]equipped with the necessary implements.

[194]Lev. 5:23	UM
[195]Dt. 15:8;	
Lev. 25:35	
-36	UM
[196]Dt. 15:14	UM
[197]Ex. 22:24	UM
[198]Dt. 32:21	UM
[199]Dt. 24:13;	
Ex. 22:25	UM
[200]Dt. 24:15	UM
[201]Dt. 23:25	
-26 UM	
[202]Ex. 23:5	UM
[203]Dt. 22:4	UM
[204]Dt. 22:1;	
Ex. 23:4	UM
[205]Lev. 19:17	UM
[206]Lev. 19:18	UM
[207]Dt. 10:19	UM
[208]Lev. 19:36	UM

Social

Stolen property must be [194]restored to its owner. Give [195]charity to the poor. When a Hebrew slave goes free the owner must [196]give him gifts. Lend to [197]the poor without interest; to the foreigner you may [198]lend at interest. Restore [199]a pledge to its owner if he needs it. Pay the worker his wages [200]on time; [201]permit him to eat of the produce with which he is working. You must [202]help unload an animal when necessary, and also [203]help load man or beast. Lost property [204]must be restored to its owner. You are required [205]to reprove the sinner but you must [206]love your fellow as yourself. You are commanded [207]to love the proselyte. Your weights and measure [208]must be accurate.

[209]Lev. 19:32	UM	**Family**
[210]Ex. 20:12	UM	Respect the [209]wise; [210]honor and [211]fear your
[211]Lev. 19:3	UM	parents. You should [212]perpetuate the
[212]Gen. 1:28	UM	human race by marrying [213]according
[213]Dt. 24:1	UM	to the Law. A bridegroom is to [214]re-
[214]Dt. 24:5	UM	joice with his bride for one year. Male
[215]Gen. 17:10		children must [215]be circumcised.
Lev. 12:3	J	Should a man die childless his brother
[216]Dt. 25:5	NA?	must either [216]marry his widow or
[217]Dt. 25:9	?	[217]release her (halizah). He who vio-
[218]Dt. 22:29	UM	lated a virgin must [218]marry her and
[219]Dt. 22:18		may never divorce her. If a man unjust-
-19	UM	ly accuses his wife of premarital pro-
[220]Ex. 22:15		miscuity [219]he shall be flogged, and
-23	UM	may never divorce her. The seducer
[221]Dt. 21:11	UM	[220]must be punished according to the
[222]Dt. 24:1	UR	Law. The female captive must be
(Matt. 5)		[221]treated in accordance with her spe-
[223]Num. 5:15		cial regulations. Divorce can be exe-
-27	NA	cuted [222]only by means of a written
	TUM	document. A woman suspected of adul-
		tery [223]has to submit to the required
		test.

(224-231 have a basic underlying principle of social justice)

[224]Dt. 25:2	UM?	**Judicial**
[225]Num. 35:25	UM	When required by Law [224]you must adminis-
[226]Ex. 21:20	UM	ter the punishment of flogging and you
[227]Ex. 21:16	UM?	must [225]exile the unwitting homicide.
[228]Lev. 20:14	UM?	Capital punishment shall be by [226]the
[229]Dt. 22:24	UM	sword, [227]strangulation, [228]fire, or [229]ston-
[230]Dt. 21:22	UM	ing, as specified. In some cases the
		body of the executed [230]shall be hanged,

²³¹Dt. 21:23   UM?   but it ²³¹must be brought to burial the
                         same day.

                         (232-234—The moral principle is not endorse-
                         ment of slavery but to limit hardship
                         and apply kindness)

²³²Ex. 21:2   UM   **Slaves**
²³³Ex. 21:8   UM   Hebrew slaves ²³²must be treated according
²³⁴Ex. 21:8   UM   to the special laws for them. The mas-
²³⁵Lev. 25:46 UM   ter should ²³³marry his Hebrew maid-
                         servant or ²³⁴redeem her. The alien
                         slave ²³⁵must be treated according to
                         the regulations applying to him.

                         (236-245—show principles of justice)

²³⁶Ex. 21:18   UM   **Torts**
²³⁷Ex. 21:28   UM   The applicable law must be administered in
²³⁸Ex. 21:33   the case of injury caused by ²³⁶a person,
  -34   UM   ²³⁷an animal or ²³⁸a pit. Thieves ²³⁹must
²³⁹Ex. 21:37-   be punished. You must render judg-
  22:3   UM   ment in cases of ²⁴⁰trespass by cattle,
²⁴⁰Ex. 22:4   UM   ²⁴¹arson, ²⁴²embezzlement by an unpaid
²⁴¹Ex. 22:5   UM   guardian and in claims against ²⁴³a paid
²⁴²Ex. 22:6-8 UM   guardian, a hirer, or ²⁴⁴a borrower.
²⁴³Ex. 22:9-12 UM   Judgment must also be rendered in
²⁴⁴Ex. 22:13   UM   disputes arising out of ²⁴⁵sales, ²⁴⁸inher-
²⁴⁵Lev. 25:14 UM   itance and ²⁴⁶other matters generally.
²⁴⁶Ex. 22:8   UM   You are required to ²⁴⁷rescue the per-
²⁴⁷Dt. 25:12   UM   secuted even if it means killing his
²⁴⁸Num. 27:8   UM   oppressor.

PROHIBITIONS

[1]Ex. 20:3	UM	**Idolatry and Related Practices**
[2]Ex. 20:4	UM	It is [1]forbidden to believe in the existence of
[3]Lev. 19:4	UM	any but the One God. You may not
[4]Ex. 20:20	UM	make images [2]for yourself or [3]for oth-
[5]Ex. 20:5	UM	ers to worship or for [4]any other purpose.
[6]Ex. 20:5	UM	You must not worship anything but God
[7]Lev. 18:21	UM	either in [5]the manner prescribed for
[8]Lev. 19:31	UM	His worship or [6]in its own manner of
[9]Lev. 19:31	UM	worship.
[10]Lev. 19:4	UM	Do not [7]sacrifice children to Molech.
[11]Dt. 16:22	UM	You may not [8]practice necromancy or [9]resort
[12]Lev. 20:1	UM	to "familiar spirits," neither should
[13]Dt. 16:21	UM	you take idolatry or its mythology [10]ser-
[14]Ex. 23:13	UM	iously. It is forbidden to construct a
[15]Ex. 23:13	UM	[11]pillar or [12]dais even for the worship of
[16]Dt. 13:12	UM	God or to [13]plant trees in the Temple.
[17]Dt. 13:9	UM	You may not [14]swear by idols or instigate an
[18]Dt. 13:9	UMJ?	idolator to do so, nor may you encour-
[19]Dt. 13:9	UMJ?	age or persuade any [15]non-Jew or [16]Jew
[20]Dt. 13:0	UM	to worship idols.
[21]Dt. 13:9	UM	You must not [17]listen to or love anyone who
[22]Dt. 7:25	UM	disseminates idolatry nor [18]should you
[23]Dt. 13:17	UM	withhold yourself from hating him. Do
[24]Dt. 13:18	UM	not [19]pity such a person. If somebody
[25]Dt. 7:26	UM	tries to convert you to idolatry [20]do not
[26]Dt. 18:20	UM	defend him or [21]conceal the fact. It is

forbidden to [22]derive any benefit from
the ornaments of idols. You may not
[23]rebuild that which has been destroyed
as a punishment for idolatry nor may
you [24]have any benefit from its wealth.
Do not [25]use anything connected with
idols or idolatry.

It is forbidden [26]to prophesy in the name of

[27]Dt. 18:20	UM	
[28]Dt. 13:3, 4	UM	
[29]Dt. 18:22	UM	
[30]Lev. 20:23	UM	
[31]Lev. 19:26		
Dt. 18:10	UM	
[32]Dt. 18:10	UM	
[33]Dt. 18:10		
-11	UM	
[34]Dt. 18:10		
-11	UM	
[35]Dt. 18:10		
-11	UM	
[36]Dt. 18:10		
-11	UM	
[37]Dt. 18:10		
-11	UM	
[38]Dt. 18:10		
-11	UM	
[39]Dt. 22:5	UM	
[40]Dt. 22:5	UM	
[41]Lev. 19:28	UM	
[42]Dt. 22:11	J	
[43]Lev. 19:27	J?	
(Ancient only?)		
[44]Lev. 19:27	J?	
(Ancient only?)		
[45]Dt. 16:1;		
Dt. 14:1; &		
Lev. 19:28	UM	

idols or prophesy [27]falsely in the name of God. Do not [28]listen to the one who prophesies for idols and do not [29]fear the false prophet or hinder his execution.

You must not [30]imitate the ways of idolators or practice their customs; [31]divination, [32]soothsaying, [33]enchanting, [34]sorcery, [35]charming, [36]consulting ghosts or [37]familiar spirits and [38]necromancy are forbidden. Women must not [39]wear male clothing nor men [40]that of women. Do not [41]tattoo yourself in the manner of the idolators. You may not wear [42]garments made of both wool and linen nor may you shave (with a razor) the sides of [43]your head or [44]your beard. Do not [45]lacerate yourself over your dead.

Prohibitions Resulting from Historical Events

[46]Dt. 17:16	J	
[47]Num. 15:39	UM	

It is forbidden to return to Egypt to [46]dwell there permanently or to [47]indulge in

⁴⁸Ex. 23:32;
Dt. 7:2
⁴⁹Dt. 20:16
(Ancient) J
⁵⁰Dt. 7:2
(Ancient
only) J
⁵¹Ex. 23:33
(Ancient) J
⁵²Dt. 7:3 JUM
⁵³Dt. 23:4 UMJ
⁵⁴Dt. 23:8 UMJ
⁵⁵Dt. 23:8 UMJ
⁵⁶Dt. 23:7
(Ancient) J
⁵⁷Dt. 20:19 UM
⁵⁸Dt. 7:21 UM
⁵⁹Dt. 25:19
(Ancient) J

impure thoughts or sights. You may not ⁴⁸make a pact with the seven Canaanite nations or ⁴⁹save the life an any member of them. Do not ⁵⁰show mercy to idolators, ⁵¹permit them to dwell in the land of Israel or ⁵²intermarry with them. A Jewess may not ⁵³marry an Ammonite or Moabite even if he converts to Judaism but should not refuse (for reasons of genealogy alone) ⁵⁴a descendent of Esau or ⁵⁵an Egyptian who are proselytes. It is prohibited to ⁵⁶make peace with the Ammonite or Moabite nations.

The ⁵⁷destruction of fruit trees even in times of war is forbidden as is wanton waste at any time. Do not ⁵⁸fear the enemy and do not ⁵⁹forget the evil done by Amalek.

Blasphemy

⁶⁰Lev. 24:16 UM
(rather) Ex. 22:27
⁶¹Lev. 19:12 UM
⁶²Ex. 20:7 UM
⁶³Lev. 22:32 UM
⁶⁴Dt. 6:16 UM
⁶⁵Dt. 12:4 UM
⁶⁶Dt. 21:23 UM

You must not ⁶⁰blasphemo the Holy Namc, ⁶¹break an oath made by It, ⁶²take It in vain or ⁶³profane It. Do not ⁶⁴try the Lord God. You may not ⁶⁵erase God's name from the holy texts or destroy institutions devoted to His worship. Do not ⁶⁶allow the body of one hanged to remain so overnight.

⁶⁷Num. 18:5 T
⁶⁸Lev. 16:2 T
⁶⁹Lev. 21:23 T
⁷⁰Lev. 21:17 T

Temple

Be not ⁶⁷lax in guarding the Temple. The high priest must not enter the Temple ⁶⁸indiscriminately; a priest with a physical blemish may not ⁶⁹enter there at all or ⁷⁰serve in the sanctuary and even if

[71]Lev. 21:18	T
[72]Num. 18:3	T
[73]Lev. 10:9	
-11	T
[74]Num. 18:4	T
[75]Lev. 22:2	T
[76]Lev. 21:6	T
[77]Num. 5:3	T
[78]Dt. 23:11	T
[79]Ex. 20:25	T
[80]Ex. 20:26	T
[81]Lev. 6:6	T
[82]Ex. 30:9	T
[83]Ex. 30:32	T
[84]Ex. 30:32	T
[85]Ex. 30:37	T
[86]Ex. 25:15	T
[87]Ex. 28:28	T
[88]Ex. 28:32	T

the blemish is of a temporary nature he may not [71]participate in the service there until it has passed.

The Levites and the priests must not [72]interchange in their functions. Intoxicated persons may not [73]enter the sanctuary or teach the Law. It is forbidden for [74]non-priests, [75]unclean priests or [76]priests who have performed the necessary ablution but are still within the time limit of their uncleanness to serve in the Temple. No unclean person may enter [77]the Temple or [78]the Temple Mount.

The altar must not be made of [79]hewn stones nor may the ascent to it be by [80]steps. The fire on it may not be [81]extinguished nor may any other but the specified incense be [82]burned on the golden altar.

You may not [83]manufacture oil with the same ingredients and in the same proportions as the anointing oil which itself [84]may not be misused. Neither may you [85]compound incense with the same ingredients and in the same proportions as that burnt on the altar. You must not [86]remove the staves from the Ark, [87]remove the breastplate from the ephod or [88]make any incision in the upper garment of the high priest.

[89]Dt. 12:13	
[90]Lev. 17:3-4	T
[91]Lev. 22:20	T
[92]Lev. 22:22	T
[93]Lev. 22:24	T

Sacrifices

It is forbidden to [89]offer sacrifices or [90]slaughter consecrated animals outside the Temple. You may not [91]sanctify, [92]slaughter, [93]sprinkle the blood of or

[94]Lev. 22:22	T
[95]Dt. 17:1	T
[96]Lev. 22:25	T
[97]Lev. 22:21	T
[98]Lev. 2:11	T
[99]Lev. 2:13	T
[100]Dt. 23:19	T
[101]Lev. 22:28	T
[102]Lev. 5:11	T
[103]Lev. 5:11	T
[104]Num. 5:15	T
[105]Num. 5:15	T
[106]Lev. 27:10	T
[107]Lev. 27:26	T
[108]Num. 18:17	T
[109]Lev. 27:33	T
[110]Lev. 27:28	T
[111]Lev. 27:28	T
[112]Lev. 5:8	T
[113]Dt. 15:19	T
[114]Dt. 15:19	T
[115]Ex. 34:25	T
[116]Ex. 23:10	T
[117]Ex. 12:10	T
[118]Dt. 16:4	T
[119]Num. 9:13	T
[120]Lev. 22:30	T
[121]Ex. 12:46	T
[122]Num. 9:12	T
[123]Ex. 12:46	T

[94]burn the inner parts of a blemished animal even if the blemish is [95]of a temporary nature and even if it is [96]offered by Gentiles. It is forbidden to [97]inflict a blemish on an animal consecrated for sacrifice.

Leaven or honey may not [98]be offered on the altar, neither may [99]anything unsalted. An animal received as the hire of a harlot or as the price of a dog [100]may not be offered. Do not [101]kill an animal and its young on the same day. It is forbidden to use [102]olive oil or [103]frankincense in the sin offering or [104], [105]in the jealousy offering (sotah). You may not [106]substitute sacrifices even [107]from one category to the other. You may not [108]redeem the firstborn of permitted animals. It is forbidden to [109]sell the tithe of the herd or [110]sell or [111]redeem a field consecrated by the herem vow.

When you slaughter a bird for a sin offering you may not [112]split its head.

It is forbidden to [113]work with or [114]to shear a consecrated animal. You must not slaughter the paschal lamb [115]while there is still leaven about; nor may you leave overnight [116]those parts that are to be offered up or [117]to be eaten. You may not leave any part of the festive offering [118]until the third day or any part of [119]the second paschal lamb or [120]the thanksgiving offering until the morning.

It is forbidden to break a bone of [121]the first or [122]the second paschal lamb or [123]to

[124]Lev. 6:10	T	
[125]Ex. 12:9	T	
[126]Ex. 12:45	T	
[127]Ex. 12:48	T	
[128]Ex. 12:43	T	
[129]Lev. 12:4	T	
[130]Lev. 7:19	T	
[131]Lev. 19:6-8	T	
[132]Lev. 7:18	T	
[133]Lev. 22:10	T	
[134]Lev. 22:10	T	
[135]Lev. 22:10	T	
[136]Lev. 22:4	T	
[137]Lev. 22:12	T	
[138]Lev. 6:16	T	
[139]Lev. 6:23	T	
[140]Dt. 14:3	T	
[141]Dt. 12:17	T	
[142]Dt. 12:17	T	
[143]Dt. 12:17	T	
[144]Dt. 12:17	T	
[145]Dt. 12:17	T	
[146]Dt. 12:17	T	
[147]Dt. 12:17	T	
[148]Dt. 12:17	T	
[149]Ex. 29:33	T	

carry their flesh out of the house where it is being eaten. You must not [124]allow the remains of the meal offering to become leaven. It is also forbidden to eat the paschal lamb [125]raw or sodden or to allow [126]an alien resident, [127]an uncircumcised person or an [128]apostate to eat of it.

A ritually unclean person [129]must not eat of holy things nor may [130]holy things which have become unclean be eaten. Sacrificial meat [131]which is left after the time-limit or [132]which was slaughtered with wrong intentions must not be eaten. The heave offering must not be eaten by [133]an uncircumcised person, or [136]an unclean priest. The daughter of a priest who is married to a non-priest may not [137]eat of holy things. The meal offering of the priest [138]must not be eaten, neither may [139]the flesh of the sin offerings sacrificed within the sanctuary or [140]consecrated animals which have become blemished.

You may not eat the second tithe of [141]corn, [142]wine, or [143]oil or [144]unblemished firstlings outside Jerusalem.

The priests may not eat the sin-offerings or the trespass-offerings outside the Temple courts or [146]the flesh of the burnt-offering at all. The lighter sacrifices [147]may not be eaten before the blood has been sprinkled. A non-priest may not [148]eat of the holiest sacrifices and a priest [149]may not eat the first-fruits outside the Temple courts.

[150]Dt. 26:14	T	One may not eat [150]the second tithe while in
[151]Dt. 26:14	T	a state of impurity or [151]in mourning;
[152]Dt. 26:14	T	its redemption money [152]may not be
[153]Lev. 22:15	T	used for anything other than food and
[154]Ex. 22:28	T	drink.
[155]Dt. 23:22	T	You must not [153]eat untithed produce or
[156]Ex. 23:15	T	[154]change the order of separating the
[157]Num. 30:3	UM	various tithes.

Do not [155]delay payment of offerings—either freewill or obligatory—and do not [156]come to the Temple on the pilgrim festivals without an offering.

Do not [157]break your word.

[158]Lev. 21:7	T	**Priests**
[159]Lev. 21:7	T	A priest may not marry [158]a harlot, [159]a
[160]Lev. 21:7	T	woman who has been profaned from
[161]Lev. 21:14	T	the priesthood, or [160]a divorcee; the
[162]Lev. 21:15	T	high priest must not [161]marry a widow
[163]Lev. 10:6	T	or [162]take one as a concubine. Priests
[164]Lev. 10:6	T	may not enter the sanctuary with
[165]Lev. 10:7	T	[163]overgrown hair of the head or [164]with
[166]Lev. 21:1	T	torn clothing; they must not [165]leave
[167]Lev. 21:11	T	the courtyard during the Temple ser-
[168]Lev. 21:11	T	vice. An ordinary priest may not render
[169]Dt. 18:1	T	himself [166]ritually impure except for
[170]Dt. 18:1	T	those relatives specified, and the high
[171]Dt. 14:1	T	priest should not become impure [167]for

anybody in [168]any way.

The tribe of Levi shall have no part in [169]the division of the land of Israel or [170]in the spoils of war.

It is forbidden [171]to make oneself bald as a sign of mourning for one's dead.

[172]Dt. 14:7	TC	**Dietary Laws**
	UM	A Jew may not eat [172]cattle, [173]unclean fish,
[173]Lev. 11:11	TC	[174]unclean fowl, [175]creeping things that
	UM	fly, [176]creatures that creep on the
[174]Lev. 11:13	TC	ground, [177]reptiles, [178]worms found in
	UM	fruit or produce or [179]any detestable
[175]Dt. 14:19	TC	creature.
	UM	An animal that has died naturally [180]is for-
[176]Lev. 11:41	TC	bidden for consumption as is [181]a torn
	UM	or mauled animal. One must not eat
[177]Lev. 11:44	TC	[182]any limb taken from a living animal.
	UM	Also prohibited is [183]the sinew of the
[178]Lev. 11:42	TC	thigh (gid ha-nashed) as are [184]blood
	UM	and [185]certain types of fat (helev). It is
[179]Lev. 11:43	TC	forbidden [186]to boil lamb in mother's
	UM	milk or [187]eat of such a mixture. It is
[180]Dt. 14:21	UM	also forbidden to eat [188]of an ox con-
[181]Ex. 22:30	UM	demned to stoning (even should it have
[182]Dt. 12:23	UM	been properly slaughtered).
[183]Gen. 32:33	J	One may not eat [189]bread made of new corn
[184]Lev. 7:26	UM	or the new corn itself, either [190]roasted
[185]Lev. 7:23	UMT	or [191]green, before the omer offering
[186]Ex. 23:19	UM	has been brought on the 16th of Nisan.
[187]Ex. 34:26	UM	You may not eat [192]orlah or [193]the
[188]Ex. 21:28	UM	growth of mixed planting in the vine-
[189]Lev. 23:14	T	yard.
[190]Lev. 23:14	T	Any use of [194]wine libations to idols is pro-
[191]Lev. 23:14	T	hibited, as are [195]gluttony and drun-
[192]Lev. 19:23	T	kenness. One may not eat anything on
[193]Dt. 22:9	T?	[196]the Day of Atonement. During Pass-
[194]Dt. 32:38	UM	over it is forbidden to eat [197]leaven
[195]Lev. 19:26;		(hamex) or [198]anything containing an
Dt. 21:20	UM	admixture of such. This is also forbid-
[196]Lev. 23:29	J	den [199]after the middle of the 14th of
[197]Ex. 13:3	J	Nisan (the day before Passover). Dur-

[198]Ex. 13:20	J
[199]Dt. 16:3	J
[200]Ex. 13:7	J
[201]Ex. 12:19	J

ing Passover no leaven may be [200]seen or [201]found in your possession.

Nazirites

[202]Num. 6:3	J
[203]Num. 6:3	J
[204]Num. 6:3	J
[205]Num. 6:4	J
[206]Num. 6:4	JT
[207]Num. 6:7	J
[208]Lev. 21:11	JT
[209]Num. 6:5	JT

A Nazirite may not drink [202]wine or any beverage made from grapes; he may not eat [203]fresh grapes, [204]dried grapes, [205]grape seeds or [206]grape peel. He may not render himself [207]ritually impure for his dead nor may he [208]enter a tent in which there is a corpse. He must not [209]shave his hair.

Agriculture

[210]Lev. 23:22	UM
[211]Lev. 19:9	UM
[212]Lev. 19:10	UM
[213]Lev. 19:10	UM
[214]Dt. 24:18	UM
[215]Lev. 19:19	J
[216]Dt. 22:9	J
[217]Lev. 19:19	J
(215-217)—Symbols of purity	
[218]Dt. 22:10	JUM
[219]Dt. 25:4	UM
[220]Lev. 25:4	J
[221]Lev. 25:4	JUM
(220-228)-Ancient Israel's law with moral principles of kindness and dependence on God in non-	

It is forbidden [210]to reap the whole of a field without leaving the corners for the poor: it is also forbidden to [211]gather up the ears of corn that fall during reaping or to harvest [212]the misformed clusters of grapes, or [213]the grapes that fall or to [214]return to take a forgotten sheaf.

You must not [215]sow different species of seed together or [216]corn in a vineyard; it is also forbidden to [217]crossbreed different species of animals or [218]work with two different species yoked together. You must not [219]muzzle an animal working in a field to prevent it from eating.

It is forbidden to [220]till the earth, [221]to prune trees, [222]to reap (in the usual manner) produce or [223]fruit which has grown wthout cultivation in the seventh year (shemittah). One may also not [224]till

planting year.
[222]Lev. 25:4	JUM
[223]Lev. 25:5	JUM
[224]Lev. 25:11	JUM
[225]Lev. 25:11	JUM
[226]Lev. 25:11	JUM
[227]Lev. 25:23	JUM
[228]Lev. 25:33	JT
[229]Dt. 12:19	JT

the earth or prune trees in the Jubilee year, when it is also forbidden to harvest (in the usual manner) [225]produce or [226]fruit that has grown without cultivation.

One may not [227]sell one's landed inheritance in the land of Israel permanently or [228]change the lands of the Levites or [229]leave the Levites without support.

[230]Dt. 15:2	UM
[231]Dt. 15:9	UM
[232]Dt. 15:7	UM
[233]Dt. 15:13	UM
[234]Ex. 22:24	UM
[235]Lev. 25:37	UM
(at real profit)	
[236]Dt. 23:20	UM
[237]Ex. 22:24	UM
[238]Lev. 19:13	UM
[239]Dt. 24:10	UM
[240]Dt. 24:12	UM
[241]Dt. 24:17	UM
[242]Dt. 24:6	UM
[243]Ex. 20:13	UM
[244]Lev. 19:11	UM
[245]Lev. 19:13	UM
[246]Dt. 19:14	UM
[247]Lev. 19:13	UM
[248]Lev. 19:11	UM

Loans, Business and the Treatment of Slaves

It is forbidden to [230]demand repayment of a loan after the seventh year, you may not, however, [231]refuse to lend to the poor because that year is approaching. Do not [232]deny charity to the poor or [233]send a Hebrew slave away empty-handed when he finishes his period of service. Do not [234]dun your debtor when you know that he cannot pay. It is forbidden to [235]lend to or [236]borrow from another Jew at interest or [237]participate in an agreement involving interest either as a guarantor, witness, or writer of the contract. Do not [238]delay payment of wages.

You may not [239]take a pledge from a debtor by violence, [240]keep a poor man's pledge when he needs it, [241]take any pledge from a widow or [242]from any debtor if he earns his living with it.

Kidnapping [243]a Jew is forbidden.

Do not [244]steal or [245]rob by violence. Do not [246]remove a landmark or [247]defraud.

It is forbidden [248]to deny receipt of a loan or

[249]Lev. 19:11	UM	
[250]Lev. 25:14	UM	
[251]Lev. 25:17	UM	
[252]Ex. 22:20	UM	
[253]Ex. 22:20	UM	
[254]Dt. 23:16	UM	
[255]Dt. 23:17	UM	
[256]Ex. 22:21	UM	
[257]Lev. 25:39	UM	
[258]Lev. 25:42	UM	
[259]Lev. 25:43	UM	
[260]Lev. 25:53	UM	
[261]Ex. 21:8	UM	
[262]Ex. 21:10	UM	
[263]Dt. 21:14	UM	
[264]Dt. 21:14	UM	
[265]Ex. 20:17	UM	
[266]Dt. 5:18	UM	
[267]Dt. 23:26	UM	
[268]Dt. 23:25	UM	
[269]Dt. 22:3	UM	
[270]Ex. 23:5	UM	
[271]Lev. 19:35	UM	
[272]Dt. 25:13	UM	

a deposit or [249]to swear falsely regarding another man's property.

You must not [250]deceive anybody in business. You may not [251]mislead a man even verbally. It is forbidden to harm the stranger among you [252]verbally or [253]do him injury in trade.

You may not [254]return, or [255]otherwise take advantage of, a slave who has fled to the land of Israel from his master, even if his master is a Jew.

Do not [256]afflict the widow or the orphan. You may not [257]misuse or [258]sell a Hebrew slave; do not [259]treat him cruelly or [260]allow a heathen to mistreat him. You must not [261]sell your Hebrew maidservant or, if you marry her, [262]withhold food, clothing, and conjugal rights from her. You must not [263]sell a female captive or [264]treat her as a slave.

Do not [265]covet another man's possessions even if you are willing to pay for them. Even [266]the desire alone is forbidden.

A worker must not [267]cut down standing corn during his work or [268]take more fruit than he can eat.

One must not [269]turn away from a lost article which is to be returned to its owner nor may you [270]refuse to help a man or an animal which is collapsing under its burden.

It is forbidden to [271]defraud with weights and measures or even [272]to possess inaccurate weights.

[273]Lev. 19:15	UM
[274]Ex. 23:8	UM
[275]Lev. 19:15	UM
[276]Dt. 1:17	UM
[277]Lev. 19:15,	UM
rather Ex. 23:3	
[278]Ex. 23:6	UM
[279]Dt. 19:13	UM
[280]Dt. 24:17	UM
[281]Ex. 23:1	UM
[282]Ex. 23:2	UM
[283]Ex. 23:2	UM
[284]Dt. 1:17	UM
[285]Ex. 20:16	UM
[286]Ex. 23:1	UM
[287]Dt. 24:16	UM
[288]Dt. 19:15	UM
[289]Ex. 20:13	UM
[290]Ex. 23:7	UM
[291]Num. 35:30	UM
[292]Num. 35:12	UM
[293]Dt. 25:12	UM
[294]Dt. 22:26	UM
[295]Num. 35:31	UM
[296]Num. 35:32	UM

Justice

A judge must not [273]perpetrate injustice, [274]accept bribes or be [275]partial or [276]afraid. He may [277]not favor the poor or [278]discriminate against the wicked; he should not [279]pity the condemned or [280]pervert the judgment of strangers or orphans.

It is forbidden to [281]hear one litigant without the other being present. A capital case cannot be decided by [282]a majority of one.

A judge should not [283]accept a colleague's opinion unless he is convinced of its correctness; it is forbidden to [284]appoint as a judge someone who is ignorant of the Law.

Do not [285]give false testimony or accept [286]testimony from a wicked person or from [287]relatives of a person involved in the case. It is forbidden to pronounce judgment [288]on the basis of the testimony of one witness.

Do not [289]murder.

You must not convict on [290]circumstantial evidence alone.

A witness [291]must not sit as a judge in capital cases.

You must not [292]execute anybody without due proper trial and conviction.

Do not [293]pity or spare the pursuer.

Punishment is not to be inflicted for [294]an act committed under duress.

Do not accept ransom [295]for a murderer or [296]a manslayer.

[297]Lev. 19:16	UM
[298]Dt. 22:8	UM
[299]Lev. 19:14	UM
[300]Dt. 25:2-3	UM
[301]Lev. 19:16	UM
[302]Lev. 19:17	UM
[303]Lev. 19:17	UM
[304]Lev. 19:18	UM
[305]Lev. 19:18	UM
[306]Dt. 22:6	UM
[307]Lev. 13:33	UM
[308]Dt. 24:8	UM
[309]Dt. 21:7	T
[310]Ex. 22:17	UM
(J-ancient)	
[311]Dt. 24:5	UM
[312]Dt. 17:11	UM
[313]Dt. 13:1	UM
[314]Dt. 13:1	UM
[315]Ex. 22:27	UM
[316]Ex. 22:27	UM
[317]Lev. 19:14	UM
[318]Ex. 21:17	UM
[319]Ex. 21:15	UM
[320]Ex. 20:10	J
[321]Ex. 16:29	J
[322]Ex. 35:3	J
[323]Ex. 12:16	J
[324]Ex. 12:16	J

Do not [297]hesitate to save another person from danger and do not [298]leave a stumbling block in the way or [299]mislead another person by giving wrong advice.

It is forbidden [300]to administer more than the assigned number of lashes to the guilty.

Do not [301]tell tales or [302]bear hatred in your heart. It is forbidden to [303]shame a Jew, [304]to bear a grudge or [305]to take revenge. Do not [306]take the dam when you take the young birds.

It is forbidden to [397]shave a leprous scall or [308]remove other signs of that affliction. It is forbidden [309]to cultivate a valley in which a slain body was found and in which subsequently the ritual of breaking the heifer's neck (eglah arufah) was performed.

Do not [310]suffer a witch to live.

Do not [311]force a bridegroom to perform military service during the first year of his marriage. It is forbidden to [312]rebel against the transmitters of the tradition or to [313]add or [314]detract from the precepts of the law.

Do not curse [315]a judge, [316]a ruler or [317]any Jew.

Do not [318]curse or [319]strike a parent.

It is forbidden to [320]work on the Sabbath or [321]walk further than the permitted limits (eruv). You may not [322]inflict punishment on the Sabbath.

It is forbidden to work on [323]the first or [324]the

[325]Lev. 23:21	J
[326]Lev. 23:25	J
[327]Lev. 23:35	J
[328]Lev. 23:36	J
[329]Lev. 23:28	J

seventh day of Passover, on [325]Shavuot, on [326]Rosh Ha-Shanah, on the [327]first and [328]eighth (Shemini Azeret) days of Sukkot and [329]on the Day of Atonement.

[330]Lev. 18:7	UM
[331]Lev. 18:8	UM
[332]Lev. 18:9	UM
[333]Lev. 18:11	UM
[334]Lev. 18:10	UM
[335]Lev. 18:20	UM
[336]Lev. 18:10	UM
[337]Lev. 18:17	UM
[338]Lev. 18:17	UM
[339]Lev. 18:17	UM
[340]Lev. 18:12	UM
[341]Lev. 18:13	UM
[342]Lev. 18:14	UM
[343]Lev. 18:15	UM
[344]Lev. 18:16	UM
[345]Lev. 18:18	UM
[346]Lev. 18:19	UM
[347]Lev. 18:20	UM
[348]Lev. 18:23	UM
[349]Lev. 18:23	UM
[350]Lev. 18:22	UM
[351]Lev. 18:7	UM
[352]Lev. 18:14	UM
[353]Lev. 18:6	UM
[354]Dt. 23:3	UM
[355]Dt. 23:18	UM
[356]Dt. 24:4	UM

Incest and Other Forbidden Relationships. It is forbidden to enter into an incestuous relationship with one's [330]mother, [331]step-mother, [332]sister, [333]step-sister, [334]son's daughter, [335]daughter's daughter, [336]daughter, [337]any woman and her daughter, [338]any woman and her son's daughter, [339]any woman and her daughter's daughter, [340]father's sister, [341]mother's sister, [342]paternal uncle's wife, [343]daughter-in-law, [344]brother's wife and [345]wife's sister.

It is also forbidden to [346]have sexual relations with a menstruous woman.

Do not [347]commit adultery.

It is forbidden for [348]a man or [349]a woman to have sexual intercourse with an animal.

Homosexuality [350]is forbidden, particularly with [351]one's father or [352]uncle.

It is forbidden to have [353]intimate physical contact (even without actual intercourse) with any of the women with whom intercourse is forbidden.

A mamzer may not [354]marry a Jewess.

Harlotry [355]is forbidden.

A divorcee may not be [356]remarried to her first husband if, in the meanwhile, she had married another.

[357]Dt. 25:5	UM	A childless widow may not [357]marry any-
[358]Dt. 22:29	UM	body other than her late husband's
[359]Dt. 22:19	UM	brother.
[360]Dt. 23:2	UM	A man may not [358]divorce a wife whom he
[361]Lev. 22:24	UM	married after having raped her or

[359]after having slandered her.

An eunuch may not [360]marry a Jewess.

Castration [361]is forbidden.

[362]Dt. 17:15	J	**The Monarchy.**
[363]Dt. 17:16	JUM	*(Jewish Ancient—with moral principles)*
[364]Dt. 17:17	UM	You may not [362]elect as king anybody who is
[365]Dt. 17:17	JUM	not of the seed of Israel.

The king must not accumulate an excessive number of [363]horses, [364]wives, or [365]wealth.

APPENDIX II

Major Writings Supporting Positions Taken In This Book

The whole of the viewpoint given in this book is the product of the author's own integrative work. He bears full responsibility for the positions outlined herein. The presentation is in *no way* an exhaustive one and the author expects that further study will add to his knowledge and cause revision of certain positions; but he has confidence in the basic thrust of the book. The author's position is one gained from study and he is indebted to many writers, as is evidenced by footnotes. However, he wishes here to list major works that suport his basic conclusions. The list could be significantly expanded; but only works predominantly in print in America are represented here. We also list various persons and statements of value. The author does not necessarily agree with these works in entirety.

B. BAGGATI, *The Church of the Circumcision*, Rome. This unfortunately hard-to-get work (although available in many Catholic university libraries) is a *seminal work*. Bagatti claims that the early movement of followers of Jesus among Jews was far more extensive than most imagine. He also argues that the Jewish Christians were faithful to Torah and that this was in accord with *apostolic example* and teaching as concerns Jewish believers. Bagatti distinguishes the Nazarenes who fully followed New Testament teaching and the Ebionites who did not.

SAMUELE BACCHIOCCHI, *From Saturday to Sunday* available from *Biblical Archaeology Review* contains a summary of the author's views (see also *BAR*, October 1978). Bacchiocchi is in accord with Bagatti's position and applies his effort to show how the Church severed its Jewish connection and how its practice differed from Messianic Jews of the first century. He emphasizes the switch from Saturday to Sunday worship in the second century as part of this study.

JEAN DANIELOU, *The Theology of Jewish Christianity* out of print in America and available in England, also in magazine *Cross Currents* (1968). Danielou examines the theological concepts of the early Jewish believers and firmly distinguishes the heretical Ebionites from the Nazarenes whom he emphasizes were true to the New Testament. He also sees the Apostles and the Nazarenes as Torah-loyal and even calls for a wing of the Church which will be liturgically Hebraic. All this from a Catholic cardinal!

GREGORY DIX, *Jew and Greek; A Study in the Primitive Christian Church*. Dix also argues that the Apostolic Church within Jewry saw itself as Torah-loyal and that this was simply part of their calling in Israel.

MARCUS BARTH, in "Jews and Gentiles; the Social Character of Justification in Paul" (Spring 1968). *Journal of Ecumenical Studies*. Barth, the illustrious son of Karl Barth, argues that Paul himself was Torah-loyal. He was not anti-Torah at all but only against the loss of the sense of open fellowship between Jews and non-Jewish Christians who were to maintain acceptance despite different identities vis-a-vis Torah.

JOHN HOWARD YODER, in *The Politics of Jesus* 1972 picks up this theme and argues forcefully that Torah loyalty among Jews was never at issue (p. 220).

W.D. DAVIES, *Paul and Rabbinic Judaism*. A *true classic* outlining Paul's debt to and difference from Pharasaical Judaism. Davies argues that Paul was *fully Torah-loyal* and never gave up his sense of being part of Israel and that Israel was still God's people with a unique calling.

DAVID DAUBE, *The New Testament and Rabbinic Judaism* outlines the interrelationship very positively. We might note in passing that it is difficult to find *scholars in the area of early Jewish Christianity* who disagree with the above positions since the early sources are so clear in regard to the Jewish loyalty of the Nazarenes.

Fuller Theological Seminary statement on Jewish-Christian relations includes a section in clear defense of Messianic Jewish Congregations. Write Fuller Theological Seminary in Pasadena, California. This is in accord with the School of World Misson at FTS which argues for the closest identification possible with any culture in reaching them for the Gospel. In line with this, see D. McGaven's *Understanding Church Growth*, sections on Jews (see index).

PHIL GOBLE, *Everything You Need to Grow a Messianic Synagogue*. Goble received his Ph.D. from Fuller and argues passionately for Messianic Judaism.

JIM HUCHINS, *The Case for Messianic Judaism*. (Ph.D. thesis at Fuller). Huchins, the former chaplain of Wheaton College, develops the case well and is in accord with most positions taken here.

JULES ISAAC, the Jewish scholar in *Jesus and Israel* argues beautifully concerning the positive Jewish identity of Jesus and His teaching to encourage such.

ELMER JOSEPHSON, in *Israel/God's Key to World Redemption*, argues strongly concerning God's continuing covenant with Israel and her call to Torah. However, Josephson evidences no knowledge of Messianic Judaism, though he says much of positive value about the Law.

RICHARD LONGENECKER is an evangelical scholar who has authored *several excellent books* that deal with issues which concern us. His first book, *Paul the Apostle of Liberty*, shows that Paul's philosophy of grace and liberty is not at all inconsistent with his practice of the Law. This book gives an appendix both describing and defending the practice of the first Jewish followers of Yeshua in keeping the Law. His books, *The Christology of Early Jewish Christianity* and *Biblical Exegesis in the Apostolic Period*, also give excellent information for interpreting difficult passages that would relate to Messianic Judaism.

PETER RICHARDSON'S *Israel in the Apostolic Church* is of importance. In this book, some of our central viewpoints on Israel and the Law are espoused—especially in understanding Romans 9-11.

The work of HUGH SCHOENFIELD, *A History of Jewish Christianity*, (out of print) gives a good summary as well as a description of the Jewish identity of the early Jewish followers of Jesus. The book does have Ebionite tendencies. Of note is that this book records the tireless efforts of Mark John Levy, the first general secretary to the Hebrew Christian Alliance, who worked for a position similar to our position on the calling of Messianic Jews. Eichorn, in *The Evangelization of the American Jew*, points to Levy as one of the few exceptions to unscrupulous behavior among Jewish Christians and praises Levy's sincerity. Through Levy's efforts, the Episcopal Church adopted in 1914 a statement which supported Levy's position as well as the establishment of Hebraic congregations.

HANS J. SCHOEP'S has written several works on the early Jewish Christians. He emphasizes Ebionite history and theology, but does recognize the Torah importance among many early Jewish Christians. The *Jewish-Christian Argument* is one of his few books in print in English.

SAMUEL SCHULTZ, a supporter of Messianic Judaism, has written the *The Gospel of Moses* and *Deuteronomy, the Gospel of God's Love*. These titles already indicate the ground Schultz is breaking.

Also of interest is CORRIE TEN BOOM's *In My Father's House*. This book is of note because it describes Corrie's brother, Casper ten Boom, of the famous family. Casper came to Messianic Jewish conclusions in his doctor's thesis in Germany. He concluded that Jewish followers of Jesus were called to maintain their heritage, perhaps in unique congregations. The ten Boom family survivors have been supportive of Messianic Judaism.

MICHAEL WYSCHOGROD, in *Evangelicals and Jews in Conversation* (ed. Mark Tannenbaum, Marvin Wilson, A. James Rudin Baker), is a Jewish scholar who concludes that Paul was Torah-loyal and expected other Jewish Christians to be Torah-loyal. His issue was not a Jew's call but forcing Judaism on non-Jewish believers. *Wyschogrod is one of the few Jewish scholars who, without following Yeshua, understands Paul and the Law.* Even his book, which was written to counter Messianic Judaism and Christian missionary efforts among Jews *(Judaism and Hebrew Christianity), fairly* presents Paul and the Law. Wyschogrod argues that the Apostles and Paul still considered themselves part of Israel and practiced Torah, although they understood justification only by grace.

ALAN COLE, *Epistle of Paul to the Galatians* (Tyndale *New Testament Commentaries*) is also excellent in these regards. See especially his introduction.

JOHN FISCHER and the author are seeking to edit a book called *Messianic Judaism Exploratory Essays*. Many scholars have written supportive essays. Included are:

H.L. ELLISON, "Paul and the Law" (England); R.N. LONGENECKER, "Jewish Exegesis in Matthew and Paul" (U. of Toronto); ARTHUR LEWIS, "Semetic Thought in the New Testament" (Bethel College); SAMUEL SCHULTZ, "Is the Old Testament a Dispensation of Law?" (Wheaton College); JAMES HUCHINS, "Divine Messiah and Triune God?" (Watchman Association); LARRY RICH, "Messianic Judaism and the Book of Acts" (Gen. Sec. Messianic Jewish Alliance); JOHN FISCHER, "*Hebrews* and Messianic Judaism" (Trinity Ev. Divinity); WALTER KAISER, "Does the Old Testament Truly Prophecy Jesus?" (Trinity Divinity); DAVID STERN, "Grace in Judaism" (independent scholar); A. GLASSER, "Congregational Growth and Messianic Judaism" (Fuller Theological Seminary); DANIEL FUCHS,

(American Board of Missions) "Reapproachment Between Traditional Missions and Messianic Jews"; D. JUSTER, "Covenant and Dispensation"; LOUIS GOLDBERG, "Messianic Jewish History" (Moody).

The book *Evangelicals and Jews in Conversation* is a helpful compendium of Jewish and evangelical views. Many articles give a sense of understanding the reaffirmed Jewish calling among the first century apostles and Jewish believers.

We should also note that the late 19th century famous scholars, F.J.A. Hort and J.B. Lightfoot came to similar conclusions, especially in writings specifically on Jewish Christianity.

APPENDIX III

Fuller Theological Seminary News Release

PASADENA, CALIFORNIA—Dean Arthur F. Glasser and the School of World Mission faculty of Fuller Theological Seminary have released the following statement:

"We of the School of World Mission faculty of Fuller Theological Seminary feel constrained to address ourselves and the Church at large concerning the Jewish people. Particularly so at this time when the third commonwealth of Israel is celebrating its 28th anniversary and when we find ourselves much in prayer that the Jewish presence in the Middle East shall become under God an instrument for reconciliation and peace.

"We are profoundly grateful for the heritage given to us by the Jewish people which is so vital for own Christian faith. We believe that God used the Jewish people as the sole repository of the history-centered disclosure of himself to mankind. This revelation began with Abraham and continued to the Jewish writers of the New Testament. Not only were the oracles of God committed to them (Romans 3:2), but it was through this people that God chose to bring Jesus Christ into the world. We believe that he is the only hope of salvation for the Jewish people, and for all mankind. Indeed, we continue

to pray that through the mercy and blessing of God, the
Jewish people shall turn to the Messiah Jesus and become
once again a light to the nations, that his salvation may reach
to the end of the earth (Isa. 49:6).

"We wish to charge the Church, as a whole, to do more
than merely include the Jewish people in their evangelistic
outreach. We would encourage an active response to the
mandate of Romans 1:16 calling for evangelism "to the Jew
first." For this we have the precedent of a great Jewish missionary, the Apostle Paul. Though sent to the Gentile world,
he never relinquished his burden for his own kinsmen after
the flesh. Wherever he travelled, he first visited the synagogue before presenting Christ to the Gentiles. So it must be
in every generation. We must provide a priority opportunity
for our Jewish friends to respond to the Messiah. They are
our benefactors and it was they who first evangelized us.
Furthermore, the Gospel we share with them must be carried to all tribes and peoples and tongues.

"We regret exceedingly that Christians have not always
shared this Gospel with the Jewish people in a loving and
ethical manner. Too often, while interested in Jewish evangelism in general, we have demeaned the dignity of the Jewish person by our unkind stereotyping and our disregard for
Jewish sensitivities. How un-Christlike we have been!

"Likewise, we have unwittingly encouraged Jewish converts to divest themselves of their Jewish heritage and culture. For this too, we would repent and express our regret
that the Western influence on our beliefs has precluded the
original Jewish context. Our Church is culturally and spiritually poorer for it.

"In our day we are encouraged that thousands of Jewish
people are coming to the Messiah. This being so, we cannot
but call upon the Christian community to renew its commitment to share lovingly the Gospel of Jesus with the Jewish
people. And we heartily encourage Jewish believers in him,
including those who call themselves Messianic Jews, Hebrew-
Christians, and Jews for Jesus, to retain their Jewish heritage, culture, religious practices and marriage customs within

the context of a sound biblical theology e pressing Old and New Testment truth. Their freedom in Christ to do this cannot but enrich the Church in our day.

"More, we feel it incumbent on Christians in all traditions to reinstate the work of Jewish evangelism in their missionary obedience. Jewish-oriented programs should be developed. Appropriate agencies for Jewish evangelism should be formed. And churches everywhere should support those existing institutions which are faithfully and lovingly bearing a Christian witness to the Jewish people."

Pasadena, California
May 12, 1976

APPENDIX IV

When Is Ritual Idolatry?

During the last several years an undercurrent of disagreement concering the place of Jewish ritual has existed among Messianic Jews. On the mild side the disagreement is expressed in non-judgmental terms—"The Spirit of God has led us to include (or exclude) these traditional rituals as part of our life and worship expression." The more radical opinion is sometimes voiced that ritual is idolatry.

Certainly God would never have given rituals if ritual in and of itself was idolatry. The most explicit directions for ritual were given for cleansings, sacrifices, priestly functions, ordinations, and other Temple procedures. The Spirit of God Himself filled the Tabernacle and the later Temple of Solomon which was the center of Jewish rituals. Hence *we can safely and forever conclude that ritual is not idolatry.*

Can ritual, however, become idolatry? Are there dangers in ritual? Are there guidelines for leaders who will by their leadership be greatly influencing the spiritual life and perspective of their flocks? The answer to all of these questions is yes.

First of all, it is crucial to define idolatry in its broad sense. Idolatry is not simply bowing down to a statue. Scripture defines idolatry as, "worshipping and serving created things rather than the creator." (Romans 1:25)

To worship is to bow down, to give our heart's allegiance. Yet God has said, "You shall love the Lord thy God with all thy heart . . ." Everything, then, that is loved must be loved *in the Lord*. Hence, idolatry can occur whenever we give an allegiance to something that is not in the Lord. In idolatry, a person derives a meaning or significance from something beyond what it is meant by God to give. These false meanings give a *false basis of self-worth*. External achievements, the pride-of-position, and even an attachment to family and friends outside of God's order is idolatry. (He that loves father or mother more than Me is not worthy of Me.) The loss of a major idol leads to bitterness, insecurity, and depression. Idolatry is often a projection of self-worship.

In the same way, of course, attachment to ritual and tradition can be idolatry. So can anti-tradition and an idolatrous attachment to spontaneity for its own sake. I have seen so-called free services that were rote and allowed no real moving of the Spirit. We can go through the motions of spontaneous worship without being Spirit-led or empowered! On the other hand a Jew may be attached to Jewish tradition and ritual or even musical style as an extension of self worship and the wrong kind of Jewish pride (as opposed to healthy self esteem).

Let us not forget that there are also Anglican idols and Pentecostal idols! Every group has the potential to spawn its own unique idolatry, a pride expressing self-worship projected into form or anti-form. Ritual can be entered into with a background of fear like unto superstition.

The avoidance of self-worship and idolatry in ritual (and in spontaneous orders of service) is simple and profound. It is the Sh'ma, to love God with our all. *The deeper we enter into the love of God with our all and enter into our position as ascended with the Messiah in the heavenlies (Ephesians 2:6), the less we will have of idolatry of any kind. The more we experience of the supernatural love and power of God, the less there is of idolatry.*

Heartless religion is idolatrous self-religion. Preoccupation with form or lack of form will never deliver us; but only pressing into depth with God will deliver. Ritual can be a valuable expression, a tool of teaching, a revealer of God's majesty and grace; or it may be idolatry, a means of avoiding the reality of God, a hiding behind the merely familiar, self-worship, a precluding of the surprise of the Spirit's revelation. Indeed, what it is for one, it may not be for another.

There *are* some ways to lead so as to avoid idolatry. We who are in leadership need to develop a keen sense of the Spirit's leading; leaders should be more keenly aware of the Spirit's prompting. What we are and do will pervade the community. We lead the services, we model spiritual life. Hence the Spirit's reality and leading must not be nebulous to us.

Under the New Covenant we must always be sensitive to the Holy Spirit; He may tell us to do something different or the same. If we assume an order without the Spirit's being free to change our direction we can fall into rote ritual; this can lead to idolatry at worst or simply be dead habit or laziness. The Holy Spirit may have a reason for telling us to do something quite unusual. Who knows the condition of someone in our midst and how this will impact upon him? Moment-by-moment obedience to the Spirit as a definite presence precludes idolatry. Hence the chief criterion for a worship leader is not his voice, bearing, diction, etc., but his ability to hear the Spirit in the context of worship. In our congregation, several sensitive men are all free to hear the Spirit in a type of team leadership. When we restrict the Spirit's moving we have taken a step that brings us closer to idolatry. He may lead us to do the Torah service the same way fifty times, but the fifty-first may be radically different. The fixed elements are not absolutely fixed; the idolatry of those seeking spontaneity for its entertainment value is also precluded by the Spirit Who may lead in repeating some things week to week. We are thus required to perceive new things in the familiar.

How well I recall an elder going to the Ark by a Holy Spirit prompting and taking the scroll out of the Ark during a praise-worship time. At first I was a bit taken aback, but then a sense of God's glory and joy pervaded the service. It was not the usual order, but thank God for this worship leader's chutzpah. Usually we are led to a similar pattern, but not always. Let us not mistake mere human creativity for the Spirit's leading either. However, one mark of Holy Spirit religion is surprise and newness in which He breaks through and manifests Himself. One mark of His absence is that all things continue always in the same way.

Secondly, when change *prompted by the Holy Spirit* produces anger, insecurity, and fear, there is idolatry. We emphasize "prompted by the Spirit" to distinguish it from our own foolishness, though the things of the Spirit may seem foolish to the flesh, the natural man, who receives not the things of the Spirit (I Corinthians 2:14)! We must not have ritual as a security blanket or as a source of false identity. Our identity is in the Spirit of the Lord, that we are in the Messiah. The same words may be penned against fleshy spontaneity. Yet the New Covenant age is an age of the Spirit who can be the leader of our worship and life. Through a genuinely "in tune" spiritual leadership, He will do fresh and sometimes unusual things demonstrating His presence. It is good to allow for such Holy Spirit leadership and freshness. Furthermore, it is good to have enough change to flush out the idolatry in midst and to be able to deal with it.

The guard against idolatry can be summarized under the concept of never entering the place where the Spirit may not say yes or no to our order, either in part or in totality from week to week. It is to enter into the deep things of God. It is to be leaders who know the reality of the Spirit and the Word. In all of this it is incumbent upon us to educate ourselves and our people so that we may be a people of the Spirit. We must have confidence in our ability to hear Him and the courage to step out in what we hear if tested by the Word. Ritual is as a frame for a picture. The picture is the manifestation of the Lord in power. Messianic Judaism is the means of conveying the power of the Gospel in the most communicative way to the Jewish community. The proper frame enhances this work. Yet let us not confuse the picture and the frame by improper valuation. God has given a structure of life to preserve our people. Within that structure the power of God is the essential thing.

NOTES

(Full reference is found in Bibliography)

Introduction

See standard Israeli Dictionary under Messianic Jews in Hebrew (Yihu-dai Mishaheem)

Chapter One

1. W.F. Albright. *From the Stone Age to Christianity* see early chapters on pre-Abrahamic religion in the Near East.
2. Several sources on this are Elmer Josephson *Israel, God's Key to World Redemption*, see Index under circumcision, and S.I. McMillan, *None of These Diseases.*
3. Albright, *From the Stone Age to Christianity* see material on Exodus and God's name.
4. Walter Kaiser, professor of Old Testament and Semitic languages at Trinity Evang. Divinity School, Deerfield, Illinois in a speech in 1975 to the American Messianic Fellowship in Chicago.
5. See especially Kenneth Kitchen. *Ancient Orient and Old Testament* and Meredith Kline *Treaty of the Great King* and *The Structure of Biblical Authority.*
6. Samuele Bacchiochi. *From Saturday to Sunday* excellent summary of views and solid conclusions.
7. Samuel Schultz. *Deuteronomy, the Gospel of God's Love. The Gospel of Moses.*
8. George Ladd. *New Testament Theology* p. 497 ff. Ladd is one of the world's most reknowned evangelical New Testament scholars.
9. Elmer Josephson. *Israel, God's Key to World Redemption.* Bible light—p. 219 ff. He is one of the few popular Christian writers who comprehend this.
10. Edwin Yamiuchi shows in *E.T.S. Journal* that the usual linguistic identi-fication of Gog, Magog and Meshech and Tubal to the Soviet Union is suspect.
11. See John Walvoord. *The Millenial Kingdom* who argues cogently for a sacrificial system.
12. On this see the excellent article by Carl Armerding—An Evangelical Understanding of Israel in *Evangelicals and Jews in Conversation.*

13. Charles Ryrie. *Dispensationalism Today*. An excellent summary of a moderate dispensational position.

Chapter 2

1. See Richard N. Longenecker. *Biblical Exegesis in the Apostolic Period*. The whole chapter on Matthew is excellent in this regard.
2. F.F. Bruce.*The New Testament Development of Old Testament Themes* emphasizes that John also used a *Moses—Jesus* parallelism in his Gospel.
3. See Wayne Meeks. *The Prophet King*—a whole book devoted to this theme.
4. Elmer Josephson. *God's Key to Health and Happiness* on the food lists.
5. Raymond Brown. *The Gospel of John*, one of the most exhaustive commentaries on John in English.
6. R.N. Longenecker. *Biblical Exegesis in the Apostolic Period*. Especially chapter on Matthew. See Krister Stendahl, *The School of St. Matthew*.
7. J.N.D. Anderson—*Christianity, the Witness of History*.
8. Ibid.
9. Meredith Kline. *The Structure of Biblical Authority*. A whole book which solidly defends this thesis.
10. I. Howard Marsual. *Luke Historian and Theologian* H. Conzelmann. *Luke the Theologian* See R.L. Harris, *The Inspiration and Canonicity of the Bible* on Luke.
11. Cf. E. Powell Davies *The First Christian*.
12. See R.N. Longenecker. *Biblical Exegesis in the Apostolic Period* on Paul and the monumental work *Paul and Rabbinic Judaism* by W.B. Davies.
13. This is known as the South Galatian theory.
14. Excellently brought out in the *Politics of Jesus* by John Yoder p. 220.
15. See W.D. Davies. *Paul and Rabbinic Judaism* on this passage—references. Also Longenecker. *Paul the Apostle of Liberty* on the same passages. See Acts 22:3, 23:6, 7.
16. See Eusebius, Ecclesiastical history Ch. 23. Josephus *Antiquities Book 9 Chapter 1*.
17. Several books bring this out. Note especially Michael Wyshogrod in *Evangelicals and Jews in Conversation*. "Judaism and Evangelical Christianity" p. 45, 46, H. Schoenfield, *A History of Jewish Christianity*, B. Bagatti. *The Church of the Circumcision*.
18. Ibid. Bagatti—See J. Danielieu. *The Theology of Jewish Christianity*.
19. Longenecker. *Paul the Apostle of Liberty*. Appendix p. 280, 281. W.D. Davies *Paul and Rabbinic Judaism* see *Conclusion*.
20. See footnote 17.
21. H.L. Ellison in "Paul and the Law" in Ward Gasque, *Apostolic History and the Gospel*. See Longenecker, Yoder, Batatti, quoted above.
22. W.D. Davies. *Conclusion*.

Chapter 3

1. This doctrine is known as Corporate Solidarity. See H. Wheeler Robins on *Corporate Personality in the Old Testament*.
2. See Appendix II on the 1050+ New Testament Commands.

3. John Calvin. *Institutes of the Christian Religion.* Book II Sec. 7 ff. especially.
4. Eric Berne. *Transactional Analysis and Psychotherapy* and Thomas Harris *I'm Okay—You're Okay* explicitly bring this out throughout their writing.
5. Rees Howell's *The Intercessor.* A classic on prayer.
6. See quoted works by W.D. Davies, Charles Caldwell Ryrie in *Journal of Evangelical Theological Society* on "The Israel of God" (Spring, '78). Also Carl Armerding "The Meaning of Israel in Evangelical Thought" in *"Evangelicals and Jews in Conversation"* p. 128. H. Berkhof "Israel as a Theological Problem in the Christian Church." Journal of Ecumenical Studies VI (Summer 1969), p. 335.
7. See the fine Article by Armerding on Romans 9-11, as a whole and H.L. Ellison's great book *The Mystery of Israel,* a truly fine exposition of Romans 9-11. This is Ryrie's interpretation above. The best explanation of this passage to my knowledge is H.L. Ellison's "Paul and the Law" in Gasque and Martin. *Apostolic History and the Gospel.*

Chapter 4
1. Most dispensational books take the non-Messianic Jewish view.
2. Alan Cole. *The Epistle of Paul to the Galatians.* See Introduction. A fine commentary on Galatians.
3. See Chapter on *Paul, Israel and the Law* on this.
4. Yoder, p. 220.
5. R.A. Cole. *The Epistle of Paul to the Galatians.*
6. See Edward J. Young. *Thy Word is Truth* on the section Nazi and Mari tablets and Patriarchal parallels.
7. See Elmer Josephson. *Israel God's Key to World Redemption* and R.N. Longenecker *Biblical Exegesis in the Apostolic Period.*
8. Ibid.
9. On this see Introductions in J.W. Bowman—*Layman's Bible Commentary* on Hebrews, R.N. Longenecker.
10. Longenecker. *Biblical Exegesis in the Apostolic Period* chapter on Hebrews, Yigael Yadin. The Dead Sea Scrolls and the Epistle to the Hebrews in *Aspects of the Dead Sea Scrolls* (Scripture Hierosoly Mitana IV) ed. C. Rabin & Y. Yadin (1958) p. 36-55. Celsus Spieq *quoted in Long.* p. 161.
11. See Danielou on Essene influence on Jewish Christianity.
12. See *Zadokite document* in T.H. Graster. *The Dead Sea Scriptures.*
13. Calvin. *Institutes of the Christian Religion*—Book II Sec. VII.
14. According to almost all dates for II Cor. 3 and the events of Acts 21 given by scholars.
15. See Kiel and Delitzch. *Commentary on Leviticus.* Also E. Josephson. *God's Key to Health and Happiness.*
16. The Talmud is very strong on requiring ritual washing and even goes so far as to suggest that failure in this regard can cause one to be precluded from the world to come.

Chapter 5
1. Josephus *Antiquities* reflects this Hegasippus in Eusebius.

2. Justin Martyr.
   H.J. Schoeps *Theologie und Geschichte des Juden Christentums* the basic book on the Ebionites.
3. Jean Danielou. *The Theology of Jewish Christianity* basic book on the Nazarenes.
4. Sources in Josephus, Justin Martyr, Epiphaneius, Hegasippus, quoted in Danilou p. 45-54.
5. Justin Martyr. *Dialogue with Trypho the Jew*—(130-150) in *Anti-Nicene Fathers* and also *Ellison* p. 82.
6. H.L. Ellison. *The Mystery of Israel* p. 82?
7. Ibid.—see also history recounted in James Chapter 4. Parks. *The Conflict of the Church and the Synagogue.*
8. Rosemary Ruether. *Faith and Fractricide.*
9. See A. Millagram. *Jewish Worship* p. 328.
10. See Parkes p. 93.
11. Justin Martyr. First Apology. Ch. 31; P.G. VI p. 375.
12. Louis Goldberg. Chairman of Jewish Studies at Moody has noted the surival of Messianic Jewish symbols in an Arab community perhaps reminiscent of conversion by force of an ancient Messianic Jewish community.
13. Rosemary Ruether. p. 123 ff esp.
14. The Hebrew word *echad* which is used of a compound unity (eg. Genesis 2 the man and woman become *one* flesh) was interpreted as *yachid*—an absolute singularity.
15. Ruether. Chapter 3 is an excellent of the period.
16. Ellison, *The Mystery of Israel* p. 82 ff.
17. Ibid.
18. Ibid. See note 27.
19. Parkes is excellent in cataloguing this legislation see chapter 6 and 7.
20. Both Parkes and Ruether deal with this well. See Parkes pps. 121-150 especially.
21. Father Flannery. *The Anguish of the Jews*—an excellent history.
22. The word Judean and Jew is exactly the same in Greek. See M. Benhayim. The American Messianic Jewish Quarterly. Spring 1979 p. 20.
23. See the Gospels and Anti-Semitism by Daniel Juster in *Messianic Judaism, Exploratory Essays* ed. to be published. John Fischer and Daniel Juster.
24. Corrie ten Boom. *The Hiding Place.*
25. Corrie ten Boom. *In My Father's House.* Her brother's conclusions are found in his PhD dissertation.
26. See for example Eichorn. *Evangelizing the American Jew.*
27. Even Eichorn, a reform Rabbi, points to such personalities.
28. For the history herein see Schoenfield, *A History of Jewish Christianity* and Louis Goldberg, *Our Jewish Friends.*
29. See Eichorn. *Evangelizing the American Jew*—p. 186, 187.
30. His Testimony in *H. Einspruch, Would I, Would You.*
31. Einspruch in the same volume in note 6.
32. See the 1909 series of books. *The Fundamentals.*
33. See E.J. Carnell, *The Case for Orthodox Theology*, Chapter on *Fundamentalism* and Bernard Ramm, *The Evangelical Heritage.*

34. See Note 25.
35. See D. McGavern. *Understanding Church Growth.*

Chapter 6

1. On these themes see George Ladd. *Jesus and the Kingdom*, and *Crucial Questions on the Kingdom of God.*
2. James Barr. *The Semantics of Biblical Language* on Interpretation, also A. Berkley Michaelson, *Interpreting the Bible.*
3. See J.N.D. Anderson. *The Evidence of the Resurrection.* Merrill Tenney. *The Reality of the Resurrection.*
4. B.B. Warfield. *The Inspiration and Authority of the Bible.* Article on "It says, Scripture says, God says."
5. See J.P. Free. *The Bible and Archaeology.*
6. Bernard Ramm. *Protestant Christian Evidences.* Chapter on "Evidence of Fulfilled Prophecy."
7. R. Laird Harris. *The Inspiration and Canonicity of the Bible.*
8. Meredith Kline. *The Structure of Biblical Authority* is the great book on this.
9. See Note 7—Harris' account on the New Testament.
10. See Elmer Josephson. *Israel: God's Key to World Redemption.* Carlson. *Oh Christian, Oh Jew!*
11. See H.L. Ellison. *The Mystery of Israel.*
12. See *Targums* on Isaiah 53, Talmud Sanhedrin 926.
13. Especially *Holy Day Prayers*, Al Het etc.
14. W.D. Davies. *Paul and Rabbinic Judaism.*
15. Kenton F. Beshore, *The Messiah of the Targum, Talmuds and Rabbinical writers*, on Genesis 3:15.
16. See Wayne Meeks. *The Prophet King.*
17. See Sanhedrin in 98B—Sukkah52 of the Talmud for two of several references.
18. See Arthur Kac. *The Messianic Hope* p. 76.
19. See Sanson H. Levey. *The Messiah: An Aramaic Interpretation* p. 63.
20. See F. Kenton Beshore. (Note 15).
21. Ibid.
22. See J.W. Montgomery. *History and Christianity*, J.N.D. Anderson. *Christianity, the Witness of History.*
23. Richard N. Longenecker. In the *Christology of Early Jewish Christianity* makes the point that in the New Testament Jewishly intended writings, Messiahship is central and explicit while divinity is only implied.
24. Talmud Sanh 11a, Baba Bartha 12:a, b.
25. See Cohen. *Everyman's Talmud* p. 42-47.
26. See G.E. Wright. *The Old Testament and Theology.*
27. Zohar. Volume III p. 288-vol. 11 p. 43.

Chapter 7

1. This is also argued by Arnold Fructenbaum, *Hebrew Christianity, Its History, Philosophy and Theology.*
2. See A. Koestler. *The Thirteenth Tribe* on the possible conversion of the Kzars.
3. Bacchiochi, *From Saturday to Sunday.*

4. Bacchiochi in "From Saturday to Sunday" Biblical Arch. Rev. September/October 1978.
5. *Jewish Catalogue* see Bibliography.
6. See A. Kac. *The Messianic Hope* p. 83, 84, 95-97.
7. See instructions in the *Jewish Catalogue*.
8. J. Danielou. *The Theology of Jewish Christianity* 339-346.
9. Ellison in "Paul and the Law" in *Apostolic History and the Gospel* by Gasque and Martin.
10. See Donald McGavern. *Understanding Church Growth* sections on Jews, etc.

Chapter 9

1. David and Lisa Loden. *Rejoice* available from House of David distributors, Box 777, Lakewood, New York, 14750.

A SELECTED BIBLIOGRAPHY

Albright, William Foxwell. *From the Stone Age to Christianity*. Garden City, New York: Double Day Anchor, 1957.

Anderson, J.N.D. *Christianity the Witness of History*. London: Tyndale Press, 1969.

Armerding, Carl. "An Evangelical Understanding of Israel" in Wilson and Tannenbaum. *Evangelicals and Jews in Conversation*. Ed, Marc H. Tannenbaum, Marvin R. Wilson, A. James Rudin. Baker: Grand Rapids, Michigan, 1978.

Bacchiocchi, Samuele. *From Sabbath to Sunday*. The Pontifical Gregorian University Press: Rome, 1977.

Bagatti, B. *The Church from the Circumcision*. Rome: Pontifical Biblical Institute, 1971.

Barr, James. *The Semantics of Biblical Language*. London: Oxford University Press, 1961.

Bowman, John W. Hebrews, James, I & II Peter: *The Layman's Bible Commentary* Richmond, Virginia: John Knox Press, 1959.

Brown, Raymond. *The Gospel of John*. Doubleday and Company, Inc. Garden City, New York, 1966.

Bruce, F.F. *The New Testament Development of Old Testament Themes*. London, 1968.

Calvin, John. *Institutes of the Christian Religion*. TR Ford Lewis Battles, Philadelphia, The Westminster Press, 1960.

Cole, R. Allen. *The Epistle of Paul to the Galatians. Tyndale New Testament Commentaries.*

Conzelmann, Hans. *The Theology of St. Luke*, London, 1960.

Danielou, Jean. *The Theology of Jewish Christianity.* London: Dartou, Longman and Todd, 1964. O.P.

Daube, David. *The New Testament and Rabbinic Judaism.* London: Athlone, 1965.

Davies, W.D., *Paul and Rabbinic Judaism.* New York: Harper Torchbooks, 1948.

Eichorn, David Max. *Evangelizing the American Jew.* Jonathan David Publishers: Middle Village, New York, 1978.

Einspruch, Henry. *Would I, Would You?* Baltimore: The Lederer Foundation, 1947.

Ellison, H.L. *The Mystery of Israel.* Grand Rapids, Michigan: Eerdmans, 1966.

Flannery, Fr. Edward. *The Anguish of the Jews.* New York, MacMillan, 1964.

Free, Joseph P. *Archaeology and Bible History.* Wheaton, Illinois: Scripture Press, 1962.

Gasque, W. and Ralph Martin (eds). *Apostolic History and the Gospel*, Exeter, England, 1970.

Gaster, Th. *The Dead Sea Scriptures.* Garden City, New York: Doubleday Anchor, 1956.

Josephson, Elmer. *Israel God's Key to World Redemption.* Bible Light: Hillsburo, Kansas, 1974.

———. *God's Key to Health and Happiness.* Bible light.

Josephus. *Antiquities of the Jews.* T.R. Whiston. Grand Rapids, Michigan: Kregel Publications, 1960.

Juster, Daniel. *Jewishness and Jesus.* Downers Grove, Illinois: Intervarsity Christian Press, 1977.

Kac, Arthur. *The Messianic Hope. Grand Rapids, Michigan: Baker, 1975.*

Kaiser, Walter. *The Old Testament in Contemporary Preaching.* Grand Rapids, Michigan, Baker, 1973.

Kitchen, Kenneth. *Ancient Orient and Old Testament.* Downers Grove, Illinois: Intervarsity Press, 1966.

Kline, Meredith. *Treaty of the Great King.* Grand Rapids, Michigan: Eerdmans, 1963.

_____. *The Structure of Biblical Authority.* Grand Rapids, Michigan: Eerdmans, 1972.

Koestler, Arthur. *The Thirteenth Tribe.* New York, 1963.

Ladd, George, *Crucial Questions and the Kingdom of God.* Grand Rapids, Michigan: Eerdmans, 1952.

_____. *Jesus and the Kingdom.* London: S.P.E.C., 1966.

_____. *A New Testament Theology* Grand Rapids, Michigan, William P. Eerdmans, 1975.

Levy, Samson H. *The Messiah. An Aramaic Interpretation.* Cincinnati, Ohio: Hebrew Union College Press, 1974.

Longenecker, Richard N. *Biblical Exegesis in the Apostolic Period.* Grand Rapids: Eerdmans, 1975.

_____. *The Christology of Early Jewish Christianity.* Naperville, Illinois, Alec R. Allenson, 1970.

_____. *Paul: The Apostle of Liberty.* Grand Rapids, Michigan, Eerdmans, 1976.

Marshall, I.H., *Luke. Historian and Theologian.* Grand Rapids, Michigan: Zondervaan, 1978.

McMillan, S.I. *None of These Diseases.* Westwood, New Jersey: Fleming H. Revell, 1958.

Meeks, Wayne. *The Prophet King.* New York, 1967.

Michaelson, A. Berkeley. *Interpreting the Bible.* Grand Rapids, Michigan: Eerdmans, 1963.

Millagram, A. *Jewish Worship.* Philadelphia: The Jewish Publication Society of America, 1971.

Parkes, James. *The Conflict of the Church and The Synagogue.* New York: Atheneum, 1969.

Ramm, Bernard. *Protestant Christian Evidences.* Chicago: Moody Press, 1953.

Ruether, Rosemary R. *Faith and Fratricide.* New York: The Seabury Press, 1974.

Ryrie, Charles C. *Dispensationalism Today.* Chicago: Moody Press, 1979.

Schoenfield, Hugh. *The History of Jewish Christianity.* New York: 1930 (O.P.)

Schultz, Samuel. *Deuteronomy, The Gospel of God's Love.* Chicago: Moody Press, 1973.

_____. *The Gospel of Moses.* New York: Harper and Row, 1974.

Schoeps, Hans J. *Theologie und Geschichte des Juden Christentums.* Tubingen, 1949.

Tenney, Merril. *The Reality of the Resurrection.* New York: Harper and Row, 1963.

Ten Boom, Corrie. *The Hiding Place. In My Father's House.* Westwood, N.J.: Fleming H. Revell, 1978.

Walvoord, John. *The Millenial Kingdom.* Grand Rapids Michigan: Dunham, 1959.

Warfield, Benjamin B. *The Inspiration and Authority of the Bible.* Philadelphia: Presbyterian and Reformed Publishing Co., 1970.

Wilson, Mark, Marc Tannenbaum, Janis Rudin. *Evangelicals and Jews in Conversation.* Grand Rapids, Michigan: Eerdmans, 1978.

Wright, G.E. *The Old Testament and Theology.* New York: Harper and Row, 1969.

Yamauchi, Edwin. "Meshech, Tubal, and Company: A Review Article." *Journal of the Evangelical Theological Society* Vol. 19, No. 3, Summer 1976.

Young, E.J. *Thy Word is Truth.* Grand Rapids, Michigan: Eerdmans, 1957.

Additional copies of this book and other book titles from DESTINY IMAGE are available at your local bookstore.

For a complete list of our titles, visit us at www.destinyimage.com
Send a request for a catalog to:

Destiny Image® Publishers, Inc.
P.O. Box 310
Shippensburg, PA 17257-0310

"Speaking to the Purposes of God for This Generation and for the Generations to Come"

LD101	Israel, the Church and the Last Days	$ 9.99
LD102	From Iraq to Armageddon	$ 7.99
LD103	Revelation: The Passover Key	$ 6.99
MJ201	Jewish Roots	$14.99
MJ202	Growing to Maturity	$ 9.00
MJ203	Jewishness and Jesus	$ 1.00
AM304	The Apple of His Eye	$ 7.99
AM305	Covenant Relationships	$14.99
AM306	Dynamics of Spiritual Deception	$ 5.99
AM307	Due Process	$ 8.99

Name _____ Phone _____

Address _____

All items available to ministries and bookstores,
in quanities of 5 or more, at 40% discount.

Please fill out the complete information for each book order: item
number; cost of the book; number of item you would like to order;
amount of each item; the amount enclosed.

ITEM	COST/BOOK	NO. ORDERED	AMOUNT
		Subtotal	
Maryland residents add 5% Sales Tax (or send tax exempt certificate for our files)			
15% P & H ($2.00 minimum)			
		TOTAL ENCLOSED	

Mail all orders with checks payable to:

Tikkun Ministries
P.O. Box 2997
Gaithersburg, MD 20886